Highlights from
the Direct and Cross-Examination
of Richard Hauptmann in
The State of New Jersey v. Hauptmann
(The Lindbergh Kidnapping Trial)

PEG *The Professional Education Group, Inc.* 12401 Minnetonka Boulevard
Minnetonka, Minnesota 55343

Foreword

Prologue

On May 20, 1927, an obscure airmail pilot climbed into the cockpit of a Ryan monoplane in New York and took off, heading across the Atlantic. The world was watching, wondering whether it was even possible to travel that far in a heavier than air craft. As the hours passed, everyone was aware that this young man was out there, alone, over endless water. When he finally landed in Paris, thirty-three and one-half hours later, the world was in love with Charles A. Lindbergh, and the United States had a new hero.

Hero may sound like a little much in these days of space exploration by committee with a supporting cast of thousands on the ground. But Lindbergh was the genuine article. He did it himself. He was the picture of the American success story, a shy and thoughtful 25 year old who had dropped out of college because more than anything he wanted to learn how to fly.

Even more important than inspiring the folks at home with his personal qualities, Lindbergh brought back American pride in aviation. While the United States was where the airplane was invented, we had treated aviation more as a novelty than a realistic method of transportation. American fliers in World War I trained in lumbering American-made Curtiss Jennies, but flew French and English fighters in actual combat.

Lindbergh seemed to turn all that around. We were the leaders in aviation once more, and Lindbergh was our goodwill ambassador to the world.

The Crime

On March 1, 1932, between 8:35 and 9:10 p.m., while Charles and Anne Lindbergh were downstairs eating dinner, their 20 month old son, Charles A. Lindbergh, Jr., was kidnaped — taken out of his upstairs bedroom in Lindbergh's new home near Hopewell, New Jersey. A crude ransom note was found in the bedroom, and a primitive home-made ladder — apparently used to take the boy out of the window of his room — was found 60 to 70 feet from the house.

There was an instant nationwide furor. It was before the FBI was automatically involved in the investigation of kidnapings, so it fell to inept local police to try to find the Lindbergh baby. Newspaper and

Foreword

radio reporters from all over the country descended on the small New Jersey town, trampling the grounds, publishing fanciful articles, and ignorantly obliterating evidence.

In a series of incredibly naive decisions, Lindbergh himself directed negotiations with the kidnapers, and actually participated in turning over $50,000 in small bills — mostly gold certificates which were still in circulation — to a man in a cemetery late at night. In return, Lindbergh got a note, supposedly telling where to find the boy, but it was a false lead.

Finally, two months after the kidnaping, a badly decomposed body of a young child was found four and one-half miles from Lindbergh's home. There has always been some speculation whether it was the Lindbergh baby. Charles Lindbergh went to the morgue, and identified the body even though the attending pathologist said the corpse was unrecognizable. Less than an hour later, after only a crude autopsy that involved no pathological or toxicological tests, the body was cremated.

After two more years of following thousands of false leads and investigating a number of individuals, including Dr. Condon, who had helped Lindbergh negotiate with the kidnapers, there was a solid lead. Some of the ransom money was spent at a filling station in The Bronx. The bill was traced to Bruno Richard Hauptmann — an illegal alien from Germany who was working as a carpenter. Hidden under a workbench in Hauptmann's garage, police found a box with $15,000 of the Lindbergh ransom money.

Hauptmann's story was unconvincing. He said he got the box from a friend, Isidor Fisch, who left it with him for safekeeping. It was not until August of 1934, said Hauptmann, that he even knew there was money in the box. There was, unfortunately, no way to verify what Hauptmann said. Fisch had returned to Germany, where he had taken ill and died.

The Trial

On January 2, 1935 the "Trial of the Century" began. It made international headlines. The courtroom was enlarged to hold 500 people. Charles Lindbergh testified, and said that the voice he heard when they turned over the ransom money at the cemetery was Hauptmann's. In addition to testifying, Lindbergh attended virtually every day of the trial.

Foreword

Not only was the case against Hauptmann largely circumstantial, it depended in many ways on what would be improper prosecutorial misconduct today. Documents were suppressed. False evidence was apparently created by the police in an effort to link the crude ladder to Hauptmann. Witnesses later shown to be testifying falsely were presented by the prosecution. A special committee of the American Bar Association decried the circus-like atmosphere of the trial. The final argument of the prosecution was an open appeal to passion and prejudice. There was no objection.

It was, of course, essential that Richard Hauptmann take the stand on his own behalf. The direct examination is by his lead defense counsel, Edward Reilly, and the cross-examination by the Attorney General of New Jersey, David Wilentz.

As you will see, he was not a good witness on his own behalf. On February 13, 1935, Bruno Richard Hauptmann was found guilty and sentenced to death in the electric chair.

Epilogue

The episodes that followed Hauptmann's conviction attracted as much attention — and more controversy — than his trial itself. Governor Harold Hoffman of New Jersey was afraid that Hauptmann's conviction was a miscarriage of justice. But under New Jersey law, Hoffman was powerless to commute Hauptmann's sentence to life imprisonment. Hoffman risked his political career (even the *New York Times* condemned his conduct) in an attempt to save Hauptmann's life.

Oddly enough, the New Jersey Attorney General did have the power to recommend clemency for Hauptmann to a special state board of pardons if Hauptmann would only confess his guilt and name his accomplices. But Hauptmann protested his innocence, saying there was nothing to confess, no accomplices to name. Clarence Darrow, who was not involved in the case, publicly asked for a new trial. The great New York criminal defense lawyer, Samuel Leibowitz, went to death row and personally pleaded with Hauptmann for more than four hours to save his life and confess — but Hauptmann still maintained his innocence.

On April 3, 1936, Bruno Richard Hauptmann was electrocuted. The headlines of the *New York Times* read, "HAUPTMANN PUT TO DEATH FOR KILLING LINDBERGH BABY; REMAINS SILENT TO THE END."

Foreword

The light of history has shown the trial of Hauptmann to be one of the great judicial wrongs of our century. Books such as Ludovic Kennedy's *The Airman and the Carpenter* (Viking, 1985) and Anthony Scaduto's *Scapegoat* (G.P. Putnam's Sons, 1976), make the convincing case that it was a true miscarriage.

It is in this light that the thoughtful lawyer should evaluate the role of direct and cross-examination in the administration of justice. Surely truth is a higher goal than victory.

James W. McElhaney
Cleveland, Ohio
October, 1988

BRUNO RICHARD HAUPTMANN, the defendant, called as a witness in his own behalf, being first duly sworn, testified as follows:

DIRECT EXAMINATION BY MR. REILLY:

MR. WILENTZ: If your Honor please, may it appear on the record with the consent of the defense that the guard standing in back of the witness is there by consent of both parties?

THE COURT: Yes.

Q. You are the defendant in this action, is that correct?

A. It is.

Q. Where and when were you born?

A. 26th of November, 1999—1899, Germany.

Q. What part?

A. Saxony.

Q. Did you go to school in Germany?

A. Yes.

Q. For how many years?

A. Well, eight years public school, and two years, two to three years, like a trading school.

Q. And in the public school did you learn to write German?

A. I did.

Q. In the regular German script, is that correct?

A. Yes.

Q. Did you learn to write any English in Germany?

A. No.

Q. And after you left school you say you attended a trade school, is that correct?

A. Yes.

Q. And what trade did you study?

A. Carpenter trade.

Q. Any other trade?

A. Yes, machinery, machinery.

Q. Machinery?

A. Yes.

Q. Were you apprenticed at any age?

1

A. No.

Q. At what age did you begin to work?

A. Fourteen.

Q. Where did you work?

A. In mine home town, Kamenz.

Q. As a carpenter's helper?

A. Yes.

Q. And for that service you received a salary of how much a week?

A. Well, approximately three marks, three or four marks, beginning.

Q. Of course, I take it that you lived with your people at that time?

A. Yes.

Q. Did you continue to work as a carpenter until the War broke out?

A. Yes.

Q. And how old were you when you went to War?

A. Seventeen and a half years.

Q. And how many years did you serve in the Army?

A. One and three-quarter.

Q. During your service, were you wounded?

A. Slightly wounded, gassed.

Q. You were gassed?

A. (Nodding head.)

MR. WILENTZ: Did he say "Yes"?

THE WITNESS: Yes.

Q. When did you come out of the Army?

A. It was around Christmas time, '18.

Q. 1918?

A. Yes.

Q. About a month after the Armistice, is that correct?

A. Yes.

Q. And then did you come home to your home town?

A. Yes.

Q. Were you able to get any work at that time?
A. No.
Q. Germany was in a very poor condition, wasn't it?
A. It was.
Q. Now, during the period of reconstruction in Germany, about 1919 and 1920, you were convicted of some offense there, is that correct?
A. I was.
Q. And when was it?
A. The spring time, 1919.
Q. Beg pardon?
A. Spring time, 1919.
Q. You will have to keep your voice up because this last gentleman, both of them, want to hear you—in the spring time of 1919, is that correct?
A. Yes.
Q. And as a result of that, did you serve any sentence?
A. Yes.
Q. Where?
A. Beutthen, B-e-u-t-t-h-e-n.
Q. And afterwards were you paroled?
A. Yes.
Q. By the Parole Board?
A. Yes.
Q. About when? Was it about March the 26th, 1933?
A. Yes, I guess that is right.
Q. And were you admitted to parole on March the 30th, 1923?
A. Yes.
Q. When did you first attempt to enter the United States?
A. Summer time, 1930—23.
Q. You boarded a steamer did you not, as a stowaway?
A. I did.
Q. Came to America and you were discovered on board the ship, were you?

Richard Hauptmann

A. Yes.

Q. Taken to Ellis Island, is that correct?

A. Yes.

Q. And returned to Germany?

A. Yes.

Q. When did you next attempt to enter the United States?

A. I guess it was August, the same year.

Q. Same year. And did you successfully enter the United States then?

A. No.

Q. You were caught again, were you?

A. Yes.

Q. And returned to Germany?

A. Yes.

Q. When was the third time?

A. In November, the same year.

Q. Were you successful that year?

A. Yes.

Q. And you entered the United States?

A. Yes.

Q. After entering the United States, did you obtain any employment?

A. Yes.

Q. About when and where?

A. About approximate one week after my landing.

Q. About a day after your landing?

A. No, a week.

Q. A week. And in what city?

A. New York.

Q. And what was the occupation?

A. I started as a dishwasher.

Q. Where, down near the South Ferry in New York somewhere?

A. Yes, that is right.

Q. How long were you a dishwasher?
A. About a month and a half.
Q. How much were you paid a week?
A. Sixteen dollars.
Q. And with what family did you live during that period?
A. With Mrs. Aldinger.
Q. Where?
A. I can't remember exactly.
Q. What portion of New York?
A. Out 96th and Amsterdam Avenue, around this neighborhood.
Q. In a German neighborhood, wasn't it?
A. Oh, no, I don't say that.
Q. Isn't that a part of Yorkville?
A. No.
Q. It is above Yorkville?
A. It is on the west side of New York.
Q. On the west side. Yorkville is on the east side, is that it?
A. Yes.
Q. Well then, where did you get a position after you left the restaurant where you were a dishwasher?
A. A position as a mechanic.
Q. That was with Washburn & Wild?
A. Washburn & Wild.
Q. As a mechanic. Do you remember how long you worked there?
A. No, I can't.
Q. Did you take a position after that as a dyer in the dying business?
A. Yes.
Q. And after that you worked as a machinist, did you?
A. Yes, in Brooklyn.
Q. And each time you would try to improve your position: is that correct?
A. Yes.

Q. Then did you finally obtain a position as a carpenter?
A. Yes.
Q. And was that at Sixth Avenue and 40th Street, New York?
A. Yes.
Q. And did you receive a salary of approximately a dollar an hour?
A. Yes.
Q. That would be how much a day?
A. Eight dollars a day.
Q. And do you recall how long you worked as a carpenter in the first place, the place you were getting a dollar a day, eight dollars— a dollar an hour, rather—eight dollars a day?
A. In the first place, approximate two months.
Q. Now, you were a professional carpenter, weren't you? You studied in Germany?
A. Yes.
Q. You got, you say, as much as eight dollars a day for your services?
A. Yes.
Q. Now, when did you first meet the lady that afterwards became your wife?
A. In 1924; 1924.
Q. 1924?
A. Yes.
Q. And was that while you lived with the Aldingers?
A. That is the time I lived with Aldingers.
Q. And her name, your wife's maiden name, was what? Anna—
A. Anna Schoeffler.
Q. Anna Schoeffler?
A. Yes.
Q. And Anna Schoeffler at that time, who did she work for?
A. Mr. and Mrs. Rosenbaum, Riverside Park.
Q. Now, after meeting Miss Schoeffler, did you move to Yorkville?
A. No, I moved first on 156th Street, before Yorkville.

Q. Well, did you finally live in some house in the neighborhood of 88th Street?

A. 88th Street, yes.

Q. Between Park and Lexington Avenue, is that it?

A. Yes.

Q. Now, that is Yorkville?

A. That is Yorkville.

Q. And Yorkville is a German colony, isn't it?

A. Yes.

Q. How long did you live there?

A. Oh, about two or three months; 88th Street.

Q. Now, one of the men, when you came over on the different ships that you tried to enter this country on, was his name Albert Diebig?

A. Yes.

Q. How do you pronounce that, Dee-big?

A. I pronounce it Die-big.

Q. Die-big. And did Diebig finally get into America?

A. Yes; he came over when I went to this colony on this second trip, when I was successful.

Q. Well then, you and he lived together for a while, didn't you, at 154th Street?

A. Yes.

Q. Between Parkway and Amsterdam Avenue, is that right?

A. That is right.

Q. Then did you and Diebig move to an apartment on 97th Street on the East Side?

A. Yes.

Q. Well now, while you were living on 97th Street on the East Side, what were you working at?

A. I was working as carpenter.

Q. Carpenter?

A. Yes.

Q. Now do you remember obtaining a position as a carpenter in

Richard Hauptmann

Lakewood, New Jersey?

A. Well, I get this position through the newspaper.

Q. Yes. And was that in October, 1924?

A. That is right—October.

Q. And did the position end the day before Christmas, 1924?

A. This position ended on Christmas Day.

Q. Christmas Day?

A. (Nodding head.)

Q. How much did you make a week on that job?

A. Around fifty dollar a week.

Q. Well, now, were you spending all the money you made or were you saving it?

A. Well, I spent very little I say.

Q. About how much a week would you spend out of fifty dollars?

A. I say around twelve dollars.

Q. Did you open a bank account at any time or did you keep the cash with you?

A. I opened right in the beginning a bank account, United States Bank.

Q. When?

A. Must be around the end of '20 or '23.

Q. By the United States Bank, do you mean the Bank of the United States?

A. Yes, Bank of United States.

Q. Was it a savings bank account?

A. Savings bank, yes.

Q. Do you recall the branch in which you opened that account, where it was?

A. Well, this was downtown district, right under the bridge, I can't remember the street anymore.

Q. Downtown Manhattan, New York?

A. Yes, downtown Manhattan.

Q. When you were working as a carpenter in 1925, do you remember what your average wages per day were?

A. '25? Well, I always get my union wages, this time I guess it was a ten-and-a-half dollar day.

Q. Had you joined the union?

A. Yes, I joined it.

Q. After that did you work for some man near Bronx Park as a carpenter?

A. Yes.

Q. Did you get the union wage for that?

A. No, not from this man; I got one dollar, near Bronx Park.

Q. How many hours a week did you work?

A. Forty-four.

Q. Did you save some of that money every week?

A. I did.

Q. Then did you work for Heinzelmann on East 9th Street, between First and Second Avenue?

A. Yes.

Q. Did you work for him until you were married?

A. Yes.

Q. When did you and Anna Schoeffler marry?

A. The 10th of October, 1925.

Q. October 10th, 1925?

A. Yes.

....

Q. Now, I think we were at the point where you had come over to Lakewood, New Jersey, as a carpenter. Do you recall when that was? You saw an ad in the paper, you said?

A. Yes.

Q. Is that right?

A. Yes.

Q. And in answer to the ad you came over to Lakewood, New Jersey: is that right?

A. No, I went to New York. It was given an address in the paper, in New York. I forgot the address.

Q. All right.

A. And this gentleman he sent me over to Lakewood to construct a one-family house.

Q. And how many carpenters worked on that job?

A. Well, that was only Mr. Diebig and myself.

Q. Was Diebig a carpenter?

A. No, he was not a carpenter.

Q. What did he do for a living?

A. I took him along as a helper.

Q. As a helper, carpenter's helper?

A. Yes.

Q. And you say it was only a bungalow?

A. Yes.

Q. And that job was finished Christmas, 1924, is that right?

A. Yes.

Q. Now, in October, 1925, I think you testified that you were married, is that correct?

A. It is.

Q. After you were married, where did you and your wife go to live?

A. Well, first I live for about one week or two weeks on 154th Street between 4th and Amsterdam Avenue. After that I moved to, I guess, 122nd Street, Park Avenue.

Q. Well then, did you about that time go to work for a man named Olson?

A. Yes.

Q. How many years did you work for Olson?

A. Oh, this is around three or four years, sometimes they got to stop for month or two months, if there wasn't much work to do.

Q. Well, when you stopped working for Mr. Olson, would you work for somebody else?

A. Yes.

Q. If you could get the work?

A. Yes.

Q. And in 1929, did you work in Mount Vernon for an Italian?

A. Yes.

Q. As a carpenter?

A. Yes.

Q. Were you out of work very often during 1925, to 1929?

A. Not very often.

Q. Well, now, do you remember during 1928 and 1929 that you worked for someone Saturdays and Sundays, some friends of yours?

A. Oh, yes. We build three houses after working time; that means after the usual working hours—Saturday afternoon and Sundays.

Q. Now these three houses were being built by friends of yours, were they?

A. Yes.

Q. What was the name of the friend?

A. Mr. Haberland.

Q. And how much did you make on the job at working overtime in your odd hours on that job of three houses?

A. Oh, it was approximate one thousand dollars.

Q. And how much of that did you save?

A. Well, I took some to the bank, and some of the money I always keep in the house.

Q. Did you keep some of the money in the house?

A. Yes, always. That is a habit I have.

Q. Now, do you remember about how much you had in your house at the end of 1929?

A. In 1929 I would say three thousand.

Q. Three thousand?

A. Three thousand, three thousand five hundred.

Q. In cash?

A. In cash.

Q. And that was money you had made as a carpenter?

A. Yes.

Q. And saved?

A. Yes.

Q. Was Anna working all the time until practically the birth of the baby?

A. Well, she worked all the time with the exception of two times she went to Jurope.

Q. When did she first go—

MR. WILENTZ: Just a minute. He said Jurope, didn't he?

MR. REILLY: Europe.

MR. WILENTZ: But I mean with a "J". All right.

Q. Where did she go?

A. To her home town.

Q. Did she go to visit some relatives of hers in Europe?

A. Her parents.

Q. When was her first trip to Europe?

A. Summertime, '28.

Q. 1928?

A. Yes.

Q. Had she worked steadily since she came to America up to the time she made the first trip to Europe?

A. With the exception of one month, one or two months, when we get married.

Q. You were married in 1925, in October?

A. Yes.

Q. You say for about two months she didn't work?

A. I say one or two months.

Q. One or two months. Then she went back to work; she worked and you worked?

A. Yes.

Q. How much did Anna make a week?

A. She makes about $20 or $25, I guess, and about five to eight dollars tips.

Q. About $30 or $33 a week?

A. Yes.

Q. Did she save most of it?

A. Well, we kept our household from the money from my wife.

Q. The running expenses of the house?

Classics of the Courtroom

A. The running expenses—

Q. The running expenses came from the money Anna made?

A. That is it. I used to save my wages.

Q. You used to save your wages. Now, when she went over to Europe in 1928, how much did she pay for her ticket?

A. I can't recall.

Q. Did she go second class, tourist class—

A. No, she went third class.

Q. —or third class? I suppose she went on a German boat?

A. Yes.

Q. And third class. Did she buy a round-trip ticket?

A. Yes, round-trip ticket.

Q. Third class round-trip ticket to Germany didn't cost any more than maybe three or four hundred dollars, if it cost that much, did it?

A. You mean the ticket alone?

Q. Yes, the ticket alone, round-trip?

A. No, the ticket alone cost around two hundred dollar, I guess.

Q. Around $200, third class round-trip?

A. (Nodding head affirmatively.)

Q. Do you remember the line she sailed on?

A. North German Line.

Q. North German Lloyd?

A. North German Lloyd.

Q. And how long did she stay over there the first trip?

A. Approximate four months.

Q. And when did she make her second trip to Europe?

A. Summer time, 1932.

Q. Four years after her first trip?

A. Yes.

Q. She went back to see her mother and father again, her parents, or whoever was over there?

A. Yes.

Q. Did she go the same way, third class?

A. No. I guess she went tourist class.

Q. Tourist class?

A. Tourist class.

Q. Was that the year she took over Mrs. Altschuler's child?

A. No, she took the child from Mrs. Achenbach.

Q. Achenbach?

A. In 1928.

Q. In 1928?

A. Yes.

Q. Did she go over with anybody in 1932?

A. No, she went alone.

Q. Do you know how much she paid for her accommodations in 1932?

A. I really don't remember.

Q. How long was she over there?

A. Three or four months.

Q. Had she worked between 1928 and 1932?

A. Yes.

Q. And you had worked?

A. Yes.

Q. And the household ran just about the same?

A. Yes.

Q. The expenses from Anna's money and the savings from yours, is that correct?

A. (Witness nods head.)

Q. Well, now, do you remember where you worked after you left Mr. Heinzelmann?

A. From Heinzelmann?

Q. Yes.

A. I guess I went right to Olson, Mr. Olson.

Q. And after Olson, who did you work for?

A. Well, in the time I worked for Mr. Olson, sometimes there wasn't much to do and I was working on another place, I really can't recall all these places where I was working.

Q. Well, you have always worked more or less as a carpenter, is that right?

A. Always as a carpenter, yes.

Q. Sometimes you worked nights, didn't you? Do you remember working nights for a couple of weeks?

A. Yes, I did.

Q. Fixing some offices at Lexington Avenue and 42nd Street?

A. 42nd and 41st, yes.

Q. And would you be paid there by the hour or by the job?

A. Well, that was a job; you got to work day and night. I guess I worked 30 or 36 hours at one stretch.

Q. 30 or 36 hours?

A. Yes.

Q. And how much would you get for that? How much did you get?

A. It was around $40 or $50. I really can't recall.

Q. Did you work for a carpenter named Gliester in 1930?

A. Yes; it was in Yonkers.

Q. In Yonkers?

A. Yes, in Yonkers.

Q. How long did you work for him?

A. About a quarter of a year.

Q. Were your wages the same, the union rate?

A. No. I guess it was in the Winter time, and he only paid me nine dollars a day.

Q. Did you save your money?

A. Yes.

Q. Now, in the early part of July, 1931, do you recall that period?

A. Yes.

Q. You decided to go and take a trip to California: is that right?

A. Well, it was decided eight years ago already.

Q. Well, did you decide to go then in 1931?

A. Yes.

Q. Can you tell us now about how much you had in cash, just before you started for California in 1931?

A. You mean by cash all the money in my possession?

Q. In the house; in the house, yes.

A. Oh, in the house. It was approximate a little bit over $4,000.

Q. Can you remember now without referring to your bank account how much you had in bank at that time?

A. Around five—five hundred or seven hundred; I really don't know exactly how much there was.

Q. Altogether you had about $5,000, didn't you?

A. I think there was more.

Q. In the bank and the house?

A. Yes.

Q. Now, when in July, 1931 did you start for California?

A. The 5th; the 5th July.

Q. The 5th of July?

A. Yes.

Q. Now had you started some years before that to go to California with Diebig?

A. Yes, it was 1925.

Q. Did you buy a car, the two of you?

A. Yes.

Q. How far did you get in that car toward California?

A. Half a block.

Q. What happened to the car, it broke down?

A. It broke down.

Q. Did anyone go to California with you and your wife in '31?

A. Mr. Kloeppenburg.

Q. And how long had you known Kloeppenburg?

A. I know Kloeppenburg since I guess the Winter time of 1929. I met him then at the firm of Lazherbacher.

Q. And where was Lazherbacher place?

A. Located on 72nd Street, East River, not far from East River.

Q. What kind of a place was it?

A. Cabinet maker.

Q. Cabinet maker?
A. (Nodding affirmatively.)
Q. Was he working there?
A. Yes, he was.
Q. And then after meeting him—of course he was a German, wasn't he?
A. Yes.
Q. And did you two become friends?
A. Yes.
Q. Was he in the habit of visiting your home?
A. Yes.
Q. Did he have a home of his own?
A. Well, he was living mit two friends together, 175th Street.
Q. Was he single?
A. He is single.
Q. Still single?
A. Still single, for all I know.
Q. Who were the friends, if you know?
A. Mr. Lambert—
Q. Lambert?
A. Lambert and Mr. Driesigazker, D-r-i-e-s-i-g-a-z-k-e-r.
Q. Anybody else in the car besides Kloeppenburg, you and your wife?
A. No.
Q. On the California trip?
A. No.
Q. Now, how long were you three away on that trip?
A. I guess three months.
Q. And that brought you back about the end of September, early October?
A. Yes.
Q. Now, when you came back, did you bring back some souvenirs of the trip?

A. A whole lot.

Q. Among the souvenirs, did you bring back some baby alligators?

A. No.

Q. Did you bring back some small bales of cotton?

A. Yes.

Q. Now, you remember this woman that was on the stand here the other day, don't you?

A. Yes.

Q. What is the correct pronunciation of her name?

A. Ah-hen-boch.

Q. Okkenbock?

A. Yes.

Q. Now, do you recall after coming back from the trip to the South and California, you came back by way of the South, didn't you?

A. Yes, over Florida.

Q. Calling at her house?

A. Yes.

Q. And did you show her some of these souvenirs?

A. I guess I showed her all of them souvenirs.

Q. Where did she live then?

A. She lived two houses farder vest of our house.

Q. On what street?

A. 222nd Street.

Q. Did you go back to work then after coming back from California?

A. I got a couple small jobs.

Q. Now, in the following year, or rather, in March 1931, did you buy a Dodge four-door sedan?

A. Which year you mean?

Q. 1931. When did you buy your Dodge four-door sedan?

A. March '31.

Q. How much did you pay for it?

A. $725 in cash.

Q. Was it a brand new car?

A. Brand new.

Q. But it was a 1930 model, wasn't it?

A. It was.

Q. And you bought it in '31?

A. Yes.

Q. And is that the car that you had when you were arrested?

A. That is the car.

Q. So you had it when you were arrested about three-and-a-half years, is that correct?

A. Yes.

Q. When was it that you first began to go to Hunters Island?

A. That was '28, twenty—I guess '28.

Q. Now will you describe the portion of Hunters Island that you German people used to use up there?

A. It is the southern shore of the island.

Q. Well, did you have houses there, or huts or shacks or what did you have?

A. Oh, no, not that. Everybody got his particular place. Some of them builded a little bit like a shack up, some put up a tent, and some got nothing at all, only got a certain space cleaned with stones; that is all. There is no regular place.

Q. And were you and other German friends of yours in the habit of visiting that portion of Hunters Island in the spring and summer time?

A. Oh, there were lots of us.

Q. When would you go up there, on weekends?

A. Usually weekends, Saturday evening or afternoon.

Q. Stay all night or would you come home?

A. Came home usually.

Q. Sometimes you would go back on Sundays, would you?

A. Yes, sir.

Q. Tell us what they would do up there, Saturdays and Sundays?

A. Well, we usually went out to the island early in the morning take a bath, cook some coffee; like the camping life, and we played soccer, cooked our meals, whatever it was, and sometimes playing cards, making music. We would keep going until eight o'clock in the evening and then went home.

Q. It was just camping?

A. Yes.

Q. Roughing it?

A. Yes.

Q. Would Mrs. Hauptmann go along with you on those parties after you were married?

A. Well, sometimes—this time she got the work on Sunday and she couldn't come and I usually went just when she got work on Sunday, I usually went home around about five o'clock. When she was quitting work, and then I was home.

Q. Now, was the reason for your wife's second visit to Germany the fact that her mother was celebrating her seventieth birthday?

A. It was the only reason.

Q. Now, did you meet in Fredericksen's bakery one of their customers who worked in an employment agency on Sixth Avenue, New York?

A. Yes; it was in the early part '32.

Q. Early part of 1932?

A. Yes.

Q. Can you tell us what month?

A. February.

Q. After meeting that man, did you go to the agency?

A. Yes.

Q. Have I the name correct: Reliable Employment Agency, or Reliance?

A. Yes, that is—

MR. REILLY: I have Reliance. Have you a different name?

MR. WILENTZ: That is all right.

Q. Did you pay the ten dollar fee there?

A. Yes.

Q. Now, that was the customary thing to do, wasn't it, to go and register and pay a ten dollar registration fee?

A. No, I went personally down to the agency.

Q. Yes. You went there.

A. And I get a job, and I got to pay them ten dollars for it.

Q. Where was the first job that you got through that agency?

A. That first job was Majestic Apartments.

Q. Majestic Apartments?

A. Yes.

Q. Now, do you remember what date it was in 1932 that you went to this agency?

A. It was 27th of February.

THE COURT: The 27th of what?

MR. REILLY: February.

THE WITNESS: February.

Q. Now on the 28th—what day of the week was the 27th, do you remember?

A. Well, I remember 27th was a Saturday.

Q. Yes. Well then, on the 29th, Monday, did you go any place looking for work as a result of being at the agency?

A. No, I, on the 29th, on a Monday, in the morning, I sharpened the tools and put the tools in the car and went down to the Majestic and put the tools in the carpenter shop and I left.

Q. Of the Majestic Apartments?

A. Yes.

Q. Where was the—you say carpenter shop?

A. Yes.

Q. Where was the carpenter shop of the Majestic Apartments?

A. Down in the cellar.

Q. Down in the cellar?

A. Yes.

Q. Now, how long a building was the Majestic Apartments?

A. I guess it is twenty-one story.

Q. Twenty-one story. Where were the Majestic Apartments?

A. Location on 72nd and Central Park West.

Q. No. 1, either No. 1 or No. 2 West 72nd Street, isn't it, on the corner of Central Park West?

A. Yes.

Q. Right?

A. Yes.

Q. Now did you go back there any time after the 29th of February, to the Majestic?

A. I went back on the 1st of March. I was down eight o'clock in the morning.

Q. 1932?

A. Yes.

Q. And when you got down there to the place, did you go to work?

A. I got to see the superintendent first.

Q. Did you see him?

A. I saw him. I got to wait a little while, about a half hour. Then he said he couldn't put me to work and I got to come back on the 15th of February, because he said he only hires men on the first and on the fifteenth.

Q. Now do you mean the 15th of February or the 15th or March?

A. The 15th of March, I mean. Excuse me.

Q. Now, in the meantime were you trying to obtain a position as carpenter at Radio City, 5th Avenue, New York?

A. I was—a couple of times I was over there for work.

Q. Did you ever get any work?

A. No.

Q. At Radio City.

A. No, I didn't get any.

Q. When do you say now that you first went to work at the Majestic Apartments?

A. It was the 15th.

Q. Of March?

A. March.

Q. And how long did you work at the Majestic Apartments?

A. I quitted on 2nd of April.

MR. REILLY: General, may I have the book that was offered in evidence?

MR. WILENTZ: What book was that?

MR. REILLY: Of Sweeny.

MR. WILENTZ: Will you give us the time book, please? Can you get it right away?

CAPTAIN SNOOK: Yes.

BY MR. REILLY:

Q. We will just pass that for a minute until we get the book. Now, April 2nd, 1932 was a Saturday, wasn't it?

A. It was.

Q. And what time did you go to work on April 2nd?

A. The usual time.

Q. What was the usual time in New York?

A. I left the house at seven o'clock in the morning.

Q. Seven?

A. Seven o'clock in the morning.

Q. And you worked until what time for lunch?

A. Lunch hour was twelve o'clock.

Q. And came back at one, is that right?

A. Yes.

Q. And then you worked until what hour in the afternoon?

A. We worked until five o'clock.

Q. Five o'clock. And the Majestic Apartment is how many miles away from your home in The Bronx approximately? A great distance, isn't it?

A. Pretty near eight miles, I figure.

Q. Eight miles.

Q. Now, you heard the timekeeper from the Majestic Apartments job testify here, did you?

A. I did.

Q. And did you hear him testify that you did not work on April the 2nd?

A. I heard it, yes.

Q. Do you say positively that you did work on April 2nd?

A. Positively.

Q. And you were paid for it?

A. Paid for it.

Q. And it is a fact, isn't it, as testified to by the timekeeper that the following day was a Sunday?

A. Yes.

Q. And the next day was a Monday?

A. Yes.

Q. And that you did not do any work after Monday, you resigned on Monday?

A. I originally resigned on Saturday; on Monday I went down to try to get my pay check, but I get answer I got to wait till the 15th.

Q. Now you were supposed to get a hundred dollars a month, weren't you?

A. Supposed to get it.

Q. Yes. As a matter of fact all they gave you was eighty, isn't that right?

A. Yes.

Q. And that is why you threw up the job, isn't it?

A. Yes.

Q. Did you get your pay check on the 15th?

A. I did.

Q. Of April?

A. Yes.

Q. So that on April the 2nd, 1932, you worked for the Majestic Apartments the entire day until five o'clock at night?

A. Five o'clock, yes.

Q. And you took what train home? How would you go home, or did you have your car?

A. No, I never take the car when I go downtown of New York. I used Bronx Park subway. That brings me on the west side, 72nd Street express station.

Q. That would be about two or three blocks west—

A. Yes.

Q. —of number 1 West 72nd Street where you were working?

A. Yes.

Q. You'd walk up 72nd Street to the express station and take a Bronx Park subway, correct?

A. Correct.

Q. And that subway would take you how near to your house?

A. This takes me to 177th Street, that is near Bronx Park. There I have to change for White Plains.

Q. And the White Plains subway takes you how near to your house?

A. 225th Street.

Q. Three blocks away?

A. Yes. Well, I got to walk nine minutes to my house.

Q. Two or three blocks, nine minutes to walk?

A. Nine minutes. It is about seven blocks.

Q. And about what time, do you recollect now, if you can, did you arrive home that Saturday night, April the 2nd, 1932?

A. Around six o'clock.

Q. Now, do you recall the evening of April the 2nd, 1932, after supper?

A. Well, when I came home, my wife was home already and around seven o'clock Mr. Kloeppenburg came in the house.

Q. Mr. who?

A. Mr. Kloeppenburg.

Q. Yes.

A. Came in the house because this is usual—our music evening is the first Saturday in every month.

MR. WILENTZ: I move that be stricken out, if your Honor please.

THE COURT: What is that?

MR. WILENTZ: He said Mr. Kloeppenburg came to his house on that Saturday because it was his usual Saturday music day or something like that. They have the—

MR. REILLY: I think that is competent.

MR. WILENTZ: I withdraw the objection.

Q. Now, did anybody else come there that night?

A. No, I don't think so.

Q. Do you recall a fellow—Did you know a fellow named Jimmy?

MR. WILENTZ: Oh, now, I—

A. I only know him by name, Jimmie; but I don't know his regular name.

Q. Well, he is a German, isn't he?

A. Yes, he is, yes.

Q. He is a German?

A. Yes.

Q. Now, do you recall whether or not Jimmy was there that night?

A. I really can't.

Q. You have no independent recollection, now, have you, whether he was there or not?

A. No, I really can't.

MR. REILLY: Now, before going into that part, may we adjourn?

MR. WILENTZ: May we have the rest of the testimony as to who was there that night?

MR. REILLY: All right, surely.

MR. WILENTZ: Before we adjourn.

BY MR. REILLY:

Q. Now, who was there that you recall?

A. My wife, Mr. Kloeppenburg, myself of course, and about Jimmy I am not quite sure if he was there or not.

Q. This is two-and-a-half years ago, almost three years ago, is that right?

A. Yes.

Q. Now, I want you to explain to the jury before you leave the witness stand, if you will, what you mean by the first Saturday of the month, music evenings; what did you do and what happened in your home?

A. Well, he was playing the guitar and I was playing the mandolin and we used to play together and enjoy ourselves for about hour, hour-and-a-half, to keep in practice.

Classics of the Courtroom

Q. Any singing?

A. Of course singing, too.

Q. What were you playing, German tunes?

A. German and American.

Q. And how late was this monthly gathering, when would it wind up, what time?

A. Not before eleven o'clock, eleven, twelve o'clock altogether.

Q. Now, on April 2nd, 1932, after you came home from work in the neighborhood of six o'clock, did you ever leave your home that night?

A. No, sir.

Q. You were in your house all the time?

A. All the time.

....

Q. The apartment from which you were arrested, what street was that?

A. 222nd Street.

Q. You will have to speak just a little bit louder.

A. 222nd Street.

Q. And how long had you lived in that apartment?

A. Two years.

Q. You had nothing to do with building that house, did you?

A. Nothing at all.

Q. Now, the time you married your wife, did she have a bank account?

A. Yes.

Q. In what bank?

A. Central Savings Bank.

Q. And did she continue to deposit money in that bank?

A. Yes.

Q. Do you remember the winter after you were married?

A. Yes.

Q. Did you buy a lunchroom at 223rd Street and Lexington Avenue?

A. I did.

Q. From Albert Diebig?

A. I did.

Q. How much did you pay for that lunchroom?

A. Nine hundred dollar in cash.

Q. How long were you in business there with Diebig?

A. Only four, six weeks.

Q. Then did you sell it?

A. I sold it, yes.

Q. For how much?

A. Thirteen hundred.

Q. Made a profit of $400 on it, is that right?

A. That is right.

Q. Now in 1929, including the mortgage of $3750, how much do you say you were worth in cash and bank accounts?

A. You mean on the end of '29?

Q. The end of '29.

A. That includes the mortgage, the money we have in the bank and my money still kept home, approximately $9,000.

Q. What year did you enter the Wall Street market?

A. I guess it was the end of '29.

Q. And you bought and sold stocks right up to the time of your arrest?

A. Yes.

Q. Now, when did you first meet Isidor Fisch?

A. Suppose the early part of March or the early part of April, 1932.

Q. Where did you meet him?

A. Hunters Island.

Q. Who introduced you to him?

A. Well, nobody, he was just on our place, where we used to be always, he was a German and we got in conversation.

Q. After meeting Isidor Fisch, how soon after that did he suggest or you suggest that he participate in the market deal?

A. That was in May.

Q. Nineteen—
A. Same year.
Q. 1929 or '30 or '31?
A. '32.
Q. '32. Did he go anywhere with you in relation to Wall Street?
A. Well, used to go to Steiner-Rouse & Company.
Q. S-t-e-i-n-e-r R-o-u-s-e and Company?
A. And to regulate this—I didn't have any account with Steiner-Rouse & Company this time; my account was by Charleton Mott & Company, Broadway. I watched the board at Steiner-Rouse & Company.
Q. Where was Steiner-Rouse's office, where you watched the board?
A. 86th Street between Third and Lexington Avenue, New York.
Q. They had a branch, is that it, of the Wall Street house up at 86th Street?
A. That is a branch office.
Q. Near the Yorkville district, is that correct?
A. Yes.
Q. And that is where you watched the board?
A. Yes.
Q. Although you say you were not trading with them, you watched their board, is that right?
A. That is right.
Q. And by the board you mean the board in the office that shows the various changes in the quotations on the Stock Exchange?
A. That is correct.
Q. The board that is there, that is, that changes during the day as the stock advances or declines in value, is that correct?
A. Correct.
Q. Did Fisch give you any money to buy stock?
A. Yes, he did.
Q. When was the first transaction that you recall Fisch giving you money?

A. It was, I guess it was around in August that year.

Q. '32?

A. Yes.

Q. Now did Fisch visit your home?

A. Yes.

Q. What business was Fisch in?

A. Fur trading.

Q. Did you afterwards become his partner?

A. Well, we kept it this way, he kept care of his line of business and I kept care of the stock.

Q. And what interest did you have in the fur business, what percentage, if any?

A. I make it half and half.

Q. And when did you go into the fur business with Fisch?

A. The first transaction was in middle of May '32.

Q. Did you advance him any money?

A. I give him $600, the first transaction.

Q. How much did the fur business—What profit did the fur business make in the first year?

A. I didn't check it up yet.

Q. Well, did you ever receive any money from the fur business?

A. Oh, yes.

Q. Large sums?

A. Small sums and large sums.

Q. What was the largest sum you say you received as your share in any one year from the fur business?

A. I guess the largest sums, over a thousand dollars.

Q. How much?

A. Over a thousand.

Q. Over a thousand dollars. Now, was the fur business carried on under any particular name, trade name or partnership name?

A. No, it is only under Isidor Fisch.

Q. Well, did he make out any invoices or did he have any invoices made out by a young woman who lived in his neighborhood?

Classics of the Courtroom

A. Well, I find it out after he is, he died.

Q. Did you ever meet a Miss Haufert?

A. Yes.

Q. In connection with Fisch's fur business?

A. Yes.

Q. When did you first meet her?

A. Well, I saw her the first time in later part of '32.

Q. Where did you see her?

A. Mr. and Mrs. Henkel's house.

Q. Where did they live then?

A. 127th Street, east side.

Q. Was Henkel a friend of Fisch's?

A. I guess he was.

Q. How did you come to meet Henkel?

A. I met Henkel in Hunters Island.

Q. Did Fisch ever live with Henkel, as far as you know?

A. He lived in the same house.

Q. Did you visit the Henkels?

A. Yes.

Q. Do you remember when Fisch went to Europe?

A. I do.

Q. When was that?

A. December '32.

Q. December 1932?

A. '33.

Q. He never returned, did he?

A. No.

Q. Now, before Fisch went to Europe, did he call at your house?

A. He called several times at the house.

Q. When was the last time he was at your house before he sailed for Europe?

A. The night before he sailed.

Q. Who was at your house, as you recall it now?

A. Mrs. Fredericksen, my wife and I.

Q. Anyone else?

A. No.

Q. Did anybody come in during the evening, any of your friends, that you remember?

A. Can't remember.

Q. Did Fisch have anything with him, any bundles, or anything with him the night before he sailed?

A. No, sir.

Q. Well, before he sailed did he leave anything with you for you to take care of while he was in Europe?

A. Well, he left two suitcases.

Q. What else?

A. Four hundred skins, Hudson seal.

Q. What else?

A. And a little box.

Q. Now the 400 skins, or what kind of skins were they?

A. Hudson seal.

Q. Hudson seal. And they were skins that were purchased in your partnership between Fisch and yourself?

A. Yes.

Q. And did you have those skins in your possession when you were arrested?

A. Yes.

Q. And are they now as far as you know in the possession of the New York City Police?

A. I guess they are.

Q. Now this little box that you described, what kind of a box was it, paper, cardboard, or wood?

A. Well, I find it later out it was a shoe box.

THE COURT: What was that?

MR. REILLY: A shoe box.

THE WITNESS: Shoe box.

Q. What was it made of?

A. Well, cardon.

Q. Carton, cardboard?

A. Yes.

Q. Now, will you describe to the jury under what circumstances it was that he left this shoe box with you, what he said and what you said?

A. Well, of Mr. Fisch request it was he was throwing a party when he left for Chermany, it was at his request in our house; we invited a couple of friends and about nine o'clock or a short while before nine o'clock, Fisch came out and got a little bundle under his arm. I answered the doorbell, my wife was in the baby's room. He came out and we went in the kitchen and he said, "I leave it, I leave it something, if you don't mind, keep care of it and put it in a tight place." I didn't ask what is in it, he only said that is paper in it. I thought maybe they are—

MR. WILENTZ: Just a minute.

A. —they are bills.

MR. WILENTZ: Just a minute. Now, I object to what he thought.

THE COURT: Never mind.

MR. WILENTZ: I object to what you thought.

Q. Tell us what you did, not what you thought.

A. I put it in a broom closet.

Q. And where was the broom closet in your apartment?

A. The broom closet was in the kitchen.

Q. In what part of the broom closet did you put it?

A. Please?

Q. In what part of the broom closet?

A. On the upper shelf.

Q. And how long did that shoe box remain there before you disturbed it?

A. The middle of August '34.

Q. '34?

A. Yes.

Q. And what caused you to disturb it?

A. I was looking for—it was Sunday, it was nasty weather outside—was looking for a broom. I took the broom. The broom is on the left side in the closet. And when I took the broom I must hit the box with the broom handle, and I looked up, and that way I saw that it is money. I damaged the box.

Q. And you saw money?

A. Yes.

Q. In the box?

A. Yes.

Q. Well, now, had there been any moisture or wet or anything in that closet?

A. All soaking wet.

Q. Were there some pipes that ran through the broom closet?

A. Yes.

Q. What kind of pipes? Were they water pipes or gas pipes?

A. No, no water or gas pipes. That is, I guess that is ventilation pipe, I guess, for toilets.

Q. Radiator pipes, is that what you mean?

A. No.

Q. For the heating system?

A. No, not for heating system.

Q. Ventilation?

A. That is for ventilation.

Q. Did you take the box down, the paper box down then, and you disturbed it?

A. I put it in the boiler and took it down to the garage.

Q. What money did you see in that box?

A. Only gold certificates.

Q. About how much?

A. I didn't count it from the beginning.

Q. Is that the money that you afterwards started to spend?

A. That is the money.

Q. Is that the money that was found in your garage?

A. It is.

Q. And was Fisch dead at that time?

A. Yes.

Q. How many satchels did he leave with you when he went to Europe?

A. Two.

Q. What did you do with those satchels after his death?

A. After his death, I opened the big satchel and searched it for bills. I couldn't find anything in there and I closed it again and left it in the garage. That means the big satchel.

Q. While Fisch was in Germany, did he write to you?

A. Yes.

MR. REILLY: May I have the exhibit known as S-1, the two mile radius map?

MR. WILENTZ: I think maybe we will have to start carrying some of these down (indicating exhibits tacked to the wall).

MR. REILLY: I think we may have to have the assistance of the State troopers. General, look out for that nail.

Q. I am pointing now to State's Exhibit 1 which shows the estate of Colonel Lindbergh as of March 1st, 1932. Hauptmann, were you ever in Hopewell in your life?

A. I never was.

Q. On the night of March 1st, 1932, were you on the grounds of Colonel Lindbergh at Hopwell, New Jersey?

A. I was not.

Q. On the night of March 1st, 1932, did you enter the nursery of Colonel Lindbergh—?

A. I did not.

Q. —and take from that nursery Charles Lindbergh, Jr.?

A. I did not.

Q. On the night of March 1st, 1932, did you leave on the window seat of Colonel Lindbergh's nursery a note?

A. Well, I wasn't there at all.

Q. You never saw baby Lindbergh in your life, did you?

A. Never saw it.

Q. Now, I want you to look at State's Exhibit 18 and the envelope in which it was contained, Exhibit 17. Did you ever see that note before?

A. Why, I saw it in Bronx courtroom.

Q. That was the first time you saw it?

A. It was.

Q. You never saw it except in the courtroom?

A. No.

Q. Did you write it?

A. I did not.

Q. Did you leave it in the Lindbergh nursery?

A. I did not.

Q. March 1st, 1932, you referred to here yesterday in a general way. Will you again tell the jury where you were from the time you got out of bed on the morning of March 1st, 1932, until you went to bed that night, your movements that entire day?

A. Well, I wake up about six o'clock, took the wife down to the bakery.

Q. About what time did you take your wife to the bakery?

A. Between half past six and a quarter to seven.

Q. How did you take her down?

A. In automobile; in car.

Q. And again I ask you how many miles would you say it was from your home to the bakery?

A. A good mile.

Q. She had to be there about seven o'clock, didn't she?

A. Yes.

Q. How long did you remain at the bakery that morning?

A. I didn't enter the bakery at all.

Q. Well, after Anna entered the bakery, where did you go?

A. I went right home, put the car in the garage, and went to White Plains Avenue subway station.

Q. Well, you testified yesterday you were nine or ten minutes walk from there.

A. Six or nine minutes.

Q. And you took the subway, as you described yesterday, the

White Plains, to some intersection?

A. White Plains to 177th Street, and there I changed for Broadway Subway.

Q. And where did you ride to?

A. To 72nd Street, Broadway.

Q. And then where did you go?

A. I went to the Majestic Hotel.

Q. And when you arrived there did you see anybody?

A. Well, I went to the carpenter shop. Of course, my tools was down there already. I took the tools down the day before and was going to start work. The foreman said, I got to see the superintendent first.

Q. Now, do you recall the name of the foreman?

A. I can't.

Q. All right. Continue now your movements.

A. When I saw the superintendent he said I can't start. Well, I showed him the letter from the agency. He said, "I am sorry, it is filled up." So I left the tools right in the Majestic and took the letter and went down to the employment agency where I get the job, trying to get them ten dollars back what I paid for it. I couldn't get it them ten dollars and he said, "Come around next day, maybe something else coming in." And after that I went to another agencies and I went over to Radio City which was under construction, trying to get a job over there, but I couldn't. And I went home around five o'clock, maybe a little later or earlier, I don't know.

Q. Now when you arrived home, who was there, if anybody?

A. There was nobody at home when I arrived.

Q. What time did you go back and call for Anna?

A. I was there around seven o'clock.

Q. When you arrived at the bakery, who was there?

A. My wife alone, my wife was alone there, but there were customers in there always.

Q. People come in and go out and buy things, is that right?

A. Yes.

Q. Did the Fredericksens at that time have a police dog?

A. Yes, they did.

Q. Did you do anything with that dog during the evening while waiting for Anna to finish her duties?

A. Oh, yes, I usually let the dog out for a walk.

Q. Did you take the dog out that night?

A. I did.

MR. WILENTZ: Just a minute, your Honor, please. I didn't want to object to the leading suggestion about the dog, but as long as the question was asked, specifically that night, the answer was, "I usually took him out." I think the next one is very leading and offensively leading, "Did you take him out that night?"

THE COURT: Yes, that is leading.

MR. REILLY: I don't see how I could otherwise direct his attention to that night.

THE COURT: You might try.

MR. WILENTZ: He did specifically before and he refused to say anything but he usually took the dog out.

THE COURT: For the moment I have excluded this question.

Q. Well, tell us what you did there that night.

A. When I came down I usually got my supper first. I took the police dog out and took it out on the street, sometimes for a quarter hour, sometimes for a half hour.

Q. On this particular night—that is what we are interested in, did you—

A. I did.

Q. —take it out that night?

A. I did, yes.

Q. Do you remember where you walked the dog?

A. I went to the corner of the Boston Road, Boston Post Road, went a little farder up, came back again to the gasoline station; it is just the corner.

Q. Did you meet anybody?

A. As far I can't remember. I met a gentleman, I guess he was put gas, gassing in the gasoline station, and he was talking about the— about this dog, und he was asking me where I get him. I told he doesn't belong to me. I don't know whether he was asking about interest from the owner, that is what I can't remember.

Q. But you remember meeting a man that talked to you about that dog?

A. I do.

Q. On March 1st?

A. Yes.

Q. At about what time of the night?

A. I would say it would be between eight and half past eight.

Q. What did you do? Did you bring the dog back to the restaurant?

A. Oh, yes.

Q. What time did you and your wife leave there?

A. Came before nine o'clock; it was after nine o'clock. I can't remember exact the time.

Q. Well, it would be fair to say it was in the neighborhood of nine o'clock, is that right?

A. Yes, that is about right.

Q. Did you drive your wife home?

A. Yes.

Q. And after arriving at the house, did you again leave your house?

MR. WILENTZ: Just a minute. Now if your Honor please, I don't want to be objecting, but I don't think counsel ought to be testifying.

THE COURT: Well—

MR. REILLY: All through the examination of his witnesses, if the Court please, we never thought of interrupting the gentleman's continuity of thought; we allowed him to testify fully and freely. I don't want to do it, but I want to simply direct this witness's thought in the channel of March 1st, that night.

THE COURT: Well, suppose you ask him what he did.

MR. REILLY: All right.

Q. What did you do?

A. I went home. We went home, took the car—

Q. Did you stay there?

A. Took the car in the garage, went right away to bed.

Q. So that on March the 1st, 1932, I ask you again, were you in

Hopewell, New Jersey?

A. I was not.

Q. And on March the 2nd, 1932, do you remember what time it was that you got up?

A. The same time again, six o'clock, a little bit later.

Q. And did you and your wife go anyplace?

A. I took the wife down to the bakery. After that I took the car down home in the garage again and went down to Sixth Avenue. In entering the subway station one, 225th Street, I read the paper and that is the first time I read about the Lindbergh case.

Q. Then you read for the first time of the Lindbergh kidnaping, is that what you say?

A. Yes.

MR. REILLY: The second letter, please.

Q. I now refer you to State's Exhibits S-21 and 20. Were you— Withdrawn. Did you mail a letter in this envelope addressed to Mr. Colonel Lindbergh, Hopewell, New Jersey, on March the 4th, 1932?

A. No, sir.

Q. Did you write that envelope?

A. I did not.

Q. Now, I show you the letter which was contained in that envelope, S-20.

A. I did not write any letter like that.

Q. You did not write that letter?

A. Did not write it.

Q. When was the first time you saw that letter, if you ever saw it before?

A. Well, I saw some of them letters in Bronx courtroom.

Q. You didn't put any marks on any in The Bronx?

A. No.

Q. You saw some letters like this?

A. Yes.

Q. You may have seen this in The Bronx and you may not have seen it: is that correct?

A. Yes.

Classics of the Courtroom

Q. When do you say for the first time you knew or learned that Colonel Lindbergh lived at Hopewell?

A. Well, I—I heard it in the paper.

Q. The morning after the kidnaping: is that it?

A. Yes.

MR. WILENTZ: That is what I object to, if your Honor please.

MR. REILLY: He has testified already he read it.

MR. WILENTZ: He hasn't testified to that. The witness was waiting to determine his answer as to the time, if he was going to answer it at all.

THE COURT: I think the question was leading, but it has been answered.

MR. WILENTZ: I understood counsel answered it. Counsel suggested the day after the kidnaping.

BY MR. REILLY:

Q. When did you read in the paper of the Lindbergh kidnaping?

A. March 2nd.

Q. Did it say in the paper that the baby was taken from Hopewell, New Jersey?

A. It did.

Q. You didn't know Colonel Lindbergh, did you?

A. I did not.

Q. You had never been in Hopewell, had you?

A. No, sir.

Q. Now, when for the first time did you read that he lived in Hopewell, New Jersey, or did you know he lived in Hopewell, New Jersey?

A. When I read from the kidnaping.

Q. Now, do I understand you, and I don't want to lead you, I think you have answered it, though, that every day between March 1st and March 15th you went through the usual routine of looking for work, except Sundays, of course?

A. On, on March the 2nd I went down to the Majestic and took my tools up again.

Q. And what were these tools in?

A. In a tool chest.

Q. This tool chest that we have here?

A. Yes, that was—

Q. Is that your tool chest, referring to State's Exhibit 191?

A. Well, I suppose it is. It looks like it.

Q. Well, you better look at it.

A. I will have to see the inside of it. (Witness examines tool chest.) That is my tool box.

MR. REILLY: "That is my tool box."

MR. WILENTZ: The answer is "That is my tool box."

Q. All right, close it, please.

MR. WILENTZ: Well, that is all right. We can have it closed afterwards.

MR. REILLY: I don't want somebody stepping on it and hurting themselves.

(The witness closed the tool box.)

Q. Now, when you took your tool box up, where did you take it?

A. Took it home to the garage.

Q. And how long did you keep it there?

A. Well, at this time I was working for National Lumber yard, sometimes in the week one day, sometimes three days, sometimes four—it depends just how the work was coming in.

Q. Was that in your neighborhood?

A. Yes, it is White Plains Avenue.

Q. How much do they pay you a day?

A. It was mostly on contract; mostly on contract.

Q. Contract. Well, then, finally on the 15th of March you did go back to Majestic Apartments, is that correct?

A. Yes—

Q. And started to work?

A. In the meantime I went a couple of times down to the agency where I get a job, and I called up the Majestic before I went down, and they said it is okay. So I went down the 15th of March. In saying so, I went down the 15th of March, there is one thing I am not quite sure about, if I did have my tools down on the 15th of March; so it is a possibility I started 15th or the 16th, either one of them days.

Q. Well, if the time book shows—May I have that, Captain. Well, the best of your recollection is that you went to work on the 15th and if your tools were not there, were not there on the 15th, then you went to work on the 16th: is that what you said?

A. Either one of them two days.

Q. And you testified yesterday that you worked right through?

A. The 2nd of April.

MR. REILLY: The next letter, Captain.

Q. I show you a letter, S-29, or S-22, S-23, and an envelope S-21, and I ask you whether or not you mailed this envelope with these two letters inside to Colonel Henry L. Breckinridge.

A. I did not.

Q. Is that your handwriting?

A. It is not.

Q. I show you S-23, a letter, and ask you whether or not that is your handwriting.

A. It is not.

Q. I show you this exhibit, S-22, and ask you if that is your handwriting.

A. (Examines carefully.) It is not.

Q. Did you ever know of a Colonel Henry L. Breckinridge in March, 1932?

A. I did not.

Q. Now, I refer to Exhibit S-42, an envelope addressed to Dr. John Condon, 2974 Decatur Avenue, and ask you whether or not on March 9th you mailed that letter to him?

A. I did not.

Q. Did you have anybody mail the letter for you?

A. No, sir.

Q. Is that your handwriting?

A. It is not.

Q. I show you a letter which was contained in this envelope and which is known as State's Exhibit 44 and ask you whether or not you wrote that letter (handing letter to witness)?

A. I did never.

Q. Did you know a Dr. Condon?

A. I did not.

Q. Did you know anybody named Jafsie?

A. No.

Q. When for the first time did you see Dr. Condon who took the witness stand here?

A. New York Police Station.

Q. Where?

A. Police Station, New York.

Q. What part of New York?

A. Downtown district.

Q. And that was after your arrest here in September, October, last year?

A. After my arrest, yes, sir.

Q. I show you State's Exhibit 43 and 45 and ask you whether that is in your handwriting?

A. It is not.

Q. I show you the letter, is that in your handwriting?

A. No.

Q. I show you State's Exhibit 47 and 48, an envelope addressed to Mr. John Condon, 2974 Decatur Avenue, and ask you whether that is in your handwriting?

A. It is not.

Q. I show you the letter that was enclosed therein and ask you is that in your handwriting?

A. It is not.

Q. I show you State's Exhibit 51 and State's Exhibit 50 and ask you whether or not the envelope addressed to Dr., Mr. Dr. John Condon, 2974 Decatur Avenue, New York is in your handwriting?

A. It is not.

Q. I show you the note that was enclosed therein and ask you is that your handwriting?

A. No.

Q. I show you a piece of wrapping paper, State's Exhibit 53, addressed to Dr. John E. Condon, 2974 Decatur Avenue, New York, and on the sides "Mr. Condon," same address, and ask you if any part of that paper, either one or the second address, was written by you.

A. It is not written by me.

Q. Was it ever mailed by you?

A. No.

MR. REILLY: May I have, General, please, the article that was in this?

MR. WILENTZ: Captain, will you please get that for Mr. Reilly.

(Exhibit S-15 produced.)

Q. I am referring now to State's Exhibit 15, a sleeping suit. Did you take this sleeping suit off baby Lindbergh at any time?

A. I never saw the Lindbergh baby, alive or dead.

Q. When for the first time did you see this suit?

A. Right here in this courtroom.

Q. Did you ever have it in your possession?

A. I never have.

Q. Did you ever mail it to Dr. Condon?

A. I did not.

MR. REILLY: Captain, let me have the thumb guard, S-16.

(Exhibit S-16 produced.)

Q. You saw the thumb guard here in court on the witness stand?

A. Well, I saw it, but I really didn't know what it is.

Q. I show you State's Exhibit 16, thumb guard, and ask you if you ever saw this before you saw it in the courtroom?

A. No, I never saw it. I really didn't know what it is for.

Q. I show you State's Exhibit 52, a letter, and I ask you to look at it, both sides.

(Witness looked at letter.)

Q. Did you write that letter?

A. I did not.

Q. I show you State's Exhibits 55, 56, an envelope, addressed to Dr. Condon, March the 19th, 1932, and ask you first whether you wrote this envelope?

A. No, I did not.

Q. I show you the letter which was contained in the envelope and ask you whether you wrote that?

A. I did not.

Q. And I show you State's Exhibit 60, State's Exhibit 61, the envelope addressed to Dr. John Condon, the 29th of March, 1932, and ask you whether you wrote that envelope?

A. I did not.

Q. I show you the letter that was contained in the envelope and ask you whether you wrote that letter (presenting same to witness)?

A. No.

Q. I show you State's Exhibit 64, an envelope, and State's Exhibit 65, the letter contained in the envelope, and ask you first if you wrote the envelope (presenting the exhibits to the witness)?

A. I did not.

Q. Or did you mail it to Dr. Condon?

A. No.

Q. I show you the letter and ask you whether you wrote that (presenting the exhibit to the witness)?

A. No.

Q. I show you State's Exhibit 67 and State's Exhibit 66, and ask you first whether you wrote the envelope (presenting exhibit to the witness)?

A. No, I did not.

Q. I show you the letter and ask you whether you wrote the letter (presenting the exhibit to the witness)?

A. No, I did not.

Q. And I show you State's Exhibits 68 and 69, an envelope addressed to Dr. Condon containing a note, and ask you first whether you addressed that envelope (presenting the exhibit to the witness)?

A. No.

Q. I show you State's Exhibit 70 and ask you whether you wrote that note (presenting the exhibit to the witness)?

A. Did not.

Classics of the Courtroom

MR. REILLY: Captain, may I have the photograph of Woodlawn Cemetery?

....

(Photograph received in evidence and marked Defendant's Exhibit D-40.)

Q. How far away from your house—

MR. REILLY: May we have the map of the Bronx put back showing different distances?

Q. (Continuing) How far away from your house would you say the main entrance of Woodlawn Cemetery was?

A. Well, I don't know where the main entrance are of Woodlawn Cemetery.

Q. You are not familiar with the cemetery at all, is that right?

A. No.

Q. Pointing to the map in evidence, S-174, map of the Bronx, on the left Woodlawn Cemetery: do you see that?

A. I see it.

Q. The main gate—

MR. REILLY: I will have to call on the General and ask the General where is the gate.

MR. WILENTZ: The gate in question?

MR. REILLY: The gate in question.

MR. WILENTZ: Right here (indicating). Jerome Avenue and East 233rd Street.

Q. Now I show you Defense Exhibit 40 in evidence, picture of a gate of Woodlawn Cemetery, which is at 233rd Street—

MR. WILENTZ: Jerome Avenue.

Q. —Jerome Avenue, where I am pointing here—

A. I see it.

Q. —Were you at that gate or inside that gate March the 12th?

A. I was not.

Q. 1932?

A. I was not.

Q. I am pointing now to 222nd Street in The Bronx and I stop on the same exhibit where someone has indicated your home, marked with an "H"; do you see that?

A. I see 'em.

Q. Now, having the position of your house in mind and Jerome Avenue and 233rd Street—the gate as indicated—how far would you say that was from your house in miles or blocks?

A. Well, I really don't know.

Q. Well, have you any idea how far your house is in miles or blocks from Webster Avenue?

A. From Webster Avenue—

THE COURT: If you have some idea about it, you might give us your best judgment.

MR. REILLY: Yes.

THE WITNESS: To Webster Avenue I figure around 40 to 50.

THE COURT: 40 to 50?

THE WITNESS: Blocks.

THE COURT: Oh, yes.

BY MR. REILLY:

Q. And then there would be the width of the cemetery or else you would have to go up to Webster Avenue, come down 233rd Street to this gate, is that correct?

A. No. When I mean Webster Avenue, I mean around this point—excuse me—around this way.

Q. This point?

A. Yes.

Q. Webster and Gun Hill Road?

A. Yes.

Q. Right. So that you say you were not in and around or near this gate house of Woodlawn Cemetery on March 12th?

A. Well, I can't remember I ever was around this point.

Q. But on that particular night were you there and did you meet Dr. Condon?

A. No.

Q. Have you any independent recollection now where you were March the 12th, 1932?

A. Which date?

Q. March the 12th?

A. March the 12th—what day in the week was it?

Q. Well, if March the 1st was on—

A. Was it a Monday or Friday or something?

Q. Tuesday—March 1st was Tuesday, the 8th would be on Tuesday, the 9th would be Wednesday, the 10th would be Thursday, the 11th would be Friday—on a Saturday night, March the 12th?

A. March the 12th Saturday night—I really don't know. I guess we was playing cards, but I can't hardly remember.

Q. But were you on the Saturday night of March 12th in Woodlawn Cemetery?

A. I was not.

Q. Did you, on March 12th, speak to Dr. Condon through the bars of any gate in Woodlawn Cemetery and particularly through the gate as indicated on defendant's Exhibit 40?

A. Was not.

Q. Or did you climb over any gate and run away from Dr. Condon?

A. Certainly not.

Q. Now, I show you a frankfurter stand, which photograph the State offered as their exhibit 49 (presenting the exhibit to the witness). Were you ever at this frankfurter stand?

A. No, I was not.

Q. Did you ever sit in the recess or doorway of that frankfurter stand and talk to Dr. Condon?

A. No, I did not.

Q. I show you now what appears to be a small shack with a bench outside, the State's Exhibit 41, in the neighborhood of Woodlawn Cemetery, and ask you whether you recognize that as any place that you had ever visited in your life (presenting the exhibit to the witness)?

A. Never was there. Really didn't know it.

Q. Did you ever sit on a bench outside of this shack?

A. No, I did not.

Q. Did you ever sit there talking to Dr. Condon?

A. No.

Q. Did you ever sit there coughing at Dr. Condon?

A. No.

Q. I show you the State's Exhibit 32 for Identification which afterwards became—

MR. REILLY: What did that become in evidence, the ladder? We have it here for identification as 32.

THE REPORTER: In evidence 211.

MR. REILLY: S-211. Bring out the ladder, Marshall, please.

COURT CRIER HANN: The ladder is right here. Do you want it stood up?

MR. REILLY: If you will, please.

(Three sections of ladder placed against wall to the right of the jury.)

Q. Now, how many years, Bruno, have you been a carpenter?

A. About ten years.

Q. You have seen this ladder here in court, haven't you?

A. Yes.

Q. Did you build that ladder?

A. I am a carpenter. (Laughter)

Q. Did you build the ladder?

A. Certainly not.

Q. You notice how it is constructed, do you?

A. Yes, I notice it.

Q. Well, come down and look at it, please.

(Witness leaves stand and examines ladder.)

A. Looks like a music instrument.

MR. WILENTZ: What is it?

MR. REILLY: He says in his opinion it looks like a music instrument.

Q. In your opinion does it look like a well-made ladder?

A. To me it looks like a ladder at all, I don't know how a man can step up.

Q. Now, did you take this ladder in your automobile or any

Classics of the Courtroom

automobile from the Bronx and convey it to Hopewell, New Jersey?

A. I never transported a ladder in my car.

Q. Did you take that ladder that I am talking about—

A. No.

Q. —and did you at any time have this ladder on Colonel Lindbergh's estate?

A. No.

Q. Did you at any time place two or more sections of that ladder against the side wall of Colonel Lindbergh's home?

A. No.

Q. And climb that ladder?

A. No.

Q. Or did you come down the ladder?

A. No.

Q. And did you take the ladder and convey it 75 feet away from Colonel Lindbergh's house and leave it in the bushes?

A. No.

Q. Did you assemble at least four kinds of wood and make this ladder?

A. No, I did not.

Q. Your house had an attic, didn't it?

A. Yes.

Q. How many families lived in the house?

A. Three families.

Q. And who were they?

A. The landlord, Mr. and Mrs. Rauch, myself—

Q. What was the first name, Dengler?

A. Yes. Well, Schuessler, a family of Schuessler.

Q. When did the Schuesslers live there?

A. They moved in in summer time, 1932.

Q. How long did they live there?

A. Well, they was still living in the house when I got arrested.

Q. And what part of the house did they occupy?

Richard Hauptmann

A. The first floor.

Q. And how many rooms did you have on the second floor?

A. Four rooms.

Q. Where did the other party live?

A. Downstairs in the rear. They got only three rooms. And the landlord he got two rooms and he lived most in the cellar.

Q. What was the landlord's name?

A. Mr. Rauch.

Q. So there was the landlord and two tenants in the house, is that right?

A. That is right.

Q. Now, there has been exhibited here a board, S-226, which a witness has testified to came out of the attic of your house. Did you take any board from the attic of your house?

A. I did not.

Q. Did you take any board from the attic of your house and carve or cut or manipulate or manufacture a side of this ladder from that board?

A. I did not.

Q. There was nothing in the attic of yours, was there?

A. You mean when we moved in?

Q. Yes.

A. No, it was empty.

Q. What part of the cellar did this landlord use to live in? Is it a cellar or a basement?

A. It is a regular cellar, the real part of the cellar has a partition between.

Q. I am showing you now Exhibit S-210 of the State's evidence and ask you whether or not on March 1st, 1932, you left this chisel on Colonel Lindbergh's estate at Hopewell (presenting exhibit to the witness).

A. Dis chisel was never in my possession.

Q. By that you mean you never owned it?

A. Never owned it.

Q. Carpenters can buy chisels, can they not, in supply houses?

Classics of the Courtroom

A. It is at every, at every hardware store.

Q. Anybody can buy a chisel, can't they?

A. Yes.

Q. You don't have to be a carpenter to buy a chisel?

A. No.

Q. You can buy a hammer or a chisel or anything you want in a hardware store, can't you?

A. As long as you can pay for it, that's all right (laughter).

Q. Now I direct your attention to another portion of the Bronx, a place known as St. Raymond's Cemetery; over here on the right-hand lower corner we find St. Raymond's Cemetery, of Exhibit S-174; and here is your house up here.

A. I see.

Q. How many miles would you say in your judgment your house is from St. Raymond's Cemetery?

A. Well, I can only figure on the scale on the wall here.

Q. Quite a distance, isn't it?

A. What is the scale on it?

Q. One inch, 480 feet.

A. (No answer)

Q. Well, you can see the different blocks here, indentations; those are blocks.

MR. WILENTZ: 132 inches to the mile.

Q. Quite a number of blocks, isn't it, as you go along here and pass all these blocks and come down?

A. (The witness nods affirmatively.)

Q. Were you ever there in your life?

A. Yes, I was there, but not on the cemetery. I only can remember I passed the cemetery about six years ago.

Q. And do you remember where you were going?

A. I was visiting a friend's house, he lives in Throggs Neck.

Q. Throggs Neck?

A. Yes.

Q. That is over on the Long Island Sound, isn't it?

A. Yes.

Q. Anywhere near City Island?

A. No, that is not City Island.

Q. Well, it is on the Sound, isn't it, City Island—

A. Yes.

Q. —is on the Sound?

A. Yes.

Q. Were you in St. Raymond's Cemetery April the 1st or April the 2nd?

A. No, I was not.

Q. 1932.

A. No.

Q. In order to go to your house—are you familiar with this portion of the Bronx, this Baychester Avenue—

A. Not familiar with this portion, but familiar with this one.

MR. WILENTZ: Let's indicate, Mr. Reilly, on the record.

Q. You are not familiar with this lower right-hand portion, but you say you are with what other portion?

A. I was there from here myself (witness indicates by drawing both hands down over map a distance apart).

MR. WILENTZ: Just a minute now indicating?

MR. REILLY: Yes.

THE WITNESS: Like that (indicating).

MR. WILENTZ: Indicating from the White Plains Road on the north and going straight down the map, and that is from the northwest, and directly in line with that opposite on the map west along—Is that west down here, or you make a line, you had better not let me do it.

THE WITNESS: No. That is not what I, I will explain it.

MR. WILENTZ: Indicating a parallel line on the other side of the map somewhere in the neighborhood of Westchester Avenue.

THE WITNESS: There is around Pelham Bay (indicating).

Q. What is out here, Pelham Bay?

A. Pelham Bay, it must be around here, yes, that is around here.

Q. Well, of course, there is a great deal of The Bronx that isn't shown on that map: isn't that right?

A. That is right.

Q. Now, on April the 2nd, Saturday night, were you in St. Raymond's Cemetery and did you receive fifty thousand dollars from Dr. Condon?

A. I did not.

Q. Is that the night you have testified to concerning the musicale?

A. That is right.

Q. The first Saturday of the month?

A. Yeah.

Q. What time did this musicale or gathering in your house start on April 2nd?

A. Between seven and eight.

Q. Did you go out at any time that night?

A. I did not. Oh, well, I went out, around half past eleven to bring—

Q. Where did you go?

A. To bring Mr. Kloeppenburg to the station.

Q. Took Kloeppenburg to the station?

A. Yes.

Q. That was the only time you went out that night?

A. Yes. That means not to the station. That is to the streetcar line.

Q. How near to your house?

A. White Plains Avenue, around nine blocks away from the house.

Q. Now you have told us that you were in business with Fisch and—can you give me your best recollection of whether you did any dealing with Fisch in the market through the firm of Mott & Company?

MR. WILENTZ: Carleton-Mott.

Q. Charles Mott, no, Carleton-Mott. Do you remember whether you did or not?

A. No, not by Charles Mott.

Q. Now it has been testified to and these exhibits have been offered in evidence that concern your wife's account under the name of Anna Schoeffler. You have heard that testimony?

Richard Hauptmann

A. Yes.

Q. It has been testified to that January 16th, 1928, when she had a balance of $411.16, that was transferred to a joint account of Anna and Richard, you have heard that?

A. Yes.

Q. And that is correct, isn't it?

A. That is correct.

Q. There is a withdrawal here after it became Anna and Richard, June 25th, 1928, $452.63 (handing the exhibit to the witness). Can you recall the reason for the withdrawal or what you did with the money?

A. Why, yes, it must have been my wife went to Germany the first time. I am not quite sure but I guess it is.

Q. Did your wife go to Germany about the end of June, 1928?

A. That is the time, about.

Q. Now I notice in 1928, September the 17th, a deposit of $720 (showing exhibit to the witness). Can you give the jury any idea how that $720 deposit was made up, where you got it, what it was from?

A. Well, I guess I can. This time I was working very hard, mostly evenings, Sundays, Saturdays, and I open an account, I open an account on White Plains Avenue, I open an account in the summer time, I think, I am not quite sure; and after a couple of months, I closed this account and forward the money to the bank of my wife. That was $720, something like that.

Q. Was that an account in the Bronxboro Bank, 230th Street and White Plains Avenue, Bank of Manhattan Company?

A. What is the street?

Q. 230th Street and White Plains Avenue.

A. Yes, that is right. I can't remember the name of the bank any more.

Q. I show you a photostatic copy of that account, which shows that it was open in September, September the 12th, 1927, with $250, and closed January the 16th, 1928, with $782. Is that the account you refer to?

A. That is the account I refer to.

(Witness examines papers and returns to Mr. Reilly.)

Classics of the Courtroom

Q. Now, there were withdrawals here from the Anna and Richard account in 1928, last—rather, the 30th of November, 29th of December and the 31st of December; you withdrew three deposits—or rather, three withdrawals, and they total $485 in all. Can you explain those withdrawals, the three there (handing papers to witness)?

A. I really can't explain them withdrawals; sometimes it was lent money to friends if they need it and give it back after a couple of months in small lots; just how I got them—

Q. Well, now, here is a withdrawal of $2,800, the 1st of November, 1929. Can you recall anything about that withdrawal?

A. Yes. That is—that is the money I put in the stock market.

Q. And in 1929 you were doing business with Steiner-Rouse, weren't you?

A. No.

Q. Or was it with the—

A. Charleton, Mott.

Q. —Charleton-Mott?

Q. Now here is a withdrawal in 1930, on the 14th of June, $500, on the 25th of June, $950. Can you recall why you withdrew that?

A. I guess I put this money in the stock market, as far as I can remember.

Q. And then after these two withdrawals there is a deposit the next month, the 14th of July, is there not, of $302.50?

A. It is, yes.

Q. Now here is a withdrawal on March the 9th, 1931, of $640.

A. March 31?

Q. March the 9th, 1931?

A. Yeah.

Q. Can you explain where that money went?

A. I guess that is the time I bought my car.

Q. How much did you pay for the car?

A. Seven, seven hundred twenty-five dollar.

Q. And here is a withdrawal of July 3rd, 1931, $450?

A. Yes.

Q. Can you explain where that money went?

A. Trip to California, I guess.

Q. When did you go to California?

A. July, 1931.

Q. You came back, I think you said, in October?

A. Yeah.

Q. Right?

A. In October.

Q. Right. Now here we have a withdrawal of $430, May 9th, 1932.

A. I guess this was one of the first money I put in Fisch's account on the fur business.

Q. In the fur business?

A. (Nodding affirmatively.)

Q. And I notice that seven days afterwards, the 16th, you deposited $200: is that correct?

A. Yes.

Q. And on the 23rd, $116: is that correct?

A. Correct.

Q. So that you were constantly depositing and constantly withdrawing: is that correct?

A. That is right.

Q. Now, come down to August 3rd, 1932. Here is a withdrawal of $837 and on the 25th of the same month a deposit of $817.35. Can you explain those two cross amounts (presenting exhibit to the witness)?

A. I got one of them slips. I marked it out. I can't really remember it if you go over it like that.

MR. WILENTZ: Let's have the answer.

THE COURT: You will have to speak up.

A. I got one of them slips and marked it, with our deposit. I can hardly read it from this one.

Q. You mean you made a slip or a memorandum?

A. Yes.

Q. Where is it?

A. I guess Mr. Fisher can get it.

Q. All right.

MR. REILLY: We will suspend with this until after the luncheon recess, your Honor. I don't want the recess now, but I say I will suspend this line until after lunch.

THE COURT: Very well.

Q. Now, do you recall when it was that you started your account with Steiner-Rouse?

A. It was August, I guess, '32.

Q. August '32?

A. (The witness nods affirmatively.)

Q. Do you recall what your initial transaction with them was?

A. I got to have my slip I marked down. I can't explain it other.

Q. So we will understand about the slip, after these—

A. Of course them accounts, some belongs to Fisch and some belongs to me.

Q. After these photostatic copies had been offered in evidence—

A. Yes.

Q. At one of the hearings—

A. Yes.

Q. —you were permitted to take, over the last weekend, were you not, a copy of them into the jail?

A. (Witness nods affirmatively.)

Q. And you went over them?

A. Yes.

Q. And you made certain memorandums from which you believe you can testify, is that correct?

A. That is correct.

Q. And you wish to testify from those memorandums, is that correct?

A. Yes.

MR. REILLY: I will hold that up until after recess.

MR. WILENTZ: We will have no objection to that procedure, if your Honor please.

Q. Now getting back to—suspending this until after lunch—getting back to Fisch's trip to Europe. You said he left certain satchels and a shoe box with you; and when was it to the best of your recollection that you discovered any money in that shoe box?

A. Middle of August, '34.

Q. And I think you testified that you took it some place, to the garage or some place?

A. Took it down to the garage.

Q. Now, what did you do with the money when you got it to the garage?

A. Put all the money in a—squeezed the water out first.

Q. Well, now, what water are you referring to that was in the money?

A. That is the waters coming through the roof.

Q. Well now, you will have to describe that to the jury, and I don't want to lead you. What do you mean by the water coming through the roof; explain it to the jury.

A. There is a leak in the closet since we moved in; I complained a couple times to the landlord, but it never get fixed. I guess it ain't fixed now, and the water was running mostly right on the pipe. On them shelves it was standing most of the time and sometimes in the shelves was water standing as deep as that (indicating with thumb and finger).

MR. WILENTZ: Indicating about an inch?

MR. REILLY: Yes.

THE WITNESS: Three-quarters inch.

Q. Now, the closet you refer to, was that the closet you call the broom closet?

A. That was the broom closet, that was the broom closet in the kitchen.

Q. Now, just where in your apartment is this broom closet?

A. In the kitchen.

Q. In the kitchen?

A. Yes.

Q. You will have to tell us what part of the kitchen it is in.

A. What part of the kitchen—well, it is right side the ice box, and I have to explain where the ice box are, do I?

Classics of the Courtroom

Q. Well, let's begin this way: you were on the top floor of the house, as far as people living in the house is concerned, is that right?

A. Yes.

Q. And over your head was this peaked roof?

A. Yes.

Q. Now, as you come up the stairs to your apartment, where was the entrance to the kitchen from the head of the stairs? We will start there; maybe that will give us some idea.

A. I could go along the hall, the end of the hall, you enter the kitchen.

Q. I see. Now, as you enter the kitchen—how large a room was the kitchen, approximately? You don't have to have it exactly.

A. Approximate 12 by—12 by 6 or 7.

Q. 12 by 6. The rear of the house or the front of the house?

A. Rear of the house.

Q. Rear of the house. Now, let us assume that that doorway in which the Crier is sitting, on the right of the courtroom, for purposes of the record, that is the entrance to your kitchen as you come along the hallway?

A. That is right.

Q. And that is the rear of the house?

A. Yes.

Q. Where was the ice box, right or left?

A. The ice box is right left to the door.

Q. On the left?

A. Yes.

Q. Was it a built in ice box?

A. Yes.

Q. It was an ice box that held ice, was it, and not a Kelvinator or a Frigidaire or one of the electrics.

A. No, ice.

Q. Now, in connection with that ice box, where was the broom closet?

A. On the left side of the ice box.

Q. And about how wide would you say the broom closet was?

A. Broom closet (indicating a measurement with his hands).

Q. General, two and a half or three feet.

A. About two feet or a little more, and deep—that is about sixteen inches (indicating the measurement with his hands).

Q. I suppose you kept other things besides brooms in there?

A. Well, there were three shelves in there, many things on the shelves.

Q. Now these pipes that ran through the broom closet, tell us where the pipes were.

A. The pipes was on the rear wall of the closet more on the left side.

Q. And where did these pipes start, if you know, and where did they end?

A. I don't know where they start but they end out of the roof.

Q. Out through the roof?

A. Yes.

Q. Did they pass through any bathroom, as far as you know, downstairs?

A. Not as I know.

Q. Now this water that you complain of, will you explain to the jury how it got into the broom closet?

A. It comes through the roof, the water.

Q. The water—you will have to explain to them how it comes down from the roof, if you can.

A. There must be a leak around the pipe.

Q. You mean in their exit to the roof?

A. Yes. It isn't, I guess them shingles doesn't cover close to the pipe so there was a space between them. I was never up to the roof and didn't see it.

Q. Well, did you get more water after a rainstorm than you did before?

A. This depends. Sometimes when it was rain we didn't get any water in at all. I guess it depends from which side the rain came.

Q. But sometimes after a rainstorm you did get water?

A. And plenty of it.

Classics of the Courtroom

Q. And it rolled down the side of these pipes?

A. Yes.

Q. There was no break in the pipes, was there?

A. No, there was no break in the pipe.

Q. The water came on the outside of the pipe, is that it?

A. Yes, yes.

Q. And flowed down into your broom closet, is that correct?

A. Yes; and some of it flowed up on the ceiling and dropped down.

Q. Now did any of that water, did you see any of that water, or did you see the effects of any of that water on the paper shoe box or cardboard shoe box that Fisch had left in your apartment and which you had placed in the broom closet?

A. I will explain it this way. When I put the shoe box on the upper shelf, there was laying them—them—how you call them? I don't know them.

MR. WILENTZ: Curtains?

Q. Curtains, shades?

A. Them shades, and them rods from the curtains was laying up there, cross-way; so I put a box over there, and them rods and them shades I put on top and laid against the back, so the water coming down the pipe was catched by them rods and running it down the rods on top of the box.

Q. And how many months had this paper or cardboard shoe box been in that closet before you disturbed it?

A. Since I get it.

Q. Yes. And you got it in December, 1933?

A. Well, it was the last Sunday before he left.

Q. When did he leave?

A. I can't remember exactly the day.

Q. What month? I don't ask you exactly.

A. In December.

Q. In December. And it was, you say, in August, 1934?

A. Yes.

Q. Before you disturbed the box?

A. Yes.

Q. Now, what was the condition of the box, what was the change in the box from the time you put it up there and the time you took it down?

A. She was practical falling apart.

Q. Now, describe to the jury without any leading from me, please, the condition of the money in the box as you saw it for the first time.

A. Well, I—when I saw the money I took the box down and took it in a pail, because the water was running round my, down my arm in the sleeves, took it in the pail and carry it down to the garage.

Q. Well, was the money flat, rolled up, divided, or tell us more about the condition of it.

A. It was, it was bundle.

Q. You will have to tell us.

A. My recollection—

Q. Describe the bundle.

A. I guess it was four bundles in there.

Q. Four bundles?

A. Dem, dem bundles was mostly mesh up, but must be wrapped in paper, not in thick paper, in thin wrapping paper, brown paper, and there was newspaper in the box too, I guess they wasn't filled up at all; it was empty space, there was some newspaper; I didn't look on the newspaper at all. I took the money out, squeezed the water out, put it in the basket, loosened it a little bit, put it in the basket, and the rest, I mean the empty box and the paper I put in the garbage.

Q. Now, when you took the money down into the garage—is this the—Well, what did you take it down in?

A. In the bail(pail).

Q. A barrel?

A. No, not a barrel, a pail.

Q. A pail?

A. Yes.

Q. What kind of a pail, tin pail, wooden pail?

A. Tin—no tin pail.

Q. Now, you got down into the garage—this was in August 1934, wasn't it?

Classics of the Courtroom

A. That is right.

Q. This garage was a one or two car garage?

A. One car.

Q. And it was across a short road, wasn't it, from your house?

A. It is around about sixty, seventy feet from the house.

Q. Well, your house was like this desk, (referring to stenographer's desk), is that correct? And then there was a short dirt road, wasn't there, over to the garage, like an alley or a street, was it?

A. Yes, there is around the house, there is a cement road, about—excuse me—about only a foot and a half, I say, maybe a little bit more, going around the house, on the east side, and on the south side from the house—when I step out the house, the front door, that is the only way to get in and out is the front door. Then there was—

Q. The garage is not attached to the house?

A. No, it was not attached to the house.

Q. It is on the side of the house?

A. On the other side from the street.

Q. Yes. And there is a dirt road between?

A. It is.

Q. That runs through to the next street?

A. It is.

Q. Is that right?

A. That is right.

Q. All right. You took the money into the garage. What did you do with the money?

A. Put it in a basket and covered it up. And then laid the basket up on the ceiling so nobody could see it—not exact lay it on the ceiling, I put it on the upper shelf which reached the ceiling and put a nail and two strips in front of it and put another basket on top of the basket where the money was laying in.

Q. What was the condition of your account with Fisch when he sailed for Europe? How did you two stand on the accounts, on the fur business?

A. Well, when he sailed we made what you say clean table because we didn't know where we are and so on and my account on the market was $12,000 and there was five thousand five hundred in

Fisch's mar—Fisch's account.

Q. You say your account was $12,000?

A. Yes.

Q. Explain, please, just what you mean by that.

A. The stock I got in possession was worth twelve thousand dollar. That was on 25th or 26th of October, 1934.

Q. Well, did you owe anything on that $12,000 worth of stock or was that a margin?

A. No, that was actual money. The stock was worth more, but the rest was margin.

Q. And how much of that $12,000 belonged to Fisch?

A. Only $2,500.

Q. The rest was yours?

A. The rest was my money.

Q. Now on the fur angle, the fur end of it, how did you and Fisch stand on that?

A. Fisch said he got $21,000 of furs and there was a fur part of it I didn't take from Fisch and there was some of the money from the stock market, I kept up for my money, them two together made $5,500, but I didn't take the money from it, because Fisch said he hasn't got any and I left it in his account.

Q. Now did Fisch owe you money when he went to Europe?

A. Well, when he went to Europe, he said if I am willing to sell some of them furs.

Q. Furs, yes.

A. Yeah. I said, "Why should you, you just bought a couple of weeks before—" he bought it, I didn't buy it—and better him leave it. He said, "Well, can you give me $2,000?" I said, "All right, I take $2,000 from my account and give it to you."

Q. Which account?

A. From the stock account.

Q. Did you give it to him?

A. I took a check out for $2,000, cashed a check and give it to him in cash.

Q. How long before he sailed?

A. It was about two or three weeks before he sailed.

Q. Well now, have you in your memoranda that you made up in the prison the other night a record of how you and Fisch stood when he sailed? Or can you tell us that now? Did he owe you or did you owe him?

A. Well, this was made out. He is interested in the stock market, in the lose or in the win. If I win he gets half and I get half; if I lose, he has to carry the half of the loss and I carry 'nother half. And the fur account is just the same way.

Q. Fifty-fifty in both, is that it?

A. Fifty-fifty in both. And each account goes of one name. For instance, the fur account goes of his name, and the stock account goes of my name.

Q. Now, when you struck your balance, before he sailed, what you call a clean table—

A. Yes.

Q. Did you owe him anything or did he owe you something?

A. Well, there was only the difference I got in his account, $5,500. But take $2,500 off, you got in mein account. That's $3,000. That's the difference.

Q. Then you cashed a check for $2,000?

A. Yes.

Q. And gave him the money: right?

A. Yes.

Q. Now, you knew, did you, that Fisch was dead when you found this money?

A. I know it, yes.

Q. Now, after drying it, what did you do with it then?

A. Well, when I took it down, I took a few of them, I guess two or three I took out, and put in circulation.

Q. Now you remember the 26th of November, every year after you were two years of age, don't you?

A. Because it is my birthday.

Q. Yes. And you remember, do you, November 26th, 1932, your birthday?

A. Trying to, yes, I remember this birthday, too.

Richard Hauptmann

Q. That was a Sunday. Were you down at the Sheridan Square theater at half past nine at night alone with one of these ransom bills folded up in eight folds, and did you throw it in to the cashier, the lady that was here the other day, and ask her for a ticket?

A. I just—

Q. Yes or no.

A. You referred for 1932?

MR. WILENTZ: Just a minute, now, you wanted an answer, and I understand—

MR. REILLY: Yes, I will get an answer.

MR. WILENTZ: I think the witness is trying to correct you on the year, maybe 1933.

MR. REILLY: '32 or '33, am I wrong in the years, General?

MR. WILENTZ: He says you are wrong. He is trying to tell you.

A. I never was down in this theater.

Q. That is what I want to know, the Sheridan Square Theater, do you know where Sheridan Square is? Have you any idea where it is?

A. I have idea about where it is.

Q. Well, about where do you think it is?

A. I hear this is Greenwich Village and I know about where Greenwich Village is.

Q. Greenwich Village is somewhere, is it not, near the New York side of the Holland Tunnel?

A. It is on the east side of New York downtown district.

Q. And you lived how many miles would you say away from Greenwich Village to the Bronx up here (indicating S-174)?

A. I would say it was around 12, 15 miles.

Q. Were you ever in that territory in your life?

A. No, sir.

Q. No matter what the date is?

A. Makes no difference, I never was there.

Q. So you couldn't, could you, have handed a bill to this woman?

A. No, sir.

....

Classics of the Courtroom

Q. In checking my notes during the noon recess I found that the date I wanted to inquire about was November the 26th, 1933, the date that Mrs. Barr, I think her name is, says you passed in a five dollar Federal Reserve Lindy bill to her window. I understand that you testified November the 26th is your birthday. Is that correct?

A. That is right.

Q. Now, have you a recollection as to where you were on the evening of November 26th, 1933?

A. November 26, 1933, I was home, have a little birthday party at home there, a couple of friends present.

Q. Do you recall who was present?

A. Mrs. Miller, his little daughter, my wife and a friend of my wife from her home town in Germany and I.

Q. And what was her name, the name of the friend?

A. I really only know her by Paul.

Q. Now, I have these different memoranda.

A. Do you want to give me all of them inside too?

Q. Yes. Do you wish to look at these too?

A. Yes.

(Examining counsel opened envelope of photostats and handed envelope and contents to the witness.)

MR. REILLY: I wonder if I might borrow, General, one of your copies from one of your assistants.

MR. WILENTZ: Yes, certainly.

Q. Bruno, it is suggested and agreed by the General and myself that as you indicate the sheet that you are testifying from in the photostats that you tell us what number of the account or what date it starts so we may check from here.

MR. REILLY: Is that all right, General?

MR. WILENTZ: Go ahead, Mr. Reilly.

Q. Now, what sheet—Let's start with August 8th. Have you that sheet there?

A. Yes, I got it in my hand.

Q. Yes. The entry of August 8th indicates a deposit, does it not, of Warner Brothers Pictures?

Richard Hauptmann

A. Yes.

Q. Do you recall when you purchased that?

A. That was 51 of Warner Pictures I bought long ago, I guess about three quarter of a year ago. I didn't mark it all down here on the sheet when I bought it.

Q. By three quarter of a year ago—

A. Yes.

Q. —you mean three quarters of a year before August 8th?

A. I will tell you in a second.

(The witness examined photostats.)

Q. Well, I will ask you this question: Did you buy it when you had your account with the other firm?

A. There was 51 of Warner Pictures left. In the same firm I bought in April '32 another 51 of Warner Pictures and 500 Curtiss-Wright.

Q. Now, you traded in the market, didn't you, back and forth, different stocks: is that right?

A. Well, that is with Steiner-Rouse & Company—

Q. I know that, but while you were dealing with Steiner-Rouse, you dealt in various kinds of stock, different companies: is that right?

A. Right.

Q. And did you know the customers' man in Steiner-Rouse?

A. Yes, I do.

Q. Did you ask him for advice at different times as to what stock he thought was a good stock to buy or to sell?

A. Oh, yes, I did; that is the usual way you ask.

Q. Now, if you will look down the sheet you are looking at, Steiner-Rouse, beginning August 8th, there is an item of cash that you put into the business or into the account on September 15th of $170: right?

A. That is right.

Q. Where did you get that cash from?

A. $170 came from the $4,300 I got in my home.

Q. Now, Bruno, on the question of cash that was deposited by you at any time in Steiner-Rouse & Company, was one dollar of that cash, was there one dollar of that cash Lindy ransom money?

Classics of the Courtroom

A. There was no Lindy ransom money at all.

Q. We will pass to the next item of $582.50 of cash put into the account by you on the 19th of September. When did you get that? Where did you get it?

A. That is the first money Mr. Fisch put in the market.

Q. May I have it? (Taking a paper from the witness.)

MR. REILLY: And this is my copy, General, that I am—

(Mr. Reilly hands witness a paper.)

Q. Now I notice the next month of September, after the trading balance, Steiner-Rouse & Company and yourself was struck off, that the balance was $1,004.50, correct?

A. That is correct.

Q. Then I notice that on October 7th a cash deposit by you to Steiner-Rouse of $860, correct?

A. I put it in my name, dis money came from Mr. Fisch to buy a hundred New York Central Railroad.

Q. When was that purchased?

A. Purchase was the 6th of October.

Q. So that on the purchase of New York Central on October 6th, a credit, or rather a debit to you against the firm of $2,412.50, you say Fisch gave you $860 to cover that transaction?

A. That is right.

Q. Which you deposited there. Will you take my pencil, please, and put on that photostatic copy opposite that item the capital F?

A. (Witness marks paper.)

Q. Now we go to October, and there was no cash put in, is that correct?

A. That is correct.

Q. But there was trading, there was buying, wasn't there?

A. There was only buying, no selling.

Q. Yes. Well then, December, there was another purchase of New York Central and no cash placed in the account, correct?

A. Yes.

Q. Now, will you turn to the next sheet? It is a short sheet, December the 31st. You have it?

A. Yes.

Q. So that December the 31st you had on hand in your account stock with the company, Warner Brothers, Allegheny, Curtiss-Wright and New York Central, correct?

A. That is right.

Q. Now, during January, 1933, there was in the early part of the month—you bought and sold, didn't you?

A. Yes.

Q. And your balance at the end of the month, your credit was $274.33, is that correct?

A. Of which month, of January '33?

Q. January, yes, where it says "To balance, $274.33."

A. I haven't got it on the sheet here.

Q. (Indicating) Here.

A. December, 1st of January—

Q. January.

A. That is right, yes, $274.33.

Q. And during that month you had sold, had you not, stock amounting to about $2,380 on the 3rd and on the 6th?

A. About, yes.

Q. That money you allowed to remain in Steiner-Rouse & Company?

A. Yes.

Q. Now, on February 27th—that is withdrawn.

Q. During the early part of February I notice several purchases, Radio, and a purchase on the 27th of Curtiss-Wright, 200 shares; correct? And later on that day, Curtiss-Wright 100 shares, Curtiss-Wright 200 shares, and 100 Radio; is that correct?

A. That is correct.

Q. And then I notice on the other side that the same day it indicates a cash deposit in to Steiner-Rouse & Company of $700.

A. Yes.

Q. Where did that money come from?

A. This money I took from my bank. Just a minute.

THE COURT: "This money I took from my bank;" that is what

Classics of the Courtroom

he said.

THE WITNESS: I am not quite sure. I will have to look it over.

Q. All right; look it over.

A. (After examining photostats at length.) Yes, this $700 I put in was—I took $500 from my bank and there was $200 was profit from furs. I put $500 from the bank and $200 from fur account, makes $700.

Q. Now will you indicate the bank account you took the $500 from?

A. Yes, it is marked in bank book—I made a mistake there. Yes, it is marked in the bank book $500 out on February 7, '33—February 27, '33.

Q. Yes. So that your answer as I understood the stenographer to get it was $700 deposited in Steiner-Rouse & Company on the 27th of February, of which $200 was profit from the fur business and a $500 withdrawal from the Anna and Richard Hauptmann account in the Central Savings Bank of the City of New York as indicated on their photostatic copy February 27th, 1933, draft $500, correct? Now, it appears by the same sheet before you that in March, 1933, there was $850 placed in Steiner-Rouse & Company, is that right?

A. Will you repeat it again, please?

Q. On your sheet before you, March 1st, you deposited with Steiner-Rouse $850 in cash, is that correct? That is this sheet here.

A. No, that is not it. $850—October—oh, this one, yes.

Q. March 1st, right?

A. March.

Q. Now, tell us, please, where that $850 came from?

A. $850 came from Mr. Fisch and he bought in January 100 New York Central.

Q. What date?

A. January 13th.

Q. 100 New York Central, 20-3/4, $2,087.50, right?

A. That is right.

Q. You must keep your head up when you are testifying. After you look down on the paper and want to give your answer, look up so the last juror can hear you.

A. All right.

Q. You said that Fisch had bought in January some New York Central. What date?

A. January 13th.

Q. For how much?

A. $2,087.50.

Q. And this $850 on March 1st you say came from Fisch?

A. It came from Fisch, yes.

Q. Will you mark that with an "F" please?

A. (Witness marks paper.)

Q. Now we come into April, the large sheet, April (Mr. Reilly hands witness a sheet) and you will notice on this sheet of April an item of March 27th, a check for $1,500, right?

A. Yes.

Q. Where did that check come from?

A. This check I took a couple days before from the Steiner-Rouse Company, I guess it was (witness examines paper), dats, I took a check out on March 24th, $1,673.90, I can't remember for which purpose, and I took part of them back, that means $1,500, on the 27th, 27th of March.

Q. Is that—

A. That is the check for thousand seven hundred dollars.

Q. Now let me see the withdrawal, please, from your bank account.

A. I took it from the stock account.

Q. The stock account?

A. (Nods affirmatively.)

Q. You drew that March the 27th?

A. Yes, I drew it here. Here is the check.

MR. REILLY: May I have that last sheet, the one before.

Q. So then, referring to the Steiner-Rouse account for March the 24th, you drew from them $1,673.80: is that correct?

A. That is correct.

Q. And $1,500 of that $1,600 check you redeposited with Steiner-Rouse & Company March the 27th?

A. Yes.

Q. So it was practically a cross entry in bookkeeping, wasn't it?

A. Yes.

Q. There was a great deal of trading during April, wasn't there?

A. There was, yes.

Q. The purchases in April were about $10,000, weren't they?

A. Yes, a little bit over.

Q. And the sales were about $7,500?

A. It is about, yes.

Q. And the check that was redeposited was $1,500. That made your deposits and sales that month as against the $8,000 or $10,000, purchase and sales and deposit, was approximately $9,000, wasn't it?

A. I couldn't follow you so quick.

Q. Well, it has been totalled up here. Maybe you can testify from this better (showing a paper to the witness). Is it a fact that April your purchases were in the neighborhood of $10,000?

A. Yes, that is right.

Q. Or $11,621. I thought that was a credit. $11,621.32, right?

A. Yes.

Q. And including the $1,500, check, which you redeposited, up to the 26th of April, your sales and deposits amounted to $9,120.90, right?

A. Yes.

Q. Now on the 28th of April you deposited in cash, did you, $2,500?

A. Yes.

Q. Where did that come from?

A. In this month I bought from Mr. Fisch a hundred New York Central.

Q. When?

A. April the 3rd and—

Q. And that purchase amounted to $1,537.50, didn't it?

A. Yes, that is right; and on the 19th of the same month, 100 Southern Pacific, amounts to $1,462.50; and on April the 25th a hundred Republic Steel, amounts to $1,062.50. And that is the reason he put $2,500.

Q. Did he give you that in cash?

A. Always in cash.

Q. Now, May was a very active month, wasn't it?

A. Yes.

Q. On May the 3rd there was a cash deposit of $2,575; right?

A. Yes.

Q. Where did that money come from?

A. Mr. Fisch got a debit balance this time, he bought too strong in April and didn't sell much, and then he bought on the 2nd of May another additional—not additional, another 100 Canadian Pacific Railroad share for $1,237.50, and he put this money of $2,575.

Q. In cash?

A. In cash.

Q. Now, continuing on to the next sheet, May 24th, 1933, no cash was placed in the account, is that correct?

A. You mean May?

Q. May.

A. No. No cash put in, but in the same month I bought for Fisch hundred shares of American Rolling Mills for a thousand five hundred eighty-seven dollars fifty cents, and—I will have to look it over—and 300 Radio shares for $2,197.50.

Q. And your account ran along in trading, with yourself and Fisch buying and selling during May down to June 7th, is that correct?

A. June 2nd.

Q. For cash.

A. Oh, for cash? Yes, June 7th.

Q. When $2,225 was put into the account?

A. Yes.

Q. Where did you get that from?

A. That Mr. Fisch bought in June, 500 Continental Motors, hundred Pittsburgh Screw & Bolt, hundred Alaska-Juneau and hundred shares New York Ontario & Western Railroad, and another hundred shares Interborough.

Q. Now the trading was very heavy in May, wasn't it, and June, buying and selling almost every day?

A. There was buying and selling every day, practically every day.

Q. Now, take the next sheet. You bought on the 21st, you bought on the 22nd, you bought on the 23rd, 26th, 27th, 28th, 29th and 30th, didn't you?

A. Yes.

Q. You sold on the 23rd, 26th and 29th?

A. That is right; that is right.

Q. At the end of the month you had a balance of $7,973.72?

A. Debit balance, yes.

Q. Debit. That is what you owed the firm as against the stocks they were holding: correct?

A. That is correct.

Q. Now, on—

A. I—

Q. —on July 3rd, you sold, did you not, 1300 shares of stock of twelve different descriptions?

A. More as that.

Q. On the 3rd, July 3rd—

A. Oh, only dis, yes.

MR. WILENTZ: How much, Mr. Reilly?

THE WITNESS: Twelve.

MR. REILLY: 1300 shares in twelve independent stocks.

Q. They are all 100 sales, except one 200: is that right?

A. Except 200 Kelvinator.

Q. And that was a sale which amounted to $16,041.46, is that correct?

A. Yes, that is correct.

Q. And there were no purchases on July the 3rd, were there?

A. No, purchases start on July the 5th.

Q. Purchases start on the 5th. The sales on the 3rd for $16,000 and you left that money in Steiner-Rouse?

A. Yes.

Q. Then on the 5th you began to buy, didn't you, right?

A. That is right.

Q. And you bought on the 6th and you bought on the 7th and you bought on the 10th and you bought on the 11th, didn't you?

A. Yes. Now excuse me, Mr. Reilly, you want to go back to month of June?

Q. Yes, I will go back with you.

A. I want to—

Q. Want to explain something?

A. I want to explain what Mr. Fisch bought.

Q. Yes.

A. He bought hundred Kelvinator for $1,100, and he bought 50 shares National Dairy Products, and I bought 50 shares this time.

Q. What date, the 23rd?

A. June 23rd. And he bought 50 shares Lorillard and I bought 50 shares to make up a full lot.

Q. And that was on the 23rd?

A. On the 23rd, yes, and on the 26th Mr. Fisch bought another additional hundred shares Kelvinator, a thousand and fifty dollars, and his buying in July was 500 shares of Budd Wheel.

Q. That was the 6th, July 6th?

A. July 6.

Q. Who bought that?

A. Well, I bought, for Fisch's account.

Q. On the 6th?

A. Yes, sir. And on the 11th, 500 shares Commonwealth Southern.

Q. Now your trading from the sheet you are reading, beginning June the 21st—the account was very active, wasn't it?

A. Yes.

Q. And your trading down through the month of June and down through the month of July to the bottom of the sheet required no cash investment, did it?

A. No, it didn't require any more cash. The account was strong enough to carry it over on margin.

Q. How many points margin were you dealing on?

A. It depends; sometimes I was on limit, which was about 50 per-

Classics of the Courtroom

cent.

Q. Whenever the house thought it required more margin to cover the strength of your purchases, did they ask you for some more money?

A. Well, I usually didn't let it come so far; I sought something out.

Q. Now your purchases in June had been heavy, and your purchases in July had been heavy, had they not?

A. Yes.

Q. July 12th you bought a hundred shares?

A. Yes.

Q. On the 17th, 500; on the 18th 300; 19th 1,000, another hundred in another block on the 19th; on the 20th a hundred, another block of 300, another one of 100. Now did you deposit on the 24th of July $4,500?

A. This date, $4,500; it was the last money Mr. Fisch put in.

Q. The last money he put in?

A. Yes.

Q. And that was July, 1933?

A. 24th of July, 1933.

Q. Will you mark that with an "F" please?

A. Because he put this money in, I bought very heavy in this month for him; I bought 500 U. S. Molasses—

Q. A little louder please.

A. Three hundred U. S. Leather, 100 Bethlehem Steel, another 500 Molasses, 100 St. Paul preferred, 25 shares Byers, and another hundred additional shares of U. S. Molasses. That is what he bought in July, from the 17th on to the 25th.

Q. Now during July is it a fact that you had purchased—go back to the last sheet, the sheet before this, please—about 4,350 shares of different stocks?

A. How many hundred, you say.

Q. 4,350.

A. That's about right.

Q. And you sold, did you not, about 3,150 shares?

A. Yes, around 3,000.

Richard Hauptmann

Q. And Fisch put in $4,500 in cash to cover the overlapping margin: is that correct?

A. Yes, because I bought very lightly this month for myself.

Q. And you did in that month about $49,300 worth of business on the books of Steiner-Rouse: is that right?

A. Yes.

Q. Where you had done the month before $50,000?

A. Yes.

Q. Your balance the month before, the debit balance that you owed Steiner-Rouse & Company was $7,973.72?

A. Correct.

Q. And it had been reduced by profits and deposits at the end of July to $4,038 debit?

A. That is right.

Q. You had quite a block of stock at the end of July, didn't you, on deposit with Steiner-Rouse? There are several blocks of individual concerns and corporations?

A. Yes.

Q. Covering about fifteen different corporations?

A. That is right, fifteen.

Q. And you had bought that on margin: Correct?

A. Well, the margin account was $4,038.04.

Q. Now you began to trade quite extensively, did you not, beginning August 1st?

A. Yes.

Q. And trading means buying and selling, doesn't it?

A. Buying and selling.

Q. Now coming down into August, I see a deposit of $7.50, what is that, a dividend?

A. Oh, I really don't know where dis comes from, $7.50.

Q. Then I find on the 10th a check for $112.50?

A. Yes, dis was a dividend check from our mortgage.

Q. And I find no more cash deposited for the balance of that sheet, am I correct?

Classics of the Courtroom

A. Correct.

Q. Now I refer you to the next sheet, which has at the top August 18th?

A. Will you mark out what I bought for Mr. Fisch, dis—

Q. Yes, please tell us what you bought for Mr. Fisch.

A. On August 1st, 100 Bethlehem Steel.

Q. Mark them with an "F", please.

A. And August 11th was 500 Warner Brother Pictures and August 14th and 15th, 500 Eitingon-Schild.

Q. Now we will pass to the next one. Now the top of the sheet shows, does it not, trading on the 18th, 21st, 23rd and 28th as to purchases?

A. Yes.

Q. And no sales?

A. That is right, there was no sale.

Q. So, from the purchases which amounted to, between the 15th of August to the 28th of August, the purchases were about $35,000, weren't they?

A. For which date you mean?

Q. The top of the sheet, the 18th down—

A. Yes.

Q. And you did in that month with Steiner-Rouse & Company $75,000 worth of business, didn't you?

A. Yes.

Q. And through sales and profits, with no cash placed into the account at all, except $7.50 and a dividend check of $112.50—

A. Yes.

Q. The balance stood as you and Fisch indebted to Steiner-Rouse on August 31st, $11,735.90.

A. Debit, yes.

Q. That you owed them, right?

A. Yes.

Q. Then they were carrying quite an extensive block of stocks, weren't they on August the 31st?

A. Yes, quite a lot.

Richard Hauptmann

Q. They were carrying, were they not, 1, 2, 3, 4, 5, 6, 7, 8, 9, 10, 11, 12, 13, 14—14 different corporations?

A. You mean in August 31st?

Q. Yes.

A. Yes.

MR. WILENTZ: May I inquire who was carrying this stock?

MR. REILLY: Steiner-Rouse.

MR. WILENTZ: I understood it was the defendant and his partner Fisch.

Q. The house was carrying this stock, was it not?

A. The house.

Q. As against your deficiency or debit balance?

A. The house was carrying everything against me.

Q. Now, so there will be no mistake, were they carrying 15 different kinds of stock?

A. Fourteen, that is right.

Q. Fourteen?

A. Yes. And going back to the month of August. I bought for Mr. Fisch 300 Alaska-Juneau and 300 shares cost $9,045.

Q. Now, I again refer you to—Are you through with Mr. Fisch's purchases for that month?

A. I am through, yes.

Q. Now, the 14 different blocks of stocks they were holding as against your debit balance on August 31st, were they holding 5900 shares of stock in those 14 corporations?

A. I count 5700.

Q. Well, I will take your word for it. The air in this room is making my glasses dizzy anyhow. Now, on September 14th did you start trading again?

A. Yes.

Q. And you bought on the 14th, the 18th, 22nd, 26th and 29th, didn't you?

A. Yes.

Q. You sold on the 14th, 25th, 26th, 28th—27th and 28th; right?

A. Yes; yes.

Q. Now, is it a fact, reading from the sheet you have before you now, that at the end of September, when the house struck a balance with you and Fisch, or with you as the party on the books buying for Anna Schoeffler, the balance, the debit balance had grown to $22,172.96?

A. That's correct.

Q. A jump of over $10,000 on the debit side in a month?

A. Yes.

Q. Correct?

A. Yes.

Q. But no cash was placed in the account up to the 29th of September, from the 18th of August: is that correct?

A. That's correct. To explain the paying in the month of September, in this month I didn't for my person—I didn't pay anything at all; the paying in the month of September was the account of Mr. Fisch.

Q. Well, it doesn't appear from my sheet that any cash was deposited with Steiner-Rouse—

A. Yes, but Mr. Fisch—it wasn't necessary for Mr. Fisch to put any cash up.

Q. The stock was carrying itself?

A. Yes.

Q. The point I make is that there was no cash deposited.

A. No.

Q. Although they allowed your balance to jump $10,000: is that right?

A. Yes. That means we was heavy on margin.

Q. Now we will turn to the next sheet, please, and on October 9th you began to trade; correct? Rather on the 9th you began to buy.

A. Yes.

Q. But on the 2nd you began to sell, is that right?

A. October 9th I bought.

Q. Now on October 2nd you began to sell, is that right?

A. That is right.

Q. Is that what they call selling off?

A. Oh, I don't say that is selling off.

Q. But you were selling anyhow?

A. I was selling.

Q. You sold on the 2nd, 3rd and on the 10th, right?

A. Yes.

Q. 17th, 19th, 23rd, 25th, 27th and 31st, is that right?

A. That is right.

Q. And your operations in buying and selling during that month?

A. It was $46,500—$46,592.93.

Q. And your balance due the firm dropped from 22,000 to 6,000, right?

A. No. Balance dropped to $1,380.

Q. What is that?

A. To $1,380.

Q. Where is that?

A. (Indicating on the exhibit.)

Q. That was a dividend. The balance then you say dropped to $1,380.16?

A. Yes.

Q. From 22,000 the month before?

A. Yes.

Q. Because of your excessive sales, right?

A. That is right.

Q. Now I notice in here on October 19th an item which says "From commodity account $1,615.35." Do you see it?

A. Yes, I do.

Q. What does that mean?

A. I guess at this time I bought cotton or wheat, I am not quite sure.

Q. Does that mean that you were dealing in foodstuffs and grain?

A. Yes.

Q. Through some other house or through a different branch of this house?

A. That is through the same house. They handled, I am not quite

Classics of the Courtroom

sure if it is silver, cotton or wheat.

Q. It was a sell-off anyhow, wasn't it, it was a sale?

A. Wait a minute. No, it is only a transfer. You handle commodities, you handle that separate from stock account.

Q. Now looking at the sheet you have before you which begins on the purchase side, September 30th, and on the sales side October 2nd, 1933, running down the column of sales, down to the end of the month of October when your balance was $1380.16, there was no cash placed in the account that month, was there?

A. Except $27.22, that is a dividend.

Q. That wouldn't be considered cash in Wall Street, would it?

A. No, I don't think so.

Q. Now, we begin the latter half of the sheet, which begins October 31st, 1933, and we find trading on November 1st, both purchases and sales, correct?

A. November 1st?

Q. November 1st.

A. You wouldn't mind to go back to October?

Q. We will go back to October, we will go back to any date at all.

A. To the 24th, that is the date I bought another additional 500 shares Eitingon-Schild for Mr. Fisch.

Q. For Fisch?

A. Yes.

Q. Was that Eitingon-Schild stock, machine?

A. No, that is a trading house in furs, Mr. Fisch was very interested in it.

Q. Do you find anything else for Fisch the upper part of the sheet there, you want to refer to?

A. No, that was only—

MR. WILENTZ: Don't lead him.

A. —only 500 shares.

Q. So now we pass to the latter half and bottom half of the sheet, don't we?

A. Yes.

Q. And the trading begins on November 1st, buying and selling, or rather, November the 1st you received a dividend, did you not, on 200 A.J., $57?

A. Yes, means Alaska-Juneau.

Q. And you began to buy on November the 1st?

A. Yes.

Q. Began to sell on the 6th: correct?

A. Yes.

Q. And the trading was quite active that month, was it not?

A. Well, I don't say so, quite active, compared with the last couple months this was.

Q. Only did about $21,000 that month?

A. Yeah.

Q. Now, I notice that your purchases and sales and your balance struck the end of November, the balance is $5,167.78—was it credit or debit?

A. That is debit balance.

Q. Debit?

A. Uh-huh.

Q. And reverting back now to the sheet before, used on October the 31st, and which began September the 30th, and ends with an item at the bottom of the page, November the 24th, I ask you to examine that sheet and tell me whether or not the only cash that was required in the account during that period was that $27.22, which was a dividend.

A. That means in month of October?

Q. That whole sheet right down to the bottom.

A. Yes; there is another dividend check for fifty-seven dollar from Alaska-Juneau, November the 1st.

Q. Yes. Well, outside of those two dividend checks there was no actual cash?

A. No; no cash.

Q. Now we come into December, the next sheet, November and December. You began to trade, did you, December 1st?

A. Yes, I did.

Q. Purchased on the 1st, sold on the 4th, back and forth, down to the end of the month; and no cash was placed in the account, was it?

A. No cash was placed. Would you mind to go back to the last sheet you got in your hands?

Q. Yes, you may go back to the last sheet.

A. There you find a check I took out for Mr. Fisch on November the 14th, $2,057.

Q. You drew that out of the account?

A. I drew it out from this account. There was a drawing on November the 2nd. That was for living.

Q. And what did you do with that check?

A. The big check, for $2,057, I cashed in the bank—I forgot the name of the bank, a bank on 86th Street.

Q. Who did you give the money to?

A. $2,000 I give to Mr. Fisch for his voyage to Germany; the rest I keep for myself, $57. There was a drawing on November 21st. That is the usual drawing I took out every month since then, a hundred or $150 a month.

Q. How much did you draw then on the 21st? $100?

A. $100 check.

Q. Now we will take this December account 1933. You did about $9,000 worth of transactions; correct?

A. That's correct.

Q. And you sold on the 4th, the 7th, the 12th, the 13th, the 14th, the 18th and the 29th?

A. Yes.

Q. And your balance, debit balance jumped to, or rather, it was only $1195.64, is that right?

A. That is right.

Q. And you used no cash that month, put no cash in the account.

A. No.

Q. But you did—

A. I took some.

Q. But you did take out some. Now is there any stock on that sheet that you want to explain or talk about?

A. No, from dis time on every stock you will find on the sheet belongs to me, there is no more paying for Mr. Fisch. From November 1st, 1933 Mr. Fisch was only interested in the loss or in the win. That is when we split.

Q. You mean November 1st, 1933, whatever stock was in the possession of Steiner-Rouse & Company, Fisch was interested in the profit and losses 50 percent?

A. Yes.

Q. But bought no more?

A. Bought no more. That is the date I said before I made a clean table.

Q. A clean table.

A. That is what I called it.

Q. Now we come to December 31st, 1933, and Fisch had already sailed for Europe, right?

A. Yes.

Q. And we find the January, 1934, account very active, don't we?

A. Yes.

Q. Buying the second, third, fourth, fifth, ninth, eleventh, twelfth, fifteenth, sixteenth, nineteenth, and twenty-fourth?

A. Yes.

Q. Selling, the third, fourth, fifth, tenth, seventeenth and eighteenth.

A. Yes, sir.

Q. And with all the trading necessary that month, you did not deposit any cash with Steiner-Rouse & Company?

A. (continuing) Yah; to correct my saying from the first, from the—

Q. Give us that again.

A. There was, I said every stock was belonging to me and nothing to Fisch there, excepting Fisch he got $2,500 left, but I can't make out without my big book which stock it was, so I left this one out.

Q. You mean he had an interest in some stock?

A. Yes, it was two thousand—

Q. $2500?

A. Yes, it was $2500. I can't make out which one it was.

Q. Now, in January when you were dealing for yourself, no cash was placed int he account was there?

A. No, there is only a little bit of eighty dollars.

Q. That was one check for $30, one for $50, that you got on the 2nd?

A. Yes.

Q. Now we come to February. The trading was quite active, wasn't it?

A. No, it wasn't active, very active.

Q. Well, on the 1st of February you sold a thousand shares, didn't you?

A. The selling was more as the buying.

Q. The selling was more than the buying?

A. Yes.

Q. The end of February your balance, debit balance, had dropped from $9,641.60 in January to $1313.03: is that right?

A. How much did you say?

Q. $1313.

A. $1,313.03.

Q. Now I notice on the 26th of February, cash was deposited with Steiner-Rouse & Company of $1350?

A. Yes.

Q. Where did that come from?

A. This cash is deposit on 26th of February and ten days before I took out a check from my account for $1,500. This money I lend to a friend of mine for paying a business but he couldn't agree, so he was giving back the money and I put it back in the market again.

Q. So the $1,350 which you deposited with Steiner, Rouse & Company on the 26th of February, am I correct in saying that that represents a portion of the $1,500 check you drew from Steiner- Rouse & Company on the 16th of February?

A. Yeah, that is right.

Q. And if you will examine your sheets that you have looked at heretofore from the last $4,500 deposited by Fisch in July, 1933, this item of $1,350 is the first cash deposited in the account with the exception of a couple of dividend checks since July 24th, the year before; is that correct?

A. That is correct.

Q. So the account was carrying itself August, September, October, November, December, January, and February without the inclusion of a dollar of your money except the dividends I have referred to?

A. That is correct.

Q. And then this item which you now explain, you say, as a matter practically of cross-bookkeeping, taking money out and putting it in again within a few days?

A. Yes.

Q. And your balance I think you have testified to. Now we come to March, 1934; and you traded beginning the first by collecting some dividends, $50, another one of 18 cents; correct?

A. Excuse me, don't go too fast; I can't follow.

Q. Take all the time you want. If I am going too fast just refer to anything you want.

A. There was on March the 1st—

Q. I said March the 1st you collected a couple of dividends, is that correct?

A. Yes, $50 and 18 cents.

Q. $50 on one and 18 cents on another, right?

A. Yes.

Q. And you began to buy on the 5th, didn't you?

A. Yes.

Q. You began to sell on the 6th?

A. Yes.

Q. And your balance at the end of the month, the 31st of March, the debit balance was how much?

A. It was $12,746.08.

Q. So that independent and irrespective of the fact that your balance which you owed Steiner-Rouse in February was only $1300, you bought stocks in March which brought your debit balance to $12,000; no cash was placed in the account; correct?

A. That's right.

Q. Taking the bottom of the sheet we find a sale on April the 3rd of 100 General Motors for $3780.50; correct?

A. That's correct.

Q. Now is there anything on that sheet, before we pass it, you would like to explain?

A. Yes, on the two checks I took out; that is for my living the monthly checks I took out. I say as I explained, since Mr. Fisch left for Germany there wasn't any more profit from the fur account coming in.

Q. From the fur account?

A. Yes. Before, I used always the money coming in for fur account for my living and for expenses; and if you follow the sheet, since he left for Europe, I drew the living out from my stock account.

Q. That explains the drawing of the check on April 2nd for $150?

A. Yes.

Q. Is there anything else on that sheet that you would like to explain?

A. No; really not.

Q. Now we will pass to the April 9th sheet, keeping in mind that your debit balance was $12,746. You traded during the month of April, buying and selling: correct?

A. That is correct.

Q. And at the end of April your balance had decreased to $11,144.94: correct?

A. That is correct.

Q. And during the month you did close on to $30,000 worth of trading, $27,000 some odd?

A. Yes, that is right.

Q. And no cash placed in the account?

A. No. I only took out a check of $50.

Q. Now we come to May, we find that you took a check for $350 May 4th.

A. Yes.

Q. And you traded on the 10th, 14th and 21st and also on the 31st— No, you didn't; those are balances struck—May 10th, 14th and 21st were your purchases: is that correct?

A. That is right.

Q. Your sales ran along the 3rd, 4th, 8th, 9th and 14th?

A. That is correct.

Q. You reduced your balance from $11,000 to $9,000, didn't you?

A. That is correct.

Q. And you put no cash into the account?

A. No, I did not.

Q. Then on June 1st you sold, rather you obtained a dividend of $25?

A. Yes.

Q. And on the 7th sold off 400 Universal Pipe, was it?

A. Universal Pipe & Rad., radiator.

Q. And you reduced your balance, or rather, you reduced your balance for the month of June to $6,511.57?

A. Yes.

Q. And put no cash in your account?

A. No.

Q. Now we come to the middle of that sheet which brings up to the end of July, 1934, and you traded on the 18th by selling off and on the 26th by purchase?

A. Yes.

Q. 27th by a purchase?

A. Yes.

Q. 30th by a purchase?

A. Yes.

Q. 26th, 31st, by a sale?

A. Yes.

Q. The balance of $6,500 as of June, 1934, was reduced to $3,800 at the end of July?

A. That is correct.

Q. And no cash in to take up the slack?

A. No cash—took out two checks, one seven-five and one check $25.

Q. You took out $175 during July, right?

A. Yes.

Q. In two checks?

A. Two.

Q. Now we come to August, 1934, and we have you selling off on the 1st, the 6th, the 14th, the 15th and the 31st.

A. Yes.

Q. We have your balance reduced from $3,800 to $2,200.

A. That is right.

Q. And no cash deposited as a set off.

A. No, there is only a liquidated dividend from National Bellas-Hess—That is liquidated dividend of $350.

Q. That was a dividend from the National what?

A. National Bellas-Hess.

Q. National Bellas—

A. Hess preferred.

Q. Preferred. So you left the dividend stay there?

A. Yes.

Q. But you didn't go out anywhere and get any Lindbergh money and put $350 in the account, did you?

A. Certainly not.

Q. Now we come to August the 31st which is a small sheet, white.

A. Yes.

Q. We find you in September selling off on the 13th and the 14th, right? It is rather hard to read it.

A. I hardly can read it.

Q. Well, if you need any help we will give you a couple of these other ones. Maybe they are a little bit better. Look at that one, please.

A. It is a little bit better.

Q. All right. You can use that one and give me the bad one. Now, looking at that month, the balance of $2,233 at the end of July had been reduced to $1242.41, hadn't it?

A. No, that is not a debit, that is a—

Q. Credit?

A. A credit balance.

Q. Well, then, the old balance, the old debit, had been wiped out, you were out of the red and you were in the black for $1,242.41: is that right? You were to the good?

A. Yes.

Q. And no cash used by you that month, was there?

A. No; only a $25 dividend from Purity Bakery.

Q. Well, of course, that was merely a bookkeeping item, wasn't it, the $25 dividend? You left it there?

A. Yes, I left it there.

Q. So now we are at the end of this account?

A. That is the end of it.

Q. And I will swap with you again, because this belongs to somebody else (handing another photostatic copy to the witness). Now, let me ask you this question: from the day that Fisch put the $4,500 in, in July 1933, until September the 14th, 1934, when this account was totalled and closed, as a matter of bookkeeping, so far as we are concerned on the sheet, isn't it a fact that the only cash that you put into this account was small dividend checks and a cross item of $1,350 of the $1,500 check that you drew?

A. That's correct.

Q. Now, I want to go back, if you will, please, to your bank account. You will need your pencil. I want you to look at the deposits made in your bank account from March the 1st, 1932—

A. March the 1st, 1932?

Q. 1932. That is the date of the kidnaping, down to date; tell the jury what those deposits are, what they represent.

Q. You have one of those there, one of these (indicating file of photostatic copies)?

A. Yes, I have.

Q. Have you the set?

A. Yes, just a second, please.

Q. Is that it?

A. Central?

Q. Central Savings Bank. I am just going to direct your attention to a few of these deposits, I want you to go down the list with me and see if I am right. We will begin with the 11th day of January, 1932,

1/11/32. Have you got it there?

A. I have it.

Q. All right, deposit of $125, right?

A. Yes.

Q. April 5th, $87?

A. Yes.

Q. The 8th, $27?

A. Yes.

Q. 16th, $166?

A. Yes.

Q. 25th, $41?

A. Yes.

Q. May 4th, $55?

A. Yes.

Q. 9th of May, withdrawal $430?

A. Yes.

Q. What was that for?

A. $430, I was giving to Mr. Fisch to buy fur and another additional $170 came from the $4,300 I left home. I got home, I mean.

Q. On the 16th a deposit of $200?

A. Yes.

Q. And on the 23rd, $116?

A. Yes.

Q. And several small deposits running all under $200 down to August, 1932, when you drew out $837?

A. Yes.

Q. What was that for?

A. $837 I put in fur to Mr. Fisch.

Q. Now on the 25th you put back $817.35.

A. Them $817.35 comes from the stock account.

Q. From the stock account?

A. Yes, if you look the stock account over you will find one check.

Q. Whose check?

A. Check deposits was over $700.

Q. On September 12th, 1932, you drew out $350, on the 19th you put back $250. Will you explain that?

A. Will you go over again?

Q. At the bottom of the page.

A. Yes.

Q. 350 out and 250 in.

A. Yes, that was $350 I put in to Mr. Fisch, to pay certain furs, and he sold that a week later, I took out the profit $250, I put the profit in the bank and left the additional $350, give to Mr. Fisch.

Q. So you drew out $350 on the 12th and you put $250 back on the 19th, one week later?

A. Yes.

Q. On the next page, on the 19th of September you drew out $500?

A. Them $500 went to the stock account.

Q. And on the 26th you put back $150?

A. On the 5th that was profit on fur for Mr. Fisch, all them three.

Q. All three. 150, 147 and 140, is that right?

A. Yes, that is right.

Q. All those three items in less than a month you say were profits from fur.

A. Yes.

Q. December 7th, 1932, you draw out $800?

A. Yes.

Q. What was that for?

A. Them $800 from the $4,300 I got in my house, I took $1,750 and $800 I took out from the bank and $1200 was from fur account, and with this money I paid a mortgage on first January on 1933.

Q. You paid a mortgage or bought a mortgage?

A. I bought a mortgage.

Q. That mortgage of $3750—

A. That is the mortgage.

Q. —which is offered in evidence here?

A. Yes.

Classics of the Courtroom

Q. All right. Now figure that up again and show us where you got the $3750 from.

A. It was thousand seven hundred fifty from the $4,300 I got home.

Q. Cash in the house?

A. Cash in the house, eight hundred dollar I took from the bank and $1200 was from fur account.

Q. From the fur account?

A. Yes. Made up them $3,750.

Q. And that is the money you took to the lawyer at the end of December 1932 and bought that mortgage with?

A. That is the money I brought to Mr. Burkard.

Q. The lawyer that was on the stand?

A. The lawyer that was on the stand.

Q. Now you put $1400 in bank on the 10th of January, 1933?

A. I put in the bank $1,400 in January, '33, 10th.

Q. Where did you get it?

A. Yes. This money Isidor Fisch said I should put it in the bank, in the stock account. But my account was strong enough to carry his buying. So I didn't put it in the stock account; I put it in my bank. That's just the same as mine, because I got money left; there was not much buying from my side on, it wasn't necessary. So I only made out a slip and deposited it.

Q. Now on March the 13th, 1933, you deposited $1250?

A. March 15th, 1933, $1250. That's the money when President Roosevelt called in all the gold certificates and the gold coin. I put in $750 in gold certificates and $500 in gold coin.

Q. And the gold certificates were not Lindy gold notes, were they?

A. Them gold certificates—that's the rest from the money, from the $4,300. I didn't put them gold certificates in the bank before, or not in the stock market either. My intention was to keep them gold certificates and them gold coin.

Q. Why?

A. Please?

Q. Why?

A. I thought I would play safe on account of inflation, but according to President Roosevelt's declaration, I put it in the bank.

Q. And when you put the $750 in gold notes in, you made out a deposit slip?

A. I did.

Q. And you handed it in the window?

A. I did.

Q. In a bank that you had been trading with for years and years, is that correct?

A. Trading for eight years.

Q. Eight years. And you made out the slip in your name, did you, Anna Hauptmann or Richard Hauptmann, when you deposited it, a deposit slip?

A. I don't know if I made out Anna Hauptmann or Richard Hauptmann. I really don't know.

Q. Well, you made it out either one, didn't you?

A. Either one.

Q. And the date?

A. And the date, yes.

Q. And the date, and handed it in?

A. Yes.

Q. And nobody came around the next day and said, "Mr. Hauptmann, you have deposited $750 gold Lindy notes," did they?

A. Nobody came around, because there was $50 gold notes and I guess two or three hundred dollar gold notes, too.

Q. Now I notice that on the 25th of March, 1933, you had a balance in bank of $2,528.35. That money was transferred then to Anna Schoeffler's account, wasn't it?

A. Yes.

Q. March 25th, 1933. Now why did you transfer your account, your joint account, to Anna Schoeffler's account in March, 1933?

A. The reason was I got in an automobile accident in New York and I run over a man, but it was entirely not my fault. This man was standing behind the elevated post, the road was very slippy and in the same moment I was going to pass the elevated post and he was stepping right in front of me and he slipped and I went over his leg, and on account of that I was afraid. This gentleman happened to be a lawyer, the gentleman I run over, his name is—I just can't get it just now—and that is the reason I transferred the account in my wife's name, the stock account and the bank account. That is the reason for it. I thought he was going to sue me. It was not my fault. I settled with the lawyer. I guess he know it himself I was right. We was going to settle for $250, well, finally we settled for $350, made an agreement and I agreed to pay him weekly according to my wages and I paid him so far I guess it is close to $300.

Q. When was the accident?

A. It was a couple day before the transfer from the accounts from my name to my wife's maiden name.

Q. Now, here is a deposit July 20th, 1933, $2,112.50.

A. From dis deposit was $2,000 I should put it in the stock account, the same transaction as before. I didn't put it in an account; I got enough money in the stock account, because I did not much trading after the July 1933, I got idle money and that is the money I didn't put it in.

Q. Who gave you the money?

A. From Mr. Fisch—So I put it in my bank account $2,000—$112.50 was a check, a dividend check from our mortgage.

Q. You drew out on the 18th of January, 1934, $2,500.04.

A. This money I drawed out and put it in the stock account to Pierce.

Q. Who?

A. Pierce.

Q. What is their name—Pierce?

A. Pierce & Company, Wall Street, No. 40. That is the account I have over here.

Q. So that $2,500 matches your initial deposit to—

A. Pierce & Company.

Q. Pierce & Company?

A. That is right.

Q. They don't put any names on these. Oh, here it is. E. A. Pierce & Company, right?

A. Right.

Q. What is their address?

A. That is 40 Wall Street.

Q. Then that is the last large withdrawal until after you were arrested?

A. Yes, that is right.

Q. And then the next one went to a lawyer, is that right?

A. The next one went to the lawyer.

Q. And he is not here?

A. He is not here.

Q. Now that explains your bank accounts, correct?

A. Explains—

Q. Is there anything else—

A. Bank account.

Q. (Continuing) You would like to point out there?

A. No, I am finished.

Q. I am calling your attention now to the young lady, Miss Alexander, who says some time in March, 1932—am I correct, General, March?

(Mr. Wilentz nodded affirmatively.)

Q. (Continued) She saw standing in a railroad station, in the upper part of the Bronx, I think she described it as the Pelham New York Central Railroad station, that Dr. Condon was in front of you, he was very much excited, he was talking to a telegrapher, and you were standing at one side of the room looking at him. Were you ever in that station?

A. I never was in this railroad station. I just happened—I know the railroad station, but I never was in there, had nothing to do in any railroad station.

Q. And you were never there when Dr. Condon was there?

A. Didn't know Dr. Condon.

Q. Did you ever see that girl before she took the witness stand?

A. Never saw her.

Q. Now just one more—

A. That is your pencil.

Q. Thank you. I want you to explain, please, to the jury about whether or not you had any money in this tin can?

A. That is about $12,000 in gold certificates in that can.

Q. Gold certificates?

A. In gold certificates.

Q. When?

A. It is about one week or two weeks before I got arrested.

Q. And did you have some money in this board that was offered in evidence?

A. I did.

Q. Rolled up?

A. I did.

Q. How much did you have there?

A. I can't remember how much it was.

Q. You said if you had a big book here you could figure your stock transactions better, is that right?

A. The accounts only on our settlement on the 1st of November, 1933.

Q. Where is that big book?

A. I guess it is in the possession of the police.

Q. Did you see them take it away?

A. No, I did not, but I suppose so.

Q. Now, when you were taken to the New York City Police station, were you beaten by the police?

MR. WILENTZ: I object to it.

A. I was.

MR. WILENTZ: Just a minute now. I object to it as not being material to this cause.

MR. REILLY: I will connect it. I will connect it.

MR. WILENTZ: Well, now just wait a minute. There is no confession or any statement in this case, if your Honor please, and the State of New Jersey does not want to be impeded or handicapped by any matters that do not concern this State. If we were presenting some document or confession that was obtained, or it was claimed was obtained in New York as the result of something that is now inferred, why, I take it that there might be some basis; but the only purpose of this question is one that is not material to this cause.

MR. REILLY: I can connect it.

MR. WILENTZ: And it cannot be connected with any instrument that is in evidence by the State of New Jersey.

MR. REILLY: Oh, yes, it can.

MR. WILENTZ: Your Honor, so far as I can recall, the only things that came in were admitted handwritings, and your Honor gave defense the opportunity then to present such testimony as they saw fit, or such testimony as they could, to indicate that those statements were not given voluntarily. If there was some duress or some alleged force or something like that, that was the time; and I take it that there is no effort made now, so far as those statements are concerned, to indicate that this was done.

MR. REILLY: The statements—

THE COURT: Well, I do not know what the purpose is now, except as indicated by the question. You will recall that when certain documents were being introduced by the police for the State, the inquiry was made by the State whether or not those papers were executed voluntarily. Now if it be competent for the State to show that they were executed voluntarily, I would think, by the same token, it would be competent for the defendant to say what he had to say with respect to their voluntary character.

MR. WILENTZ: Up to that time, with reference to those statements.

THE COURT: Yes.

MR. WILENTZ: I have no objection to that if your Honor please.

THE COURT: All right. Now you may proceed.

MR. WILENTZ: If it is limited to that extent, up to the date of the taking of those papers, or any other things that we did.

THE COURT: Yes.

BY MR. REILLY:

Q. Well, what date were you arrested?

A. September 19th, 1934.

Q. 1934?

A. 1934.

Q. And in time you landed in the Greenwich Station House, didn't you?

Classics of the Courtroom

A. Yes.

Q. How long were you there before anybody asked you to write anything?

A. My recollection, my best recollection is it was night time.

Q. What time were you brought in, in the day time?

A. Yes.

Q. Now, during the period between the time you were brought in and the time you were asked to write and give certain exhibitions of your handwriting and samples, were you beaten in that station house?

A. Not in this time.

Q. Well now, when were you beaten?

MR. WILENTZ: I object to that, if your Honor please.

MR. REILLY: We have in evidence here a certain transcript of a statement he is supposed to have made to an Assistant District Attorney in the Bronx. Read by some stenographer.

MR. WILENTZ: If the question is as to any beating made in the Bronx at that time, I will withdraw that objection.

MR. REILLY: He might have been beaten downtown and taken to the Bronx.

MR. WILENTZ: I am talking about statements made in the Bronx.

MR. REILLY: Beatings, not statements.

MR. WILENTZ: If statements were made in the Bronx and they were the result of beatings in the Bronx or the result of beatings downtown preceding the statement, I will withdraw the objection.

MR. REILLY: Let's find out when he got the beating. (Laughter.)

MR. WILENTZ: No. I object to that question: if he had any.

THE COURT: It is the business of the officers to take those folks that are interrupting this trial out of the room. Where are the officers? I want the officers to be diligent. If I were down there on the floor I could identify these people that are making this confusion and are laughing at times when I don't think there is any occasion for laughing at all. I want the officers to take those people out of the courtroom and, in flagrant cases, I want them brought up here in front of the desk and I am going to deal with them and I may mark them up quite some considerable, before I get through with them. I won't have this ribald stuff in this courtroom.

THE COURT: Now Mr. Attorney General.

MR. WILENTZ: Now if your Honor please, particularly with reference to the statements in the Bronx. Now, we are away from the statements that are in evidence as admitted writings. Now counsel is up to a statement made in the Bronx, and my recollection is that the statement with reference to the Bronx was given by a stenographer here, an official stenographer.

Let me refresh counsel's recollection about that. Specifically in that statement were the questions and answers with reference to his treatment by District Attorney Foley.

THE COURT: Yes.

MR. WILENTZ: "Hauptmann, have you been treated all right? Have you gotten everything you wanted? Have you had your lawyer here? Have you had your wife here? Have you had all the freedom that you wanted?" All of which was, "Yes."

Now, if it is contended that in making that very statement, and that is the statement we were talking about, that is the statement, apparently, counsel refers to, that that statement was brought about by duress, by intimidation, improperly, in any way, then certainly I wouldn't object and wouldn't want to use the statement, but if this is just an effort to talk about some alleged beating at some other time, merely for the purpose of attempting to attract some sympathy to this defendant, that has absolutely nothing to do with this case.

MR. REILLY: No, that has nothing to do with that at all.

MR. WILENTZ: Under those circumstances, I object. I do not object to any statement that we produce here or proving whether we got it through intimidation, beating, force or anything else.

THE COURT: Well, that I understand to be Mr. Reilly's proposition, to prove that these statements were not voluntarily made, because they were made through some sort of threat or intimidation.

MR. WILENTZ: I don't understand that to be the fact.

THE COURT: I don't know. I rather suppose—

MR. REILLY: I have to find out—

THE COURT: I rather suppose that is so.

MR. REILLY: I have to find out what hour it was.

THE COURT: Now, Mr. Reilly, suppose that you limit your present examination to finding out at what point of time it is that you think your man was under duress.

MR. REILLY: That is what I asked him: at what time you were beaten if you were beaten.

THE COURT: Yes. Well, now, let him tell.

MR. REILLY: It is a simple question.

BY MR. REILLY:

Q. Were you beaten—yes or no?

A. Yes, sir.

Q. When did it start?

A. The second night when I got arrested.

Q. Where were you?

A. New York Police station.

Q. After that were you taken to the Bronx?

A. After that I was taken to the Bronx.

Q. How long were you in the station house and how long did they beat you?

MR. WILENTZ: I object to that, if your Honor please, until it is connected.

MR. REILLY: Withdrawn.

Q. What did they do with you?

MR. WILENTZ: I object to that, if your Honor please.

MR. REILLY: He says it was before he went to the Bronx.

MR. WILENTZ: All right. He is up in the Bronx—

MR. REILLY: He is not up in the Bronx. I want to know what they did to him.

MR. WILENTZ: You had him up in the Bronx—

MR. REILLY: I asked him how long after he went to the Bronx. Don't let's quibble.

MR. WILENTZ: I am not quibbling. I object to the question unless it is connected to the statement in this case.

MR. REILLY: He certainly was down in New York and he went to the Bronx after he was beaten.

THE COURT: The proposition as I understand it is to prove duress preliminary to some of these statements.

MR. WILENTZ: All right. May I reserve my right to strike out the answers if they are not connected in that way?

THE COURT: Surely you may.

MR. WILENTZ: All right, then I won't interfere.

BY MR. REILLY:

Q. Tell us what they did to you in the Greenwich Street station, if that is the station in which you were beaten.

MR. WILENTZ: I submit the matter of time is the thing.

THE COURT: The matter of time is important, Mr. Reilly.

MR. WILENTZ: Yes.

Q. You were arrested—I will go back now, I tried to take a shortcut, but apparently it won't do—you were arrested on the street, weren't you?

A. I was.

Q. And you were held for some hours in your car, is that right?

A. Yes.

Q. Then they put handcuffs on your hands, didn't they?

A. Right away.

Q. Then you were searched, were you?

A. Yes.

Q. And in your wallet what did they find?

A. Twenty dollar bill.

Q. Then where did they take you?

A. Took me Gun Hill Road and White Plains Avenue.

Q. Then did they take you back to your house?

A. Yes.

Q. Then did they search the house?

A. Yes.

Q. Then were you told it was Lindbergh money?

A. It was told me in the house. That is the first time I hear it, I got Lindbergh money in my possession.

Q. Never knew it before?

A. Never know it.

Q. Then where did they take you from your house?

A. To the Central Savings Bank.

Q. They searched your safe deposit box, didn't they?

A. Yes.

Q. No money was there?

A. No money.

Q. Then where was the next place they took you?

A. The next place was, it was a police station, Greenwich Street.

Q. That was that night, the first night?

A. It was the first night.

Q. You hadn't been to the Bronx yet?

A. No, sir.

Q. Now, in the station the first night, what did they do to you, if anything?

A. The first night they required the request writing.

Q. Yes. Now, in writing did you spell the words of your own free will or did they tell you how to spell the words?

A. Some of them words they spell it to me.

Q. How do you spell "not"?

A. N-o-t.

Q. Did they ask you to spell it n-o-t-e?

A. I remember very well they put a "e" on it.

Q. How do you spell "signature"?

A. S-i-g-n-u-t-u-r-e.

Q. Did they tell you to spell it s-i-n-g?

A. They did.

Q. —n-a-t-u-r-e?

A. They did.

Q. "Singnature"?

A. They did.

Q. So when they were dictating the spelling, that was not your own free will in spelling, was it?

A. It was not.

MR. WILENTZ: That is Mr. Reilly's witness and his testimony, and I object to it.

THE COURT: Well, Mr. Reilly, that is rather leading.

MR. WILENTZ: Yes.

THE COURT: You see, this man is your witness.

MR. REILLY: Yes.

THE COURT: I will request you to refrain from leading.

BY MR. REILLY:

Q. Well, when you wrote s-i-n-g-, "singnature," it was not the way you usually spelled it, or ever spelled it: is that correct?

MR. WILENTZ: I object to the question as being leading, and offensively leading.

MR. REILLY: That isn't leading. He has already spelled "signature."

MR. WILENTZ: That is not the fact.

THE COURT: You may ask him whether or not the writing that he did was his voluntary act.

BY MR. REILLY:

Q. As far as the spelling of these words that I have indicated, and other words that are misspelled in these request writings of yours, was that your voluntary spelling or your voluntary act, or was it the act and spelling dictated to you by policemen and officials who wanted you to write it that way?

A. It was because of the dictation.

Q. Now some written that night, were they?

A. Yes.

Q. And in that writing, they kept on for how many hours?

A. I can't remember exactly the time of the request writing, but I know real well it was late, it was really late in night time, probably after 12 o'clock. I refused to write.

Q. What did they do to you?

A. They forced me. They said, "You won't get any sleep, you got to write."

Q. Did they do anything to you physically?

A. Not exactly, but they didn't give me any chance to sleep.

Q. Did they give you any chance to eat?

Classics of the Courtroom

THE COURT: Sleep, as I understood.

THE WITNESS: Sleep.

MR. REILLY: I am asking now about any chance to eat.

Q. Did you get anything to eat?

A. I can't remember if I was asked for anything to eat at all or not.

Q. Over what period did the so-called request writings, how long a period was it in all before they finished with you as far as the writings were concerned?

A. From the hour of my arrest to I'd say around two o'clock in the morning the next day.

Q. And how many times did he request you to write?

A. I can't recall how many times.

Q. Many times?

A. Many times. I fell asleep on a chair when they poked me in the ribs and said, "You write."

Q. Who poked you in the ribs?

A. I can't recall.

Q. What with?

A. With the hand.

Q. While you were in that room or in that station house, were you hit with anything else besides the hand?

MR. WILENTZ: Before the writing or after the writing, may we know?

THE COURT: Yes, this is before the writing.

MR. WILENTZ: Before the writing.

Q. Were you hit with anything before the writing?

A. No.

Q. Were you hit during the writing during the different periods that you wrote?

A. I got a couple knocks in the—in the ribs, when I refused to write.

Q. After the writing, before you went to the Bronx, did you get any knocks of any kind?

A. Well, that is—I got the treatment, it wasn't home at all.

Q. Well, tell us about it and when was it.

A. It was in the evening, the next day.

Q. Where?

A. The 20th.

Q. What station house?

A. New York police station—at the Greenwich Street—

Q. Greenwich Street?

A. Greenwich Street.

Q. Before you went to the Bronx?

A. yes.

Q. Now, what was the treatment?

MR. WILENTZ: Just wait one minute. If your Honor please, I just want to say to your Honor unless counsel feels and knows that this is going to connect up with the statements that were made by him in The Bronx, I don't think that the question should be permitted and the answer should be permitted, and I think counsel knows that they are not connected with the statements in the Bronx. If he doesn't that is different.

MR. REILLY: I think that any man who is taken into custody as he was, who was subjected to the treatment that he is about to testify to, in the belief that he also falsely confessed to some things that he is not guilty of, and then he is taken before a District Attorney in another County, with a mind that remembers his treatment below and his physical condition, that any statement, no matter what he made in the Bronx, should be excluded after he got the treatment that he received in Greenwich Street.

THE COURT: You are now proposing to move for the exclusion of these statements?

MR. REILLY: Well, I will leave that to Mr. Pope, who knows the law of this State much better than me, when we get to that, sir.

THE COURT: Well, is there any such motion as that pending?

MR. POPE: No, your Honor. Our contention will be that it will be for the jury to consider the treatment that this man received at the hands of the police, and then it will be for them to say how much credit they will give to the treatment, after he receives that treatment.

THE COURT: What statements are you referring to now?

Classics of the Courtroom

MR. POPE: The statements which were made in the Bronx and which were read here, question and answer, in evidence.

MR. WILENTZ: That particular statement is the statement, if your Honor please, in which the specific questions were read to him, "Have you been treated all right here? Did you make this as your voluntary statement? Haven't you been permitted all these various liberties" and so forth and so on. That is the statement.

MR. REILLY: Now, to my mind that is—pardon me, General.

THE WITNESS: I—

MR. WILENTZ: Just a moment now.

THE COURT: No.

MR. REILLY: To my mind that indicates nothing, because a man who has undergone one set of those treatments might be asked those questions and in fear he would say "Yes," not wanting a second treatment, still in the custody of the police.

THE COURT: I think that anything that has a reasonable relation to these statements and made prior thereto in the nature of showing duress is admissible, and that will be admitted. But I am asking counsel to confine themselves to the limitation that I have made.

MR. REILLY: I accept.

Q. Now, I ask you what you say the treatment was that you received before you went to the Bronx and made any statement to any District Attorney or anyone in the Bronx.

MR. WILENTZ: I object to the question, if your Honor please, and may I suggest rather than continue this controversy that I should have no objection to a question as to whether or not any statement he made in the Bronx was the result of duress or improper treatment. I have no means of controlling counsel's questions, of course, but I make the suggestion very respectfully.

MR. REILLY: They are delightful and will always be accepted in line with the good taste in which they are offered.

Q. I will ask you, Bruno, was the statement in the Bronx that you made, were you mindful and fearful of the treatment that you had received downtown in New York when you made the statement in the Bronx?

A. To explain this: When Mr. District Attorney Foley was asking me how did they treat me, the coppers in the Bronx, only the treatment in the Bronx jail and in the Bronx court house, but that did not cover the treatment in the New York police station. I said the treatment in the Bronx jail and in the court house to Mr. District Attorney Foley was fair, but it covers only the Bronx, but the treatment in the police station in New York, it was entirely different, it was just the opposite way. I got the effect from this treatment for two months, that is the reason I lost over thirty pounds.

Q. Well, did you have that in mind when you made the statement in the District Attorney's office in the Bronx?

MR. WILENTZ: I object to it.

A. I only got in my mind the treatment from the Bronx, not the treatment from the police station.

MR. REILLY: I think that is his answer.

....

CROSS EXAMINATION BY MR. WILENTZ:

MR. WILENTZ: May we proceed, if your Honor please?

THE WITNESS: Mr. General, may I go back to my financial, on my financial transaction?

MR. WILENTZ: Yes.

THE WITNESS: All I said about my financial transaction, that is to be how I remember, because there is no exact bookkeeping to keep Mr. Fisch and myself apart, that is the way I remember.

MR. WILENTZ: Yes.

THE WITNESS: And it may be some difference in one way or another way.

Q. Yes. What you mean is that everything that you have said about your financial transactions, all that testimony, you mean that that is your best recollection; there may be a difference here or a difference there, is that what you mean?

A. The difference isn't very big, but that is the best recollection I have.

Q. Yes, all right, we will get to that.

Q. (Continuing) Mr. Defendant, you came into this country, when you came here, illegally, didn't you?

A. Yes, sir.

Q. And you have been in the United States of America since 1923, haven't you?

A. Yes.

Q. You have enjoyed the privilege and opportunity of earning a livelihood, haven't you?

A. Yes.

Q. You have received police protection during those years.

A. Not quite; not quite.

Q. Not quite?

A. No, sir.

Q. You married in this country.

A. Yes.

Q. You saved money.

A. Yes.

Q. You bought stocks.

A. Yes.

Q. The State of New York and the State of New Jersey and the United States of America have been working on your case as you know; you know that, don't you?

A. I suppose so.

Q. Yes. You have had an opportunity in this court today, and you still have an opportunity this minute to tell the whole truth. Have you told the truth?

A. I told the truth already.

Q. All right. So that you stand now on the story that you have given today?

A. I do.

Q. You stand on the story that you gave in the Bronx, in the courthouse.

A. To a certain extent.

Q. Well, I am talking about the story that you swore to before a court in the Bronx. Do you stand on that?

A. To a certain extent, yes.

Q. And to a certain extent, no?

A. To a certain extent, no.

Q. And the statements that you made to District Attorney Foley, where you say you were treated properly, do you stand on those statements?

A. I was properly treated in the Bronx.

Q. Do you stand on the statements you made to District Attorney Foley or do you want to change those—

MR. POPE: Object to the question. That is not a proper question.

THE COURT: I will overrule the objection.

Q. Answer the question, please.

A. You have to—

Q. Did you lie to District Attorney Foley or did you tell him the truth?

MR. POPE: Object to that question.

THE COURT: Well, perhaps you—

A. I—

THE COURT: Perhaps you had better call his attention to the things that you think—

Q. You say you told the truth today?

A. I told the true to District Attorney Foley about my treatment in the Bronx; that is correct.

Q. About this case, not about the treatment, about the Lindbergh case, the murder, did you tell him the truth about that?

A. To a certain extent.

Q. And to a certain extent you didn't tell him the truth, is that it?

A. I was—

Q. Did you tell him the truth only to a certain extent and lie to another extent?

MR. POPE: I object to this question and I object to this method of examination and I submit to the Court that the proper question is to direct the witness's attention to any question or answer or statement which he made to the District Attorney and interrogate the witness as to whether that statement was correct or not, not to say broadly, "Do you stand on this or do you stand on that or what?" The witness will have some explanation of some of the statements.

MR. WILENTZ: Well, he may not have an explanation and I don't want counsel to give it for him. If the question is objectionable, I will withdraw it.

THE COURT: I think it is.

BY MR. WILENTZ:

Q. But there is no question in your mind but that the story you told today is the truth, is there?

A. There is no question.

Q. Today and yesterday?

A. Today and yesterday.

Q. Now Mr. Reilly asked you about the time that you were convicted in Germany and you told him yes and that you were paroled?

A. Yes.

Q. That was true, was it?

A. It was true.

Q. Now when was it that you were paroled, 1919?

A. (Witness shakes head.)

Q. 1923?

A. '23.

Q. 1923. What month?

A. Can't remember.

Q. Well, all right. About how long before you came to the United States?

A. It was in the Spring time.

Q. All right. I think the exact question to you was, "During the period of reconstruction in Germany, you were convicted of some offense there, is that correct?" And you said you were, Spring time of 1919. You served how many years?

A. That means four years, isn't it?

Q. About four years. And when you came out as the result of that conviction and as the result of that parole, what did you do to follow a livelihood, as a means of livelihood?

A. I was trying to sell some goods, later I find out it was stolen.

Q. You were trying to sell some goods which later were found to have been stolen, is that it?

A. Yes.

Q. Now, let me refresh your recollection. In the County of Bautzen you were released on June 3rd, 1919, under parole: you remember that now?

A. It is—I can't remember the date.

Q. About that?

A. About that.

Q. Now, what happened then? You went and you sold some things that were stolen: is that it?

A. Yes.

Q. And then what happened? Did you go back to jail again?

A. I got arrested.

Q. And went back to jail again: is that right?

A. It was like police station, not quite a jail.

Q. All right. How long did you stay there?

A. I stayed only a couple days.

Q. And what happened?

A. They was working in the garden or in the yards, and I went out; the door was open and everything.

Q. You escaped jail?

A. Yes.

Q. Now, you were in jail for four years, and the Parole Board let you out on a parole?

A. Yes.

Q. You understood then, didn't you, that you were to behave yourself?

A. Yes.

Q. You were back again in jail on the 19th of June?

A. Yes.

Q. Within ten days anyway, or fourteen days?

A. (Witness nods.)

Q. And being in jail you ran away from jail, you escaped from jail: isn't that right?

A. That is right.

Q. When you left jail you had on a prisoner's uniform, didn't you?

A. No, sir.

Q. When you were in jail you had a prisoner's uniform, didn't you?

A. No, sir.

Q. What sort of clothing did you wear?

A. My civil clothes.

Q. Civilian clothes?

A. Yes.

Q. In jail?

A. It wasn't in jail, it was—

Q. Whatever it was, a lock-up.

A. I was for questioning there. I wasn't convicted.

Q. Well, you didn't give them a chance to convict you, did you? You ran away?

A. That is right, I ran away.

Q. Sure. And after you ran away didn't you take the clothes that you wore in the jail, pack them up in a bundle, come back to the jail and leave them in a package marked "Best wishes to the police"?

A. From where you got this story?

Q. Didn't you do that?

A. No, sir.

Q. So you mean you were only convicted of one crime, is that it?

A. Yes, sir.

Q. Only convicted once?

A. Convicted once.

Q. Only once?

A. Only once.

Q. Is it not a fact that on March the—that you were convicted of breaking and entering—

MR. POPE: What year?

Q. On March the 14th and 15th, 1919, breaking and entering into a home through a window in Reichowitz (?) on the night of March the 14th and 15th, 1919—wasn't that one charge you were convicted of?

A. It was a charge.

Q. Isn't it a fact that you were also convicted of breaking and entering into the Mayor's home on March the 15th and 16th, 1919?

A. It is about right. I can't remember.

Q. Breaking in through a window—you went through a window, didn't you?

A. Yes—

MR. POPE: I object to that question. He may ask him if he was charged with the crime and convicted. He may not go into the detail.

THE COURT: There is a limitation there.

A. I was present but I can't remember I went through the window.

Q. You don't remember that?

A. No.

Q. Isn't it a fact that you were convicted, you and another man were convicted of holding up two women with a gun?

A. It is.

Q. Wheeling baby carriages.

A. Everybody wheels baby carriages—

Q. Everybody wheels baby carriages, and you and this man with the gun held up these two women wheeling baby carriages, didn't you?

MR. POPE: We object to the question.

MR. WILENTZ: He has answered the question.

THE COURT: He has answered the question. He says he was convicted. That is enough of that matter.

BY MR. WILENTZ:

Q. Weren't you convicted afterwards of stealing some things out of a restaurant in Kamenz which you sold for thirty marks?

A. That is one I can't remember.

Q. All right. We will pass that over then. In December 1918 or January 1919, weren't you convicted of stealing some clothing from a guest room in Kamenz and then exchanging that coat with your brother for another one?

A. I can't remember that coat.

Q. Weren't you convicted of stealing some driving belts which you then later tried to sell to a policeman?

A. I will say what you are reading is something new to me.

Q. Then you weren't, were you?

A. No, sir.

Q. Now, when you escaped from jail you at that time had lived in your country, up to that time you had lived there all your life, hadn't you?

A. Yes.

Q. Everybody that was near and dear to you in the world lived in that land, didn't they?

A. (No answer.)

Q. Did you know anybody in the United States of America?

A. Yes.

Q. You did? Did you have any relatives here then?

A. Yes.

Q. Who?

A. My sister.

Q. Out in California?

A. Yes.

Q. Where is she now?

A. I don't know.

Q. You don't know. And you got on a boat then in 1923—

A. Yes.

Q. —without the invitation of the United States of America, didn't you?

A. Didn't have any money to come over in the regular way.

Q. And you sneaked on a boat and tried to sneak into this country, didn't you?

A. That is true.

Q. And they sent you back?

A. Yes, sir.

Q. Then you sneaked on another boat and tried to sneak into the country and they sent you back again, didn't they?

A. Yes, sir.

Q. And finally, you sneaked in the last time?

A. Yes, sir.

Q. And you have been here ever since?

A. Yes, sir.

Q. You didn't take any trips back to Germany, did you?

A. No, sir.

Q. And when you told Mr. Reilly that you were in this country under parole, you knew very well then, didn't you, that Germany wanted you for years, didn't they?

A. No, sir, because when I entered the United States the first time I did, I was writing my mother a letter I am safe over here and if the German Government have any interest to convict me or have me back, they always got my address on hand, they only have to go to my mother.

Q. Yes. All they have got to do to get you is to go to your mother in Germany; that's right?

A. It was, it was—

Q. You have been planning to go back to Germany, haven't you, for the last few years?

A. I was planning to go back go Germany this year.

Q. Yes. And you were trying to make arrangements through your mother with the police so that you could go back, isn't that so?

A. It was what they call over-quota, so I could enter Germany without fear, wouldn't be arrested.

Q. Yes, that's right. And you were communicating with your mother so that she would make arrangements with the government of Germany so you wouldn't be arrested when you got there, isn't that right?

A. It was not necessary to communicate with my mother in this case. I could go over to Germany as it was cut out automatically.

Q. Well, whether it was your mother or who it was, you were making arrangements to return to Germany, weren't you?

A. Yes.

Q. And just about then you were arrested, isn't that right?

A. Just about—my arrangement covered about this year, some of this year.

Q. Yes. Now I want to show you a little book and ask you if it is yours. Is that your handwriting? Take your time about it. Look at it.

A. Yes, that's my handwriting.

Q. That is your handwriting?

A. Yes.

Q. Take a look at this word particularly. Tell me if that is your handwriting, that one word there.

A. (No answer.)

Q. Or did some policeman write it?

A. I—I can't remember every word I put in here.

Q. Just the one word, that's all. There are only a few words on the whole page. That one word; tell me if that is in your handwriting?

A. It looks like my handwriting, but I can't remember I ever put it in.

Q. You can't remember what?

A. No, no.

Q. Don't mix it up now. Just stay with that word there for a minute; two dollars and fifty cents. You see that word?

A. Yes.

Q. Alongside of it?

A. Yes.

Q. Are they your figures?

A. They must be my figures.

Q. They must be your figures. Now let's get to this word that you use.

A. Yes.

Q. Yes. That is your word then, isn't it?

A. I can't remember if I ever put it in.

Q. Well now, this isn't a joke. You know either it is your handwriting or it isn't. Is it your handwriting?

A. It looks like my handwriting.

Q. It looks like your handwriting?

A. Yes.

Q. Now, tell me, how do you spell "boat"?

A. B-o-a-t.

Q. Yes. Why did you spell it b-o-a-d?

A. You wouldn't mind to tell me how old this book is?

Q. I don't know how old it is. You know; I don't know.

A. Let me see it.

Q. Why did you spell "boat" b-o-a-d?

A. This book is probably eight years old.

Q. All right. Why did you spell b-o-a-d?

A. Well, after you make improvements in your writing.

Q. All right. So that at one time you used to spell "boat" b-o-a-d?

A. Probably eight or ten years ago, and I am not quite sure if I put it in.

Q. All right. At one time you used to spell "boat" b-o-a-d, didn't you? Isn't that right?

A. No, I don't think so.

Q. Eight years ago, six years ago, ten years ago, whenever it was, you used to spell "boat" b-o-a-d, isn't that right?

A. I don't know.

Q. You spelled it in there, didn't you?

A. I—

Q. You tell the truth, now. Didn't you spell it in there?

A. Now, listen. I can't remember whether I put it in there.

MR. FISHER: That is objected to.

MR. POPE: That is objectionable.

MR. WILENTZ: Well, it isn't twice objectionable.

MR. FISHER: Yes, it is twice objectionable.

THE COURT: One moment. I don't think it is necessary for the Attorney General to ask him to tell the truth. I will sustain the objection.

MR. FISHER: That is all we objected to, sir.

THE COURT: I understand, sir.

BY MR. WILENTZ:

Q. Will you please look at this one word (presenting a small note book to the witness). We will come to the rest of the book—

A. I looked at it already.

Q. You said yes and maybe and yes and maybe. Now will you tell us what you really mean?

A. I told you I can't remember putting this one in the book.

Q. Is the whole page in your handwriting?

A. I don't know.

Q. Look at it?

A. No.

Q. What isn't in your handwriting?

A. Some handwriting I can't even make out.

Q. But the word "boad" in there you won't say that is not in your handwriting, will you?

A. I wouldn't say yes either.

Q. You don't say yes or no?

A. I don't say yes or no because I can't remember ever putting it in.

MR. WILENTZ: Mark this for identification for a minute.

(The book was marked State's Exhibit S-252 for Identification.)

Q. The reason you don't say yes or no is because you know you wrote "boad" when you got the fifty thousand from Condon, isn't that right?

A. No, sir.

Q. Boad Nelly. Look at it (handing the exhibit to the witness).

A. No.

Q. Do you see the word "boad Nelly"?

A. I see it, certainly.

Q. Look at it again right underneath there, again "boad", do you see that?

Q. B-o-a-d?

A. I see it.

Q. Let me see this exhibit for identification (referring to S-252 for identification, and handing same to witness). Do you see that?

A. I see that.

Q. Same spelling?

A. Same spelling.

Q. All right, let me have it for a minute.

Take a look at the "o" will you in the book, your book, exhibit 252 for identification? Do you see it is open on top? You see it isn't closed on top, don't you, the "o"?

A. What makes a difference? I don't know if I put in—

Q. We are going to find out. Just tell me if you find the "o" not closed on top.

A. It is a little bit open.

Q. Take a look at the "o" here. Is it a little bit open?

A. Well, there is one "o" not open at all, another quite a bit open.

Q. Quite a bit open.

A. Yes.

Q. One is a little bit open in the book and one "o" here is quite a bit open.

A. It is quite a bit open.

Q. Now, take a look at the "b". Is it separated from the "o", doesn't touch it at all?

A. It is separated.

Q. Take a look at these b's, are they separated from the "o"?

A. That is separated.

Q. Separated. Take a look at the "d". Do you see where that curve comes on this "d" and the "d" on the ransom note?

A. I see it.

Q. Take a look at the "d" here. Does it curve again?

A. Oh, gee, that is entirely different what you told me.

Q. Entirely different?

A. Sure.

Q. You come from Saxony in Germany, don't you?

A. Yes.

Q. In Saxony they use the "d" instead of the "t", don't they? All the words are "boad" instead of "boat" and things like that, isn't that a fact?

A. Some of them, yes.

Q. Yes.

A. That is a fact.

Q. And you use the word, you spelled the word "boat" b-o-a-d, because that is the way they would spell it in Saxony, isn't that it?

A. Oh, no—

Q. That isn't?

A. They spell it maybe mit "d" but they write it in "t".

Q. Now, will you take a look at these copies of these checks to the brokers—just two of them for tonight. Is that your handwriting, the word "Bronx"?

A. Yes.

Q. Do you see those x's?

A. Yes.

Q. Did you see them on the ransom notes?

A. I didn't notice—

Q. You didn't see them on the ransom notes?

A. No, I didn't look for it.

Q. Take a look at the other "x".

A. I see it.

Q. See that "x"?

A. Yes.

MR. WILENTZ: Give me the motor vehicle license, please.

Q. You see the "x" on exhibit—I don't seem to have the number—

THE REPORTER: It is down in the corner—S-88.

Q. Take a look at that exhibit S-88 and tell me if it is isn't the same kind of an "x".

A. That is the same "x" as on the two brokerage slips.

Q. Did you see the same "x" when the handwriting experts had it up in the ransom notes—

MR. POPE: Well now, we object to that.

A. Well, now, I really can't remember it—

MR. POPE: This witness is not a handwriting expert. We don't object to the Attorney General showing him any two of his own handwritings and asking him if they look alike.

THE COURT: I think it is proper cross examination and I will allow it.

MR. POPE: Not to make him examine—

Q. Well, now—

MR. POPE: Wait a minute.

MR. WILENTZ: The court has already ruled on the question. I don't have to wait for other argument.

MR. POPE: (Continuing) with something that a handwriting expert made himself and put on the board.

THE COURT: I overruled the present objection. Counsel may proceed.

MR. WILENTZ: Question or objection?

THE COURT: The present objection.

MR. WILENTZ: Yes, sir.

THE COURT: Counsel may proceed.

MR. POPE: May I have an exception?

THE COURT: Take your exception.

(Exception allowed, and the same is signed and sealed accordingly. Judge.)

Q. So you are a carpenter?

A. I am.

Q. When was the last time you did carpenter work?

MR. WILENTZ: Where is that board, please? Oh, yes.

Q. When is the last time you did carpenter work?

A. Last time?

Q. Yes.

A. About four or six weeks before I get arrested.

Q. But you didn't do any work regularly as a carpenter since April 1932, did you?

A. That is correct.

Q. You have been a stock market trader, haven't you? That has been your business?

A. Trading in stock market, trading in furs, and through some mortgages coming in.

Q. Well, you were a partner in the fur business, but you didn't buy and sell furs?

A. No.

Q. But your business really was trading in the stock market?

A. Yes.

Q. That is what you really did?

A. Yes.

Q. That is where you spent your days, isn't that a fact?

A. Yes.

Q. And every dollar of money that went into those brokerage accounts that you have talked about today, every dollar that went in there you took yourself and gave to the brokers, didn't you? You delivered it to the brokers, didn't you?

A. Yes, I delivered to the broker.

Q. Every dollar that you said that Fisch gave you or anybody else gave you, so far as delivering it to the broker, you are the one that gave it to him, aren't you?

A. Yes, sir.

Q. And the only man that knows about any moneys between you and Fisch, so far as the stocks are concerned, is the man that is dead, Fisch: isn't that right?

A. I don't know; I guess he said to me he is keeping book.

Q. He is the only man, though?

A. As far as I know.

Q. Just between the two of you?

A. As far as I know, yes.

Q. Yes. And he is dead?

A. Unfortunate.

Q. He was your best friend, wasn't he?

A. Well, I don't say best friend, but—

Q. You don't say so?

A. He was very good friend.

Q. Did he help you kidnap this Lindbergh child and murder it?

A. I never saw—

Q. You never saw?

A. —Mr. Lindbergh's child.

Q. But Fisch didn't help you, did he?

MR. FISHER: Objected to, your Honor. He has a right to finish his answer.

MR. WILENTZ: Yes, I suppose he has. I thought he had finished it.

MR. FISHER: You knew he hadn't.

THE COURT: Mr. Fisher, you need not shout in that fashion. Make your objections in a quiet and orderly fashion and we will deal with them in a quiet and orderly fashion.

Now then, what is the objection?

MR. WILENTZ: The objection was that I hadn't permitted the witness to finish his answer.

MR. FISHER: That is right.

MR. WILENTZ: That was the objection.

MR. FISHER: That is correct.

MR. WILENTZ: He said he never saw the Lindbergh child, I think.

Q. You have seen this board before, haven't you (showing the witness)?

A. I saw it.

Q. Did you take a look at the symbols on the ransom notes, the round circles? Did you see that when it was up here?

A. I saw it.

Q. Circles like these, that you put the money in, weren't they?

A. Well, when you drill a hole, it has got to be round.

Q. Yes, I know that. But you don't need a round hole to put money in, do you?

A. Well, it wasn't prepared for money.

Q. Didn't you tell District Attorney Foley that you drilled five holes to hide money in?

A. I told him I drilled five holes in for to put small bits in; and later I used it for money.

Q. Didn't you tell District Attorney Foley in the Bronx and the other officers, when they presented you with this exhibit, 197, that you drilled those holes to put money in it, this money?

A. I drilled holes in for bits.

Q. What I want to know is whether you told District Attorney Foley that you drilled it for money.

A. That can be impossible to say.

Q. Can be impossible?

A. Is impossible.

Q. What did you have this other hole for?

MR. REILLY: I object to that.

MR. WILENTZ: Just wait a minute now.

MR. REILLY: I think that has been ruled on by the Court.

MR. WILENTZ: Oh, no, it hasn't. On my case there was a suggestion and I complied with it.

MR. REILLY: I object to it now upon the ground that it might be under the Mollineau case objectionable, and the cases that are being followed in this State.

THE COURT: What is the precise question?

MR. WILENTZ: He says he drilled these five holes and I am asking what he drilled the other hole for. It is a part of this very transaction, if your Honor please. This isn't our board.

MR. REILLY: You offered it.

THE COURT: I will admit that question.

MR. REILLY: May I have an exception?

THE COURT: You may have an exception.

(Exception allowed and the same is signed and sealed accordingly. Judge)

BY MR. WILENTZ:

Q. What did you drill the other hole for?

A. To put something in.

Q. What did you put in?

A. It wasn't money.

MR. REILLY: If it wasn't money I say it is objectionable.

MR. WILENTZ: If your Honor please, I can't see why this jury has to take this piece of lumber out and guess, why they should be permitted or required to guess about the rest of this structure. It is not the Court's act, it was not the prosecution's act that bored this hole. Why do we have to protect any information that came as the result of the work in the hand of this defendant and conceal it from the jury?

MR. REILLY: May I say to your Honor that we are bound, I take it, by the law of the State of New Jersey and I feel, under your Honor's supervision of this trial, that will be the rule, by the laws of evidence of the country.

It might well be that this man now charged with murder in the first degree might have had in that receptacle drugs, which he didn't; he might have had counterfeit money of a foreign country; he might have had letters of information that might charge him with separate and distinct crimes that this jury have nothing to weigh in this particular case, and yet in their minds there might grow a prejudice subconsciously, which would react in this particular murder case.

I say that unless ransom money was in that particular hole of which he speaks, the admission of what he made it for or what he did is incompetent, immaterial and dangerous.

THE COURT: What is the present question?

MR. WILENTZ: I will ask the question again. I think the last question I asked him was what did he bore this larger hole for and he said not for money. My next question is, "What did you bore it for?"

THE COURT: He may answer that question.

MR. REILLY: May we have an exception?

THE COURT: Take your exception.

(Exception allowed and the same is signed and sealed accordingly. Judge.)

THE WITNESS: I put something in there.

Q. Answer the question.

A. I put something in there.

Q. What did you put in it?

MR. REILLY: Now again I object to it for the same reason. There isn't any doubt but that the Attorney General knows better than anyone in this court room what was in that hole has no more to do with the kidnaping of the Lindbergh baby than anything that is foreign in Africa and because of his knowledge as the investigation officer of this State, since he has come into this case, I say he is deliberately asking this question because he expects an answer which will prejudice this defendant before this jury on an object that has nothing to do with this case and is improper, and when we move then to strike it out, the effect is registered on their minds and their memory, and I press the objection that I made before.

MR. WILENTZ: May I respond to it if your Honor please?

THE COURT: Yes.

MR. WILENTZ: I am not asking this question because I don't expect to use the answer, if it is permitted. I think it is material. I think that the things that this man did at the very time and in connection with the hiding of this ransom money cannot be separated in one part and another. I want to show the nature of the man by his own act, not mine, and it is material, and I do expect to use it to his prejudice, yes, but only because of his own act.

Now, if your Honor please, if he did something when he was hiding this board, we may content and we believe the jury would have a right to infer that when he was getting this money, whatever was in here was with him, that when he was down there at the Lindbergh estate, he was there with whatever was in it. I think it is very material.

MR. REILLY: It is not a—

MR. WILENTZ: Further than that, if it isn't why should the defense worry about showing what his man did, if he was innocent, why should they worry about what was in this garage?

MR. REILLY: Ah—

MR. WILENTZ: Now, just a minute. How can anything be prejudicial of a nature like this, hidden with this money, if there is nothing to conceal from the jury and the court?

MR. REILLY: That isn't the question.

MR. WILENTZ: Well, the other question, I don't think he answered.

MR. REILLY: We are not hiding anything, Mr. Attorney General.

MR. WILENTZ: No.

MR. REILLY: Nor are you going to put me on the spot by saying we are hiding anything, but I do say this, that I am in a court of law presided over by a Justice of your Court in your State, and I still maintain that you will be bound by the rules of evidence of this State, and every other state of the United States.

MR. WILENTZ: We submit the question is proper, if your Honor please.

MR. REILLY: I cannot see, sir, how anything that he did in nineteen hundred—when this money was found on him—in '34 can connect him circumstantially with an act which they charge March the 1st, 1932, in Hopewell, when there isn't a living soul so far that ever saw him on the grounds or ever had such an object presented to them either through fear, force or favor.

THE COURT: Well now, the question is what?

MR. WILENTZ: The question is: What did you bore this hole for? He was asked for—

MR. REILLY: No, what did he put in it.

THE REPORTER: "What did you put in it?"

MR. WILENTZ: That was preceded by the question what other—

THE COURT: He may answer that.

Q. What did you put in it?

MR. REILLY: May we have an exception?

THE COURT: Take your exception.

(Exception allowed, and the same is signed and sealed accordingly. Judge.)

BY MR. WILENTZ:

Q. Answer the question.

A. I put a small pistol in it.

Q. Small pistol?

A. Yes.

Q. So that you had the pistol hidden in here?

A. Yes.

Q. And you had the five rolls of bills there?

A. Yes.

Q. And when you fixed this board up you fixed this pistol part with different depths, didn't you, so that the handle would go way in and so that the other part would be flush along here, didn't you? Isn't that the truth?

A. Will you repeat it again, please?

....

Q. Mr. Defendant, have you ever been up in an aeroplane?

A. Yes, one time.

Q. Where?

A. Los Angeles.

Q. Was that on the trip that you took to California?

A. That is right.

Q. Tell me something about that trip: you left in July 1931, did you not?

A. Yes.

Q. And you went by automobile?

A. Yes.

Q. It was a pleasure trip, was it?

A. Yes.

Q. Who went with you, Kloeppenburg and your wife?

A. My wife and Mr. Kloeppenburg.

Q. How many times did you go up in the airplane?

A. One time.

Q. What did you pay to go up?

A. I can't remember what we paid for it.

Q. Did you cross any boats?

A. No, we wasn't over the water at all.

Q. Did you hire a motor boat any place?

A. No, I can't remember.

Q. Well now, just think for a minute. Were you on a boat anywhere at all on that trip? Take your time and think it over.

A. I can't remember.

Q. You can't remember?

A. (Shaking head negatively.)

Q. Do you remember paying 75 cents apiece for a ride on a boat, you, for yourself 75 cents, for Mrs. Hauptmann 75 cents and for Mr. Kloeppenburg?

A. (No answer)

Richard Hauptmann

Q. Altogether $2.25?

A. No, can't remember.

Q. You can't remember?

A. No.

Q. You wouldn't say that you didn't, will you?

A. Well, I can't remember.

Q. You can't remember. You kept an account of your expenditures and expenses on this trip to California, did you not?

A. Yes, we did.

Q. Every cent that you spent, you accounted for in a book, isn't that so, groceries and everything?

A. Yes.

Q. And from the very day that you started to earn any money in this country, you kept books of account, didn't you?

A. Not the first day, I was here about—I guess I started a year or two years after.

Q. Once you started to keep an account, you kept every item listed in your books, in your accounts, didn't you?

A. No, not every item.

Q. Well, you kept the money that your wife earned and you kept an account of the money that you earned, did you not?

A. Yes.

Q. You kept account of the monies that you loaned to people and you kept an account of the monies that you spent?

A. Yes.

Q. You kept an account every year of how much money you and your wife were worth, did you not?

A. Yes.

Q. At the end of the year, if you had stocks and if you had monies and if you had other things of value, if people owed you money, you kept an account of it?

A. Yes.

Q. Did you not? You have always been very careful about figures, have you not?

A. Well, I say so, yes.

Q. Yes. You have always been very careful about money, too, haven't you?

A. Yes.

Q. I mean, you have tried to save money.

A. Of course.

Q. You have tried to accumulate money and you have saved it in order to take care of yourself and your family, I suppose.

A. Yes.

Q. And you made a real hard effort to do it, too; I mean, you tried, didn't you, to accumulate money.

A. Yes.

Q. And you were doing it too, right along, up to about 1931, weren't you?

A. Well, all the time.

Q. Yes.

A. Up to the present time.

Q. But in 1931, as the result of the gambling in the stock market, you lost some money, didn't you?

A. I lost money in 1930.

Q. 1930?

A. Yes.

Q. So that getting back to the books again and the books of account again, you say you kept your accounts, I suppose when you put the figures in the books that you put the correct figures in, didn't you?

A. Well, I saved about every week, about ten dollars.

Q. No. Never mind; we will get to that.

A. I did not put—

Q. No. Just one minute now. You just answer the question. You see, you know what I am going to ask you, but I will come to that later. What I asked you was, did you, when you put the figures in the book, did you put correct figures in? Were they truthful figures; were they honest figures when you put it in the book, in your books?

A. You mean—

Q. When you wrote in the book, the books that you kept, we were just talking about the books that you had: you said you kept an account of your expenses and your income. The figures that you put and wrote in those books, were they honest figures, were the correct figures, were they true figures?

A. I said he was, them figures were true, but I will—left out some of it.

Q. Well then, you mean they weren't true?

A. That doesn't mean the figure weren't true.

Q. Let me ask you: Supposing you put $5,000 in stocks, would that be correct, if you put it in the book? Would it be correct?

A. It would be correct.

Q. If you said $500 in the bank, would it be correct, if you had that in the book in your own handwriting?

A. Yes.

Q. If you said John Jones owed you $150, would that be correct?

A. Yes.

Q. If you put in the book that you had $100 home, would that be correct?

A. Yes.

Q. So that the figures in the book, whatever the figures are in those books, they are correct, honest, and true, isn't that right?

A. Yes.

Q. All right. Now, you don't want to change that, Mr. Hauptmann, do you, your testimony now, what you are just telling me now about the figures in your book? You are willing to stand on that?

A. I stand on that.

Q. That when you wrote into your own books in your own hand, you didn't try to fool anybody but you were putting the truth in there?

A. Yes.

Q. All right.

A. But there is only one thing I did not put—

Q. No "buts". Is it the truth—

MR. FISHER: I submit, your Honor, he is entitled to answer that. He has tried three times to explain that situation and the Attorney General stops him each time. He is entitled to make a full answer and explanation, sir.

Classics of the Courtroom

MR. WILENTZ: The truth doesn't need any explanation.

MR. FISHER: He says "I put it in the book but—"

MR. WILENTZ: Just a minute now.

THE COURT: Well, I think he had better be permitted to make his explanation now, if he has any.

Q. All right; but what?

A. I saved money besides that my wife should not know. I put nothing in the book.

Q. Oh. In other words, you were hiding it on your wife.

A. (Witness nods.)

Q. Well, you were hiding a lot of things on your wife, weren't you?

A. No, sir. It is only the money I kept.

MR. FISHER: I object to this.

THE COURT: Why do you object?

MR. FISHER: Because it is improper cross examination, "You are hiding a lot of things from your wife."

THE COURT: Well, you insisted upon his making that explanation, he made it and now I think the Attorney General has a right to cross examine further about it.

Q. You were hiding a lot of things on your wife, weren't you?

A. Only the money question.

Q. When is the first time you met Mrs. Henckle?

A. Summertime, '32.

Q. Where?

A. Hunters Island.

Q. Bathing?

A. Oh, I can't recall the first day how it happens.

Q. Well, was it while you were out bathing? I am not asking you the first day.

A. I was out bathing.

Q. You were out bathing. That is the first time.

A. Yes.

Q. Was Mr. Henckle there when you met her?

A. (No answer.)

Q. What are you thinking about? You know whether he was or not.

A. I guess her sister was there.

Q. I am asking you about Mr. Henckle, not her sister.

A. I can't remember if he was there.

Q. Well, don't you know that two weeks later she introduced you to her husband when you went up to the house?

A. I can't remember this, when she introduced me.

Q. Can't you remember whether or not Mrs. Henckle met you at Hunters Island and two weeks later, or some time later, she introduced you to her husband?

A. I can't remember the date, how long afterward she introduced him.

Q. Well, forget the two weeks. I didn't mean to impress the time.

A. Yes.

Q. But it was after you met Mrs. Henckle at Hunters Island that you met her husband at his home?

A. I guess that is correct.

Q. Who introduced you to Mrs. Henckle: nobody?

A. Well, it doesn't need much introducing out there.

Q. I see.

A. It was—

Q. That was when your wife was away, wasn't it, she was in Europe then?

A. Yes, that is right.

Q. All right. Now we will get back to the accounts again. So the books were absolutely accurate except where you tried to keep it away from your wife?

A. Yes.

Q. You did say before that when you put $5,000 in stocks, that was right, you didn't try to keep that away?

A. I didn't put $5,000 in stocks.

Q. Whatever the correct amount was in the books, you had it in there and you didn't try to fool her about that?

A. No; did not.

Q. Let me ask you: when you found $14,000 or more in gold, how did you feel, did you cry? Did you laugh? Were you happy or were you sad?

A. I was excited.

Q. You were excited?

A. I was.

Q. Did you say anything, did you holler out, "Anna, look what I found," or anything like that?

A. No, I did not.

Q. Did you tell your wife?

A. I did not.

Q. You didn't tell your wife?

A. No.

Q. Have you ever seen $14,000 in gold before in your life?

A. No, I did not.

Q. Well, when you say you were excited, what do you mean you were excited?

A. Well, I guess everybody is excited if he finds $14,000.

Q. Yes.

A. Like dat.

Q. Well, you are not very excited now, are you?

A. Why should I?

Q. No, it is quite a joke with you, isn't it?

A. No, it is not a joke, I am very earnest.

Q. Oh, I see, you are very earnest. Were you earnest with your wife when you found the $14,000?

A. That has got nothing to do with my wife.

Q. Were you earnest with her?

A. I guess.

Q. Didn't she work and slave in a bakery and bring to you, when you and she got married, her earnings and her savings?

A. That has got nothing to do with them $14,000 at all.

Q. Didn't she do that? Please answer.

A. Yes.

Q. Didn't she buy the furniture for you and herself when you started your home?

A. This was my wife's money, and my money.

Q. For the furniture; didn't she pay every dollar for the furniture?

A. That comes from our bank account.

Q. Comes from your bank account. She gave you every dollar she had in the world, didn't she?

A. So did I.

Q. Yes.

A. Except these $14,000.

Q. You were partners, weren't you, both working hard?

A. Yes.

Q. But when you found $14,000 in gold, no more partnership with the wife?

A. Absolutely not, why should I make my wife excited about it?

Q. Oh, I see. Well now, let's see. When you were keeping your books and you were cheating her with the books of accounts, and you wouldn't tell her about your monies, why did you stop her from knowing about that? Why did you hide that?

A. Should it be a pleasant surprise for her sometimes.

Q. I see. You were keeping a surprise for her?

A. Yes, because my attention was to pay her house, build her a house sometimes.

Q. Do you know Mr. Brent, stock exchange business? You met Mr. Brent in your stock exchange operations, didn't you?

A. Brent?

Q. Brent, yes. Isn't he the man that introduced you to the stock broker or something like that?

A. What is his first name?

Q. I don't know. I will try to find out. What is Mr. Brent's first name (addressing associate counsel)? Well, you remember Brent's wife—she is the lady that introduced you to the brokerage firm, I think, Steiner Rouse, to E. A. Pierce & Company, I think, one of your accounts. Do you remember the lady that introduced you to the stock

Classics of the Courtroom

broker?

A. Oh, yes, that is right.

Q. That is her husband.

A. That is right.

Q. Do you know him?

A. Yes, always—

Q. Do you remember saying to Mr. Brent, "Mr. Brent, if my wife ever asks you where I was some night, tell her I was with you."

A. No.

Q. You didn't do that?

A. No.

Q. You only kept the money business away from her, is that it?

A. (No answer.)

Q. Well, anyway, getting back to your accounts again, you were telling us the other day, when I showed you a little book with some words in it, that "well, the book is maybe eight years old," and maybe you have learned since that time; something like that. Do you remember that?

A. Yes.

Q. Tell me, when you came to Flemington, New Jersey, and you got into the jail here, you knew something about ransom notes being written to Colonel Lindbergh, you knew that was one of the things in the case, didn't you?

A. It is only what I hear in the Bronx, Bronx courtroom.

Q. Yes. Did you send out for a German-American dictionary while you were here?

A. Yes.

Q. To study up the correct spelling of the words?

A. No, sir.

MR. WILENTZ: Where is that dictionary?

(Book produced by counsel for State)

Q. Is this the dictionary that you sent for, and is it your dictionary (showing to witness)?

A. I guess that is the dictionary I got over here.

MR. WILENTZ: I offer it.

Q. Is that where you learned to spell the word "singnature" correctly?

A. No, sir.

MR. POPE: We object to the introduction of the book. It is merely a book which the defendant had sent in to him after he was incarcerated. It certainly can have no effect upon this case. Perhaps he had a reason for sending for it; but it is in no way connected with the case; it is entirely too remote.

THE COURT: Well, I am inclined to think, in view of the state of the proof, that it is evidential.

MR. POPE: The book itself?

THE COURT: Yes.

MR. POPE: We don't see what it can prove, but if that is your Honor's ruling, of course we must bow to it.

THE REPORTER: S-255.

(The dictionary was received in evidence and marked State's Exhibit S-255.)

THE COURT: I suppose the book speaks for itself, and it may contain matters that are pertinent.

Mr. Attorney General, what is your theory about the admissibility of the book?

MR. WILENTZ: Why, if your Honor please, I take it that there isn't any great importance to it. I believe there is no question about its admissibility; and the reason I believe it is admissible is because counsel told this gentleman about his spelling, with particular reference to words involved in these ransom notes, and I think it is very material to show that he learned how to spell these things as the result of a dictionary in his possession since his arrest, which he has already admitted, so far as the possession of the dictionary.

MR. POPE: That is not the way to prove he learned to spell.

MR. WILENTZ: He says so himself.

MR. POPE: I suppose almost every ordinary word is to be found in a dictionary.

THE COURT: Well, I have already indicated that I think it is admissible.

MR. POPE: May we have an exception?

THE COURT: Yes, take your exception.

Classics of the Courtroom

(Exception allowed, and the same is signed and sealed accordingly. Judge.)

THE WITNESS: Do you want me to explain this dictionary book?

THE COURT: The lawyers will examine you. Your counsel after a while will enable you to make any explanations you have to make.

THE WITNESS: Thank you, your Honor.

BY MR. WILENTZ:

Q. Mr. Defendant, I want to show you this word "sing" and "singnature" on this Exhibit No. S-109. You see it, do you not?

A. I see it.

Q. You remember the testimony of the handwriting experts about the "n" being before the "g", you remember that?

A. I can—oh, yes, I do.

Q. That is a habit of yours, isn't it, putting in "n's" where they don't belong?

A. No.

Q. You do it often, don't you?

A. I can't remember. I don't remember doing it at all.

Q. You don't remember doing it at all?

A. No.

Q. Would you be surprised to find out that you had done it? Well, take a look at this just for a minute and see if this is yours (handing the witness a paper). Is that your check? You ought to be able to tell whether it is your check by this time.

A. Yes, that is my check.

Q. It is.

A. Let me see it a minute.

Q. Have you had a good look at it?

A. No.

Q. Then keep looking at it. Is that your check?

A. Yes.

MR. WILENTZ: Please mark it for identification.

(The check was marked S-256 for identification.)

Q. How much is the amount of that check?

A. $74.

Q. $74?

A. Yes.

Q. How do you spell "seventy"?

A. "Seventy"? I guess—

Q. Well, read it from here. You wrote it: Seventy. Read it. Nice and loud, please.

A. That is—

Q. Loud, now.

A. S-e—

Q. Loud, now. S-e—what?

A. S-e-n—

Q. S-e-n?

A. Yes.

Q. Senvety?

A. Senvety, yes.

Q. You have an "n" in there, haven't you?

A. Yes.

Q. All right. Now let me have it, please. The same "n" as you have in "singnature." Isn't that right?

MR. POPE: Object to the question. That is not true. I object to that question. How he spells "singnature" and how he spells "seventy" are two entirely different things. Whether the "n" is before or in the wrong place or not the check itself will show.

THE COURT: Oh, I think it is legitimate cross examination.

MR. POPE: Yes, but he is asking the witness if it isn't the same "n" that he has in "singnature."

MR. WILENTZ: That he put in the "singnature," if I haven't got that in, I want it in.

MR. POPE: Wait a minute. If he wrote the word "singnature," manifestly it isn't the same "n" that is on the check.

MR. WILENTZ: I withdraw—

THE COURT: No. No, I suppose the question better be modified in that respect and, if so modified, I think it is permissible.

Classics of the Courtroom

BY MR. WILENTZ:

Q. Didn't you place the "n" in "senventy" just like you placed the "n" in "singnature" and for the same reason?

MR. POPE: Now, I object to the question because the witness has testified that he did not place the "n" in "singnature," that he did not write the word "singnature," that he did not write the ransom note. If he wants to ask him if he placed the "n" in "seventy," where it appears on that check, we think that is a perfectly proper question, but "Didn't you place the 'n' in 'senventy' the same as you did in 'singnature,'" is either a catch question or one which is manifestly improper.

THE COURT: The objection is overruled. You may have your exception.

MR. POPE: May we have an exception?

THE COURT: You may have your exception.

(Exception allowed and same is signed and sealed accordingly. Judge.)

BY MR. WILENTZ:

Q. Answer the question, sir.

A. What is the question?

Q. (Question read as follows: "Q. Didn't you place the 'n' in 'senventy' just like you placed the 'n' in 'singnature' and for the same reason?")

A. No.

Q. All right. Now, take a look at this exhibit. You see that "N" in "New York"?

A. Yes.

Q. And that "N" in your handwriting?

A. Yes.

Q. Did the police tell you to put that little hook up on top, or did you do it yourself?

A. I do it myself; but I say there is a lot difference between them two N's.

Q. There is a lot of difference between that hook up there?

A. Hook up there like that.

Q. That "N" and that "N"?

145

A. Yes.

Q. There is a lot of difference between the two?

A. I guess there is a whole lot.

Q. A whole lot. Do you see the "York"?

A. Yes.

Q. That York (indicating).

A. (No answer.)

Q. Do you see that "York" in the ransom notes and papers (indicating)?

A. I see it.

Q. Now take a look at this book and see if this is yours, right there, that page. Don't turn the page; just look at that page.

A. No, no. I won't turn it.

Q. All right.

A. (After examining page) Yes, I wrote that.

Q. All of it. Now take this pencil and put a line under the New York, the first New York you have got there; just underneath it.

A. (The witness complied.)

Q. Then take it again and put it under the next New York.

A. (The witness complied.)

Q. Then under the next one.

A. (The witness complied.)

Q. And under the next one. Right here.

A. (The witness complied.)

Q. Now those lines are your lines, aren't they, under New York?

A. Yes.

MR. LARGE: Refer to that.

MR. WILENTZ: Referring to exhibit—just put the stamp on that page.

THE REPORTER: In evidence?

MR. WILENTZ: Well, mark it for identification, for the time being.

THE REPORTER: S-257 for identification.

MR. WILENTZ: Well, I will offer that in evidence rather, that page.

THE COURT: Any objection to that?

MR. POPE: Well, we would like to see it.

MR. WILENTZ: Just that page (handing to counsel for defendant).

(Counsel confer.)

MR. WILENTZ: Will you get the "gh."?

MR. PEACOCK: All right (placing another photographic enlargement on wall to the right of jury).

MR. WILENTZ: There is apparently no objection.

THE COURT: If there is no objection, it will be admitted.

THE REPORTER: Exhibit S-257.

(Page of memorandum book received in evidence and marked State's Exhibit S-257.)

MR. WILENTZ: Now just leave that s"New York" there for a minute. May I ask the Court's indulgence for a minute, until I exhibit these "New Yorks" to the jury?

THE COURT: Yes.

....

Q. Will you take a look at page 5 and tell me whether or not that is your writing—page 5.

A. (Examining book) It is.

Q. It is.

A. (Nods affirmatively.)

Q. It is a little weak. I want you to say it so the jury and stenographer can hear it.

A. It is.

MR. WILENTZ: I offer page 5 of this book in evidence. (Conferred with defense counsel) I will offer the whole book.

THE COURT: Is there any objection? It will be admitted.

(Book received in evidence and marked State Exhibit S-258.)

Q. Were you in court when—Well, you were in court, weren't you, when the handwriting experts were testifying about the peculiarities in the ransom notes?

A. Yes.

Richard Hauptmann

Q. You were here, weren't you?

A. Yes.

Q. Do you remember their testimony about the g's and the h's being transposed in "right" and "light" and things like that?

A. Gee, there were so many talking, I really can't remember.

Q. You can't really remember?

A. (Nods.)

Q. Well, I guess you are right about that. I want to call your attention on Exhibit 108 this word "light" l-i-h-g-t. Do you remember that?

A. I see it.

Q. You see it.

A. Yes.

Q. Then on Exhibit—I can't tell the number here, maybe it is written on the back.

MR. WILENTZ: Mr. Stenographer, will you please come over here and give us some aid?

THE REPORTER: It is on the bottom, I think.

MR. WILENTZ: Yes, S-134.

Q. I want to point out to you another thing, r-i-g-t-h, and n-i-h-g-t, do you see those?

A. Yes.

Q. This is your standard writing?

A. Yes.

Q. And this is your disputed writing?

A. Yes.

Q. And the other one I just indicated to you, you see those, don't you?

A. I see 'em.

Q. One in your standard writing and two in your disputed writings. Now, you had a habit of doing that, didn't you?

A. A habit.

Q. Yes, a habit of making mistakes with "night" and "right" and "tight" and anything that had "gh" and "hg" in it?

A. Well, I say maybe I made mistakes, I was not so—

Q. That was one peculiarity, you didn't make any mistakes with "signature," you could spell that, couldn't you?

A. You see I am not so very perfect in writing English.

Q. Yes, but you could spell "signature" without the "n", couldn't you?

A. Sure I can.

Q. But little words here like "right" and "night" and "tight", you didn't have any trouble with those, did you?

A. That is what I say, I write really very, very seldom.

Q. Very seldom.

A. Yes.

Q. As a matter of fact, you write very, very often, don't you? You do a lot of writing, don't you?

A. No, sir.

Q. You are quite a bookkeeper, you keep a big set of books, don't you?

A. That is only—

Q. You write long letters, too, don't you?

A. That is what I say, very, very seldom.

Q. Well, this page that you said is in your handwriting, you bought some Curtiss-Wright Aviation stock.

A. Yes.

Q. Spell Wright, as you have got it in here, so that the jury will know just how you wrote it.

A. That is H-g-t.

Q. Never mind the h-g-t—start at the "W".

A. W-r-i-h-g-t.

Q. W-r-i-h-g-t?

A. Yes.

Q. Just like you have the h-g-t here in light, isn't that right?

A. Yes, that is right.

....

Q. In 1932 and particularly in March 1932, you had a German-American dictionary in your home, didn't you?

A. Had it home for long years.

Q. For long years. Take a look at these (handing pamphlets to witness) and see if they are your dictionaries.

A. Sorry; isn't mine.

Q. Isn't yours?

A. No.

Q. What kind of dictionary did you have?

A. About as thick as that (indicating with fingers).

Q. As thick as that, but not these words, these printed words, just the plain dictionary?

A. I never saw them (pamphlets).

Q. You never saw them?

A. Never saw them.

Q. They don't come from your home?

A. No, sir; I never saw them.

Q. All right. If they are not, we will just put them away.

MR. WILENTZ: Before we do, I will ask that they be marked for identification as one exhibit.

(Pamphlets were marked State Exhibit S-259 for Identification.)

....

Q. When is the first time that you heard about Colonel Lindbergh, that you knew there was such a person living as Colonel Lindbergh?

A. Well, right after his flight to France.

Q. You remember that, don't you? How do you say "Colonel Lindbergh"? Will you pronounce it for me, please.

A. Linborg.

Q. Yes. Say it, "Mr. Colonel Lindbergh."

A. Mister Colonel Linborg?

Q. Yes. A little louder.

A. Mister Colonel Lindenborg.

Q. Lindenborg?

A. Linborg.

Q. You have another "n" in there, haven't you?

A. No, Linborg.

Classics of the Courtroom

Q. Lindbergh. Not Lindenbergh?
A. No.
....
Q. Now, you kept accounts of all of your transactions in July 1930, did you not?
A. I can't remember the day when I stopped.
Q. Why did you stop?
A. I can't give any reason for it, why I stopped.
Q. When did you start again?
A. Must be around 1925.
Q. When did you start again after stopping in 1930?
A. (No answer.)
Q. You did start again, did you not?
A. I started only on the trip to California.
Q. Well, you stopped when you came back from California, didn't you? You didn't keep any more accounts in 1931, did you?
A. No, I guess there wasn't any account in '30 or '31 either.
Q. Either in '30 or '31?
A. Yes.
Q. But from 1928 or '27 you kept it right up until July 1930, didn't you?
A. '29 or '30. I don't know when I stopped.
Q. And then you began again in 1932, didn't you?
A. Only on brokerage accounts.
Q. Only on brokerage accounts?
A. Yes.
Q. Fur accounts; how about those?
A. No, did not.
Q. You didn't keep fur accounts?
A. No.
Q. You didn't keep fur accounts in your book?
A. I keep the little bit of it.
Q. Didn't you keep fur accounts in your books?

A. I keep a little bit of fur accounts.

Q. Then, why did you say you didn't keep fur accounts?

A. Well, this doesn't include all the furs, only a little bit of it.

Q. Didn't you keep an account of it, of the furs that Fisch bought and that was held between you and Fisch, the amounts, the kind of furs, the cost, the sales price?

A. Part of it.

Q. Part of it?

A. Part of it.

Q. Who were you hiding the rest from?

A. He was keeping care of the fur account.

Q. But you kept the account, too, did you not?

A. No, sir.

Q. At any rate, you kept an account in 1932 of your stocks and your furs and your monies again, didn't you?

A. Not furs.

Q. Not furs?

A. Not furs, only a little bit of the furs, not quite all of it.

Q. How many pages would you say of fur accounts?

A. I guess it is only one or two.

Q. From 1932 until Fisch died, only one or two pages?

A. No, it is, it is only after the last time, it covers the last time for 1933, I guess.

Q. I show you Exhibit 23 and I want you to read this sentence.

MR. POPE: Tell us what Exhibit 23 is.

MR. WILENTZ: It is one of the ransom notes.

Q. Can you read it?

MR. POPE: I object to the question. I object to this witness being shown any document which he says is not his, does not emanate from him, is not his handwriting. We object to his being asked to read anything like that. This is not one of his admitted handwritings he is now being shown.

THE COURT: What is the question, Mr. Attorney General?

MR. WILENTZ: I ask him to read a sentence in one of the ransom notes, Exhibit 23. I have a purpose for it, if your Honor please.

THE COURT: He may answer that question.

MR. POPE: May we have an exception?

THE COURT: Yes.

(Exception allowed and same is signed and sealed accordingly. Judge.)

BY MR. WILENTZ:

Q. Read it.

A. "The baby would be back long ago—"

Q. "You would not—"

A. Oh, go farther?

Q. Yes. Further. Just the rest of the paragraph: "The baby would be back long ago—" Then go ahead.

A. Well, I have to—

Q. Sure; take your time. It is hard for you to read, isn't it?

A. You bet it is.

Q. All right; then take your time.

A. What is this word?

Q. "Would."

A. "Would"?

Q. Yes.

A. "You would not get any result from police."

Q. Go ahead: "Because—"

A. "Because—" what is that?

Q. "This."

A. "Because this—"

MR. POPE: No. Let him read it.

MR. WILENTZ: He asked me what that was and I said "this."

MR. POPE: Well—

MR. WILENTZ: If you have an objection, will you please make it to the Court, without instructing counsel?

MR. POPE: Yes; I do.

We object to the Attorney General suggesting to the witness anything that is in it. He has asked him to read it. Now if he can read it he can read it; if he can't read it, the Attorney General can't prompt him and correct him and tell him how to read it.

THE COURT: Well—

Q. Please read it.

A. "Because this kidnaping"—I can't make out the next, the next word.

Q. Yes. What is the next?

A. "plan for a year already."

Q. Go ahead.

A. "but we"—can't make out the next one.

Q. Isn't it "was"?

MR. POPE: He says he can't make it out.

Q. Take a look at it.

A. I don't know what the next word means.

Q. All right. What is the next one after that? "But we—"

A. "afraid".

Q. "Afraid" yes. What is next?

A. "the boy".

Q. Yes.

A. "would not"

Q. Yes.

A. Can't make out the next two words.

Q. "Bee," what is that? "would not bee".

MR. POPE: he says he can't make it out.

A. I can't—

MR. WILENTZ: He doesn't need the help of counsel, if your Honor please. This is cross examination, and I think the interruptions are just for the purpose of suggestion.

A. The last word is "enough".

Q. That word is "strong" isn't it? Look at it; see if you can tell. "not be strong enough," isn't that what it is?

A. When you tell me, I can make it out.

Q. Yes. Now you make it out.

A. Yes.

Q. "strong", "not be strong enough."

A. Yes.

Q. So that you have read "the baby would be back long ago. You would not get any result from police because this kidnaping"—then a word you couldn't understand—"planned for a year already, but we was afraid the boy would not be strong enough."

Now did you hear the testimony in court that the Lindbergh child was born in June, 1930?

A. I can't remember.

Q. You can't remember. You stopped keeping accounts in July, 1930, and didn't start again until after the ransom money was paid, isn't that correct?

A. I don't know when I stopped.

Q. Didn't you stop keeping these accounts as soon as you got the idea of kidnaping this child just as is set forth in that letter?

A. I never got any idea to kidnap any child.

Q. Didn't you stop keeping accounts within two weeks of the birth of the Lindbergh child, and didn't start again until a couple of months after the ransom money was paid?

A. I even didn't know the Lindbergh child was born.

Q. But this is the fact about the dates, isn't it—July, 1930 to August 1932, you kept no accounts; that's true, isn't it?

A. I can't remember the day when I stopped.

Q. You can't remember the day?

A. No.

Q. I want to show you a little book (presenting same to the witness). Is it yours, is that handwriting on that page, 1930, yours, at the top of it is the word "Anna"?

A. Yes, that is mine.

Q. On the other side is the word "Richard"?

A. Yes.

Q. Are those pages yours?

A. Yes.

Q. Do they represent some financial account of yours and your wife? Look at the whole book, if you want.

A. Yes.

Q. Start right at the first page, right up here at the beginning, and as you come to a page that is not yours, you say so.

A. (The witness examines the book.)

Q. Is that your handwriting? I don't want you to study all the figures, I want you to tell me if it is your handwriting. Will you please tell me if it is your handwriting. Will you please tell me if that is your handwriting on that page?

A. It is.

Q. All right then, turn over. Never mind studying it, please. Now the next page? Is that your handwriting?

A. It is.

Q. Is the next page your handwriting?

A. It is.

Q. All right, sir. The next page?

A. It is.

Q. The next page? I want you to look long enough at it to know if it is your handwriting?

A. It is.

Q. All right, sir, the next page?

A. It is.

Q. The next one?

A. It is.

Q. The next one?

A. It is.

Q. The next one?

A. Wait a minute.

Q. All right, sir.

A. It is.

Q. It is. If it isn't, you just say so, and we will take it out. The next one?

A. It is.

Q. The next one. Well, you said this one was; will you please look at the next one.

A. It is.

Q. It is. The next one.

A. It is.

Q. How about the next page?

A. It is.

Q. The next one.

A. It is.

Q. The next one, please.

A. It is.

Q. The next two pages, this and that. You are not looking at this page at all. Why not look at them and see if this is your handwriting?

A. Well, I am finished with that.

Q. There are only a few letters on that. Look at this, see if that is your handwriting.

A. Exclusive of this.

Q. Is that not yours? Cross it out with the pencil.

A. Oh, no.

Q. Is it yours?

A. Yes, that is mine.

Q. All right, then; turn to the next page: is that yours?

A. That is mein one.

Q. All right now. Look at this one.

A. That is mine.

Q. How about this one?

A. It is mein one.

Q. This one, a loose page.

A. Yes, that is mein one.

Q. Is that yours too?

A. Yes.

Q. How about this page?

A. Belongs to me, too.

Q. Is this your handwriting; is it, sir, that one page?

Richard Hauptmann

A. Wait a minute—Yes, it is.

Q. The whole page is yours, is it?

A. Yes.

Q. Are you sure about it?

A. (Examines page again.)

Q. You said it was. You see, I want you to be sure about it.

A. I guess not the first one.

Q. You don't think that is? Take the pencil and cross out the first one you don't think is yours.

A. (Witness marks on book.)

MR. PEACOCK: I can't hear it.

MR. WILENTZ: He said the first one is not his.

Q. Is this yours, where the word is crossed out and is this page yours?

A. Yes.

Q. The next page, that is yours?

A. Yes.

Q. Two pages?

A. Yes, they are mine.

Q. Is this page yours?

A. Yes.

Q. The next page, is that yours, the next two pages?

A. Yeah, they are mine.

Q. The next page, is that yours?

A. This one?

Q. Yes.

A. I don't know.

Q. You don't know?

A. I don't know, no, sir.

Q. "You don't know, no, sir," is that it? You say it isn't yours? You said at first you don't know. Now do you know or don't you know?

A. That is not my writing.

Classics of the Courtroom

Q. It is not yours?
A. It is not mine.
Q. It is in your book, isn't it?
A. Yes.
Q. In the middle of the book?
A. It is.
Q. Is there writing afterwards?
A. It is.
Q. "Richard 1930"?
A. Yes.
Q. Then it is January, 1931, there, isn't it—1932, isn't it?
A. It isn't mine handwriting.
Q. The "January" isn't it?
A. (Nodding negatively.)
Q. Cross it out, please.
A. This one?
Q. Cross out whatever isn't your handwriting on that page.
A. This one isn't, this one isn't either. That is mine.
Q. That is yours?
A. Yes.
Q. Just one minute, now. This writing here—read it.
A. Well, that is in German.
Q. Well, read it in German.
A. "Erhalten from Harry Roeder am 24 January, $10.00."
Q. That means you received $10 from Roeder on January 24th, doesn't it?
A. Yes.
Q. That is January, 1932, isn't it?
MR. POPE: Is that Roeder?
MR. WILENTZ: Yes.
A. I can't make it out.
Q. All right. Maybe the next page will tell the story. There is a blank there and a blank there. There are some drawings there. Are

they yours?

A. No, they are not mine.

Q. Is this yours?

A. No, sir.

Q. Well, we will throw that away, it is loose. All right?

A. Yes.

Q. These drawings aren't yours?

A. No, they are not mine.

Q. How about the picture of that window—that isn't yours, the drawing of that window?

A. That should be a window?

Q. Well, what is it? I don't know. Isn't that a ledge there?

A. I even can't make out what it is.

Q. You can't make out what it is?

A. No.

Q. But you can make out the ladder there with the dowel pin?

A. What is that?

Q. Doesn't that look like a ladder? Does it?

A. It doesn't look like—

Q. What is it, a book, a picture of a book shelf or what?

A. No, I don't know what it is.

Q. You said before when you started, you didn't know whether you put that in or not. Now here on the next page is an account of monies you received from some man by the name of Roeder.

A. Yes.

Q. And on the next page is a picture of something. What is that?

A. You are asking me? I don't know what it is.

Q. You don't know?

A. No.

Q. Well, doesn't that look like a drawing of a window with some sort of dots or marks on it for something? You don't know what it is?

A. I don't know what it is.

Q. It is not yours?

Classics of the Courtroom

A. It is not my window.

Q. Is this a loose one here? We will take that out. The one with the window on it is not loose.

A. It is not loose.

Q. Now we still continue on with accounts in that book, don't we? What is that? Is that your handwriting?

A. That is my handwriting.

Q. Is the next your handwriting?

A. Yes.

Q. And that?

A. That is my handwriting.

Q. Then a few blank spaces again; some torn sheets; then some funny drawings like a child would draw, isn't that it?

A. (No answer.)

Q. That isn't yours, is it, a picture of a—that is not yours, is it; a picture of a star and those other things?

A. No, they are little child's drawings.

Q. A child's drawings, that is right?

A. A little child used to come in our house and play inside and he put them in.

Q. Just put an "R" on top there.

A. (The witness complied.)

Q. And an "R" on top here.

A. (The witness complied.)

Q. Now, those two pages represent drawings that some child drew in that book, isn't that right?

A. Yes.

Q. All right; just so we don't get it confused. Now, what is this: a pinochle score or some game you played—you and your friends?

A. That's a kind of a card game.

Q. Well, it is a score of a card game?

A. Yes.

Q. That is at the end of the book?

A. Yes.

Q. That is what both of them are?

A. Yes.

Q. But it is your handwriting, or somebody's handwriting keeping the game?

A. It is somebody's handwriting.

Q. You can't tell?

A. I can't tell.

Q. You won't say it wasn't yours or it isn't?

A. No, I can't tell.

Q. But it is a book you kept home, and you kept the score of the game, isn't that it?

A. Yes.

Q. All right. Now, is the next page yours?

A. That's my handwriting.

Q. The next page is your handwriting too?

A. That is in my handwriting.

Q. That is an account of all the hours you worked, isn't that it?

A. That's overtime.

Q. Overtime, yes. And that is the same thing from time to time, your handwriting (indicating another portion of book)?

A. Yes.

Q. The number of hours you worked during those years and the employer for whom you worked?

A. That's only for overtime.

Q. Yes. It is all your handwriting, is it?

A. Yes.

Q. All right, we are almost to the end. Now see if the rest of it isn't your handwriting. That at the bottom isn't your handwriting, is it?

A. (Witness shakes head.)

Q. The name Captain Hans Mueller?

A. No.

Q. Cross it out, will you please? Somebody else wrote that in there, it doesn't look like your handwriting, does it?

A. No, it is not my handwriting.

Classics of the Courtroom

Q. You can tell your handwriting easy, can't you?

A. Well, many people have got, German people got about the same handwriting.

Q. About the same, many people?

A. Yes.

Q. That is the end of the book, isn't it?

A. Wait a minute.

Q. The last page you didn't write then, the last page, did you write it? You didn't write it, did you?

A. I can't make out this one.

Q. Well, if there is any doubt about it cross it off. The last page is not your signature, your writing. (Witness marks on page.) Except for that?

A. All right, if you say except for that,

Q. Well, I am going to give you all the exceptions.

A. Uh huh.

Q. Except for that—Just let me have the book a minute please.

A. I guess that is for a little child too.

Q. You think that is a little child too?

A. I guess.

Q. All right. Put an "r" on that page which you say you think is the drawing of a little child? (Witness marks page.) Put a circle around that "r" will you, please, because we have got r's in the back of the book—a circle around it. (Witness writes in book.) Now, is this also the drawing of a little child, this other piece, do you think that is too?

A. It is not my drawing.

Q. Well, I know, do you think that is also the drawing of a little child?

A. Looks like the drawing of a child.

Q. All right. Put an "x" there, an "x" with a circle around it. (Witness marks book.) That "x" with a circle also indicates that you consider to be the drawing of a child in your book. But, it is not yours anyway, it is not your drawing.

A. It is not my drawing.

Q. You are sure of that?

A. I am sure.

Q. All right, sir.

MR. WILENTZ: Now we offer this book.

Q. And, as I understand it, everything in this book except the page with the "x" on top of it, the "r" with the circle around it, and two more r's in back here, those two?

A. Yes.

Q. The drawing of the child, you said, and the last page, the hard page?

A. Well—

Q. And some things you crossed out?

A. There are marks from the card game on there either.

Q. Well, the marks from the card game—all right. Put an "h" on each one of these pages. The "h's" are not yours either?

A. (Witness marks.)

Q. That is right and the other page.

A. (Witness marks.) Which now?

Q. All right, take your time. Now look over it.

Q. If there is anything on the outside of the covers, we will charge that off. Everything else then is your handwriting except those things you have just indicated: is that correct?

A. That is correct.

MR. WILENTZ: And all those things we have been talking about as to the book—

I offer that very book now in evidence, if your Honor please.

MR. POPE: No objection.

(Memorandum book referred to received in evidence and marked State Exhibit S-261.)

....

Q. Now on April the 2nd, 1932, you remember that is the date that there has been testimony by Dr. Condon that he paid you $50,000?

A. Me $50,000?

Q. Yes. You recall that was his testimony. Now with particular reference to that date, April the 2nd, 1932, you had in your brokerage accounts 50 shares of Warner, isn't that right?

Classics of the Courtroom

A. That's right.

Q. That is all the stocks you had?

A. That is all the stocks I had.

Q. At that time?

A. Yes.

Q. On April the 2nd, 1932?

A. Yes.

Q. And you had in your bank account a balance of $200—$202.26?

A. That's about right.

Q. That is correct. That is all the money you had in the bank; that is all the stocks that you had?

A. Yes.

Q. Now you also had a mortgage which you and your wife purchased before you started buying stocks, isn't that right, about 1927 or 1928?

A. That's right.

Q. For $3,700 or $3,750 something like that, is that right?

A. Yes.

Q. April the 2nd, 1932, cash, $202, stocks 50 shares of Warner.

A. Yes.

Q. Is that right?

A. (Nods affirmatively)

Q. And the mortgage.

A. (Nods affirmatively)

Q. Now, in 1929, you had, you said, about $3,500 in cash at home, $3,000 or $3,500 I think you said. Is that correct?

A. '29?

Q. Yes. Well, if I am mistaken about it you tell me.

A. It is about right.

Q. About three thousand or thirty-five hundred. And in 1932 you had about $4,000.

A. Yes.

Q. Cash at home?

Richard Hauptmann

A. Cash at home.

Q. That was the cash you were hiding from your wife?

A. Yes.

Q. $3,500 in 1929, $4,000 in 1931—something like that.

A. Something like it.

....

Q. How much do you say you were worth in everything at the end of 1929?

A. Not even—I have to figure out.

A. (continued) On the end of '29.

Q. Yes, the beginning or the end; I don't care which it is, in the middle, any time in 1929, how much were you worth?

A. Oh, I figure around ten thousand, nine thousand, ten thousand.

Q. Nine or ten thousand?

A. Yes.

Q. Well, if it was nine, you wouldn't only have fourteen thousand, you have got $7600 total assets. When you put $7666 in this page for the year 1929, that was your total as you put it into this book of the assets: isn't that right?

A. Yes; except the money my wife—

Q. Except the money you were hiding on your wife?

A. Yes.

Q. All right. Now, let's come down to 1930. You still had quite some money in 1930, didn't you?

A. (No answer.)

Q. And so you keep up this record, that is, the number of hours you worked in 1927, isn't it, or the monies—what is that, the amount of monies you earned?

A. Let me see it.

Q. What does that German word mean, how do you pronounce it and what does it mean?

A. Weeks, week end, that is always the end of the week.

Q. The end of the week?

A. End of the week.

Q. Does that mean how much money you earned or got the end of the week, forty-five dollars?

A. Yes, sir.

Q. Twenty dollars, and so forth?

A. Yes.

Q. Those are monies that you earned when you worked.

A. Yes.

Q. On the other side you have got the monies Anna earned.

A. Yes. I didn't put the overtime in.

Q. You didn't put the overtime in?

A. No, doors put up, screens and things, I didn't put in.

Q. Were you hiding that from your wife?

A. Money I made I didn't show the wife.

Q. Most of the money you made that way you wouldn't show your wife?

A. No.

Q. Then the next page, the same thing, week after week you have got the amount of money you earned and the amount of money Anna earned, isn't that right?

A. Yes.

Q. Right from week to week, correct and accurate, right to the penny, isn't that right? And then you come down at the end of 1928 and you total again the amount of money you have got in the bank, how much of it is yours, how much of it Anna put in, how much Haberland owes you, how much Diebig owes you and how much Ernest owes you and how much you have got in the house, $112, isn't that right, in cash?

A. Yes, right.

Q. And so you are through with the end of that year. And you have $5,780. Did you ever have that much money when you were in Europe?

A. I got billions.

Q. Billions in Europe?

A. Yes. Inflation it was.

Q. What is it?

A. Inflation time.

Q. Inflation time?

A. Yes.

Q. You had billions.

A. Yes.

....

Q. That is a sort of a hallucination with you, isn't it, this billions business?

....

Q. You didn't really have billions, inflation or otherwise, in Germany or in Europe, did you?

A. Well, this was inflate money.

Q. Well, how much is the most money, inflated or otherwise, that you ever had in Europe, and when was it?

A. Very little.

Q. Very little. So this business about billions you think is a great joke, don't you?

A. No, I guess it is not a joke at all.

Q. Then you don't mean billions at all, do you?

A. (No answer.)

Q. How much would you say was the most money you ever had in your life before you came to the United States?

A. That only amounts to about a hundred dollars.

Q. About $100. So after you worked very hard and your wife worked very hard, you finally, at the end of 1928, got $6,666 saved together, didn't you?

A. Yes.

Q. And then at the end of 1929, you are still keeping an account of every dollar that you earn and every dollar that your wife earns, and what you did with it, and you take the inventory at the end of the year and you have done much better; you have saved some more money in the year and you have got up to $7,666?

A. Now may I explain?

Q. Yes, sir; you may explain.

A. This is marked in my wife's name, she earned every week $25, but it doesn't say exactly the full $25, because my wife, she was working as a waitress in a bakery at the counter, and she always got tipped, and so sometimes it was $30, sometimes more than that, but we put it every week $25 in.

Q. I see. Did she hide any money on you?

A. Well, I am not—I don't know.

Q. Well, you don't think she did, do you?

A. Well, of course, everybody got his secret, I guess.

Q. Everybody has got his secret. Do you think your wife was hiding money on you?

A. I never asked her.

Q. Do you think she was hiding money on you?

A. I really don't know.

Q. You wouldn't say she wasn't, would you?

A. I can't say anything about dat.

Q. You wouldn't give her the benefit of the doubt?

A. I don't tink so.

Q. You don't think so.

A. Yes.

Q. Well, all these amounts aren't $25, some are twenties, aren't they, and some are fives?

A. They are all twenty-fives, is it?

Q. Well, take a look at the third one, that is twenty, isn't it?

A. Maybe there was a holiday there.

Q. Well, maybe there was a holiday, but it is twenty just the same, holiday or no holiday, isn't that right?

A. That is a twenty there, yes.

Q. There is a five, and a five, that is not two twenty-fives, is it?

A. Well, that is for the whole, for the whole month. It would be only $10 for the whole month. I don't know, I can't remember exactly—

Q. That is—

A. —what was—

Q. That is why you put it in the book, because you couldn't remember, so you put it in from week to week, isn't that right? Isn't that right?

A. I put it in the week, to give me a showing in general how we are standing.

Q. Yes. Now, it was so general, that when you came to it and you earned $49.50, you put $49.50 in the book and not $49, isn't that right, isn't that so?

A. That $49.50, yes, sir.

Q. Yes, you even put the cents in you had earned, $29.25, is that exact or is that just general?

A. That is was always been the bay (pay) I got from my boss, but not extra bay.

Q. Not extra pay?

A. No.

Q. And so on.

A. Except the big ones, Haberland & Deuchstorff.

Q. So if you come to May, June, July, 1931, and on July the 11th, 1931, the book closes, no more accounts.

A. No, you are mistaken.

Q. 1930.

A. That is 1930.

Q. 1930. That is right. 1930. How many weeks after the Lindbergh child was born?

A. I don't know.

Q. You don't know?

A. (Nods negatively.)

Q. And the book stops then, doesn't it? And then you go into some other figures in the back of the book, monies—what is that? Monies that you loaned to Diebig and to Brill, or monies that they owe you or you owe them?

A. Let me see.

Q. Hours of work, I guess that is, the hours that you worked for them.

A. That is hours.

Q. Who did you build the three houses for that you talked about where you made this extra money?

A. Mr. Brill.

Q. Mr. Brill?

A. Mr. Haberland. Mr. Deuchstorff.

Q. And this is the Brill hours that you worked building the house, isn't it?

A. Yes.

Q. So you got your extra hours in here, haven't you?

A. Yes, that goes to a big amount because them people couldn't pay me right away, so—

Q. But you have got the extra hours in your book for Brill, haven't you?

A. Yes.

A. And you have got the extra hours in the book for Haberland.

A. Yes.

Q. So you weren't hiding that from your wife, the extra hours.

A. No, I got to keep this in the books.

Q. Sure you got to. That is why you kept it. But you haven't in there, in it, Haberland and Brill's extra hours.

A. Yes.

Q. Yes. Now that is the end then, July, 1930—that is the end of the account.

A. Yes.

....

Q. That is the beginning of 1928?

A. Yes.

Q. And you have got—how much cash have you got in the house then? "zu Hause, $112." What does that mean?

A. We got $112 home there.

Q. In cash?

A. In cash.

Q. All right. Now, then, I showed you the 1929 entry a moment ago, in the little book where it was written in pencil, and you have it in here again, $6,666: is that right?

A. Yes.

Q. Exactly the same; it is a copy, isn't it?

A. It is a copy.

Q. Surely. While you are looking at it, will you take a look at that "D" in "Deutschland."

A. Yes.

Q. Will you look at this "D" in the disputed handwriting (referring to chart on wall).

A. I see it. And I see a whole lot difference.

Q. You say they are different?

A. Oh, yes.

Q. All right, sir. Now we will come to the next page, 1929; and you copy again, don't you, from that little book, to make sure you will be able to keep it in pen and ink, now you have got it—$7,666 on January 1st, 1930; is that right?

A. Yes.

Q. Is that your handwriting?

A. Yes.

....

Q. Now in July, 1931, of course, in May, 1931, you had $3500 at least at home, didn't you?

A. Yes.

Q. That is May, 1931.

A. No, I guess I got a little more as that.

Q. A little bit more?

A. (Nods affirmatively.)

Q. In 1931 I think you did say about $4,000, in July, 1931.

A. Yes.

Q. That was your testimony. I want you to refresh your recollection now.

A. Yes.

Q. Now, in May, two months before that, I suppose you had a little bit less or something like $4,000, is that so?

A. What was the last date you said?

Q. July. Let me read your testimony just to refresh your recollection. Mr. Reilly asks you: "Can you tell us now about how much you had in cash just before you started for California in 1931?" Your answer was: "You mean by cash all the money in my possession, in the house?" Question: "In the house." Answer: "Yes. Oh, in the house was approximate a little bit over $4,000."

That is just about when you went to California. You remember that?

A. Yes.

Q. July the 5th.

A. Yes.

Q. So you had about $4,000. I want you to go back about two months to May, 1931. How much money did you say you had then, about? You don't have to be exact, $3,700, $3,800, or $3,900?

A. No. Probably a hundred dollars less. I really don't know.

Q. Yes, that is what I say, about 39.

A. No bookkeeping about that.

Q. Somewhere between $3,500 and $4,000, in between?

A. It is somewhere between 3,900 and 4,000, better put it that way.

Q. You had this cash. Now, don't forget that.

A. Yes.

Q. That is May, 1931?

A. Yes.

Q. Now, you got a letter from the broker for $74.89?

A. Yes.

Q. You weren't doing as well in the brokerage accounts as you did in your carpenter work, were you?

A. Well, I couldn't—

Q. In 1931?

A. This time I couldn't watch the broker, because I was working the same time.

Q. And so you were losing money?

A. Yes, that is correct.

Q. In other words, you found out you couldn't do the brokerage business and the carpenter work both and do them well, is that right?

A. That is right.

Q. And while you were trying to earn a few dollars as a carpenter, Wall Street was taking away hundreds, right?

A. That is right, that is right.

Q. So you, of course, got to the point where you were losing money?

A. Yes.

Q. You lost money until April 2, 1931, in your brokerage accounts, didn't you?

A. Yes, I did.

Q. About $3,000 or something like that?

A. That is about.

Q. $3,000 that you earned as a carpenter and that your wife earned as a waitress?

A. Yes.

Q. Is that right? You lost in the stock market?

A. Yes.

Q. Until April 2, 1932, is that right?

A. That is correct.

Q. And you were losing it right along up to, say, May 31, 1931, the market was bad, stocks were down, and the broker said to you, "Mr. Hauptmann, we need $74.89," isn't that right?

A. Yes.

Q. And so you wrote him a letter and said "Wait a few days for it"?

A. Yes.

Q. Now, you waited a few days, and did you send him the 74?

A. Oh, I can't remember. I suppose I did.

Q. Well, I am going to refresh your recollection then. Where did you get the $74 if you did give it to him? You had $3,500 in your home in cash?

A. As a rule I never touched—

Q. Not as a rule. I want to know, that money—

A. If he—

Q. That money, May, 1931, you got a call for $74 and some cents from the broker?

A. Yes.

Q. You had about $4,000 in cash in that trunk—

A. Yes.

Q. They were going to sell your stocks out if you didn't put it up; you went and got the money. Where did you get it from?

A. From my work.

Q. Where, from the trunk?

A. No, sir, never touched the trunk.

Q. Never touched the trunk?

A. No.

Q. Where did you go to get it?

A. It was probably a pay check coming.

Q. You didn't take it from the trunk, though, did you?

A. Did not.

Q. And the reason you didn't take it from the trunk was because you didn't have anything in the trunk, isn't that it?

A. No, as a rule I never touched the money in the trunk.

Q. Yes. You wanted to make sure that you would hide it on your wife?

A. That is right.

Q. So you went and paid the broker. You must have paid him all the $74; you didn't pay him less, did you, because you had a lot of money, you paid 74, didn't you, whatever he wanted?

A. I suppose—

Q. When you got the letter, you finally paid him the $74, four days afterwards, didn't you?

A. Well, I am not quite sure if I paid him them $74.89 four days after. I said I was going to pay him four days after, but if I did, I am not quite sure.

Q. Why did you write him when he asked you for $74.89 and you were worth $10,000, why did you write him and ask him to wait four days?

A. Because I ain't got them $74 not quite handy, and I was not going to touch the money I got at home.

Q. Not quite handy?

A. Yes.

Q. Thousands of dollars in cash laying in a trunk, money in a bank, stocks, mortgages, and not quite handy?

A. Yes.

Q. Is that the best explanation you can give?

A. Why should I take it for an amount for $74 and probably sell a mortgage or something?

Q. Well, you didn't have to sell the mortgage.

A. Sure.

Q. Because Anna wouldn't let you, would she?

A. No, that's right, too.

Q. Certainly that's right.

A. Sure.

Q. And that is why you didn't use the mortgage, is because Anna wouldn't let you, isn't that right?

A. (No answer.)

Q. Well, at any rate she wouldn't let you use the mortgage. Now forget the money in the trunk for a minute.

A. Yes.

Q. Anna won't let you sell the mortgage in 1932 and the only thing you have got besides the mortgage and the trunk is 50 shares of Warner and $212 in cash, isn't that right?

A. Yes.

Q. That is all you were worth that day, outside of those two items, isn't that right?

A. That again.

Q. On April the 2nd that's all you were worth outside of the money you say was in the trunk and Anna's mortgage, the $212 and the 50 shares of Warner.

A. Yes. There was a little bit money that amount to a few dollars that was outstanding; I don't know who it was.

Q. Outstanding?

A. Yes.

Q. And the 50 shares of Warner.

A. Yes.

Q. You know, of course, what it was worth; you were a stock market operator. You know it was selling for about $200 a share.

A. That's right.

Q. A hundred dollars. You had lost seven or eight hundred dollars on that one transaction alone.

A. Yes.

Q. Fifty shares of Warner Brothers.

A. Yes.

Q. You weren't such a good stock market operator, were you?

A. Well, you have to—the first time you got on the stock market you have to pay for it.

Q. And the first time you build a ladder you don't build a good one, do you?

A. I never build a ladder.

Q. You never built a ladder, did you?

A. No, sir.

Q. You built windows, though, didn't you?

A. No, sir.

Q. You built doors, didn't you?

A. No, sir.

Q. Did you build floors?

A. I lay floors, yes.

Q. You laid floors.

A. Yes.

Q. What did you build?

A. I build houses.

Q. You did?

A. Yes.

Q. You were a carpenter in Germany, weren't you?

A. For one year, yes.

Q. For one year?

A. Yes.

Q. You were a machinist, too, there, weren't you?

A. Yes.

Q. You used to make designs, didn't you, and drawings?

A. Well—

Q. Did you make designs and drawings as a machinist in Germany?

A. No.

Q. None at all?

A. Nothing at all.

Q. No blueprints?

A. No, no blueprints.

Q. Do you remember the circles in the Krupp, the symbol in the Krupp Company, the three interlocking circles?

A. I saw it.

Q. You saw that?

A. Yeah.

Q. But at any rate, when you first went into the market you weren't so good at it?

A. That is right.

Q. And you never built a ladder: that is sure?

A. That is positive.

Q. If you did build a ladder, the first one wouldn't be so good, would it?

A. I guess the first one would be very good.

Q. Very good, hey? Well, let's take a look at this $74 again. Do you remember whether you paid the $74 or whether you let him sell the stocks?

A. I can't remember, the amount is so little.

Q. Let me refresh your recollection. Didn't you then pay $50 on account of the $74.89 and take that $50 from your bank account?

A. I don't know.

Q. Well, let me show you. Possibly this may show it if anything does. Do you see the Warner Brothers—You owe them $74.89. That is the item, isn't it?

A. Yes.

Q. Now, that is May 20th—You owe that money?

A. Yes.

q. Now, you see May 25th: you write him you are going to pay him the money May the 25th, then you see the entry, "May the 25th, $50"?

A. Yes.

Q. That is what you paid him?

A. Yes.

Q. You didn't have the $74 to pay him, did you?

A. Oh, I did have the $74, I only have—

Q. You did?

A. I only have to go to the bank and take the money out.

Q. And then you got a telegram from the broker to pay the $24, didn't you, in December 1931, December—

MR. POPE: What year was that?

MR. WILENTZ: 1931.

Q. Two months before the Lindbergh child was kidnaped, didn't you get this telegram, December 2nd, 1931—or three months before: "Having no response—" Pardon me. Just take a look at that registry receipt. Is that your signature?

A. Yes.

Q. Did you sign for that telegram? Look at it.

A. (Examines carefully) Well, that is December 2nd, 1931—

Q. That is right. Did you get that telegram?

A. Well, I can't remember, but if there is my name on—

Q. Well, there it is, December the 3rd, 1931, you signed a registered receipt for it.

A. Then I got it.

Q. Now, does that refresh your recollection so that you know you received it? Not only a telegram but you got a registered letter too, didn't you?

A. Yes, I get a couple of them.

Q. Did you get a telegram like that?

A. It is signed—I can't remember a telegram, but I signed on this here.

Q. Or a letter?

A. And so I suppose I—

Q. You suppose you received it?

A. —I received it.

Q. And you remember from that now, do you not, that they sent you a telegram and wrote you a letter for the $24?

A. Must be this way.

Q. Must be that way. Now, read that telegram.

A. "Have no response—"

Q. "Having no response—"

A. "—to our previous—"

Q. "—to our previous—"

A. "—communication—"

Q. That is right: "communication, this—"

A. "—this is to advise you—"

Q. Yes.

A. "—that we intend—"

Q. "—that we intend—"

A. "—selling—"

Q. "—selling—"

A. "—sufficient stock—"

Q. "—sufficient stock—"

A. "—to liquidate the balance without further notice."

Q. "Carleton & Mott," isn't that it?

A. "Carleton-Mott."

Q. You don't have any trouble with the word "liquidate" since you have been in the market, do you?

A. Never read it.

Q. Never read the word "liquidated"?

A. Never write it.

Q. So you got a telegram for the $24 and some cents? You got letters anyway, didn't you?

A. (Nods.)

Q. And do you remember what you just read, "Having no response to our previous communications—" You had already received letters before that and notices to put up the $24, hadn't you, and you didn't put it up, did you?

A. Because the amount was too little. I really didn't much care for it.

Q. Oh, the amount now was too little?

A. Yes.

Q. How about $74.89? You didn't put that up: it was too big, wasn't it?

A. Well, you said I put up $50 of it.

Q. Yes, the $74.89, but the $74.89 was too big, so you only put up $50?

A. I explained it. Maybe I received the letter, probably on beginning of the week and I was not going—not willing to go to the bank to take the $74 out, so I sent him a letter to wait till Saturday and probably my pay check on Saturday was only $50, I suppose, and I sent him the $50.

Q. Well—

A. That is how I explain it.

Q. As a matter of fact, at the end of 1931 you were running very low for money, weren't you?

A. No, I wasn't exactly running low for money.

Q. You were losing money in the market heavily, weren't you?

A. I guess I didn't play in 1931 at all. There was—

Q. You had lost your money then. You had only 50 shares of Warner?

A. Yes.

Q. You had lost already a lot of money?

A. I lost a lot of money, yes, that is right.

Q. You took Annie Hauptmann's money out and ran it down from thousands of dollars with yours until at the end of December 1931, when they called for this money, you had a little over $100 in cash in the bank between you, and no cash: isn't that right?

A. I don't know how much money I got.

Q. Let me show it to you. What is your balance on the first of December, 1931?

A. Hundred dollars.

Q. And 96 cents?

A. Yes.

Q. That is all the cash that you had in banks, isn't that right?

A. Yes.

Q. And that $25, you finally went down on the 3rd day of December, when you got this telegram, just like the receipt shows, and you drew that $25 out, didn't you?

A. I can't remember if I drew it out.

Q. You see it shows, doesn't it?

A. It shows.

Q. And then that left you with $75.96?

A. That is right.

Q. And that is why you took some time to pay this $78, because you were getting down to where there was no more money left, isn't that right?

A. No, I was willing to take some of my money out from the trunk, so I pushed it out as far I could.

Q. When it came to losing money, you were losing Annie's money?

A. Just the same my money.

Q. But, what you were saving was your money from the trunk, isn't that right?

A. Yes.

Q. Did you want to get away from Mrs. Hauptmann?

A. No, it just happens that—

Q. Didn't you say when Mrs. Hauptmann came back from Germany that you couldn't live with her any more, that was when you had all these thousands of dollars at home?

A. What?

Q. Didn't you tell that to Mr. Brent that you can't get along with

Annie any more? Well, you did or you didn't?

A. Do you know what you are talking about?

Q. Yes, I know what I am talking about. You answer the question.

A. You are talking about my wife and me?

Q. I am talking about you and your wife, yes. Did you say that to Mr. Brent?

A. No.

....

Q. Now Fisch, he was your best friend, wasn't he?

A. Not my best friend.

Q. Now you say he wasn't your best friend?

A. I can't say the best friend, he was—

Q. Will you say that you didn't tell people he was your best friend?

A. He was my best friend, what I say, in business.

Q. Didn't you tell people that he was your very best and closest friend?

A. I got friends dey are just as good, I would say.

Q. Yes.

A. Just as dear to me as Mr. Fisch.

Q. All the friends you got have known you only since you are in this country, isn't that right?

A. Yes.

Q. Nobody that you know in this country today, none of them outside of your sister did you know in Germany, did you?

A. Oh, yes.

Q. Who?

A. Mr. Heim.

Q. Mr. Heim?

A. Yes.

Q. Who is he?

A. He lives right in New Jersey.

Q. But not Fisch, not Kloeppenburg?

A. No.

Q. None of those people?

A. No.

Q. Didn't you write letters saying that Fisch was your best and closest and dearest friend?

A. Closest?

Q. Well, best friend, I think that is the expression we used before.

A. Probably he write a letter.

Q. Probably he write a letter?

A. Yes.

Q. But it wasn't true, is that it?

A. It is true.

Q. It is true, so you wrote a letter he was your best friend and you think he was, well, one of your best friends?

A. One of my best friends.

Q. All right. And he told you to keep this money in the box.

A. Not money.

Q. Not the money, the box in a safe place.

A. Yes.

Q. He was very sick, you knew that.

A. Well, he was sick, but I really—

Q. You thought he would come back?

A. That is true.

Q. But you knew he was suffering from tuberculosis, or something like that, you knew that, didn't you?

A. I—now, listen. I was asking a couple of times about his sickness; he always said, "Never mind, I am all right."

Q. All right.

A. So I think he is O.K.

Q. Well, did you know it? Did you know it?

A. I know he was a little bit sick, but I never took it so serious.

Q. Well, he was sick anyway?

A. Yes.

Q. You didn't expect him to die, though?

A. No, sir.

Q. And here was your sick friend going home, and he asked you to keep this box in a dry place?

A. Yes.

Q. You knew from the day you moved into that house that that closet was a wet place, didn't you? You had complained about it all the time, isn't that the fact?

A. Complained a couple of times, yes.

Q. From the day you moved into that house you knew it was a wet closet, didn't you?

A. Oh, I wouldn't say from the first day.

Q. Well, from the six months or so?

A. Yes.

Q. You had complained about it?

A. Yes.

Q. But even though you knew that was a wet place, it was a wet closet, even though Fisch told you to keep it in a dry place—

A. Yes.

Q. He told you there were papers in it, you put it in the closet?

A. Because I couldn't go in the front room and I couldn't go in the middle room either, when Fisch gave me this package.

Q. You mean that night?

A. That night.

Q. Who was going to stop you? Weren't you the boss of the house? Weren't you the master of the house?

A. Yes, but I got somebody in the front room; my wife was in the baby's room; and so I put it in this closet, and I forgot all about it.

Q. You didn't want to show it to your wife and you didn't want to show it to your baby, is that it?

A. Oh, no.

Q. Well, why couldn't you take it right there, that very night— why didn't you take it there?

A. I didn't like to disturb the baby.

Q. You didn't like to disturb the baby?

A. Yes.

Q. Well, you didn't have a baby then, did you?

A. Yes.

Q. You did?

A. Yes.

Q. You didn't want to disturb the baby and you didn't want to disturb your wife?

A. That is right.

Q. Is that right?

A. Yes.

Q. And you forgot all about it afterwards?

A. Yes.

Q. Well, finally you found it?

A. Yes.

Q. You made a mistake, you put it in a wet place; Fisch asked you to put it in a dry place, you put it in a wet place, but you finally found it?

A. I found it, that is right.

Q. You found the money?

A. Yes.

Q. And you found it because a broom hit it, isn't that right?

A. Yes.

Q. There is no mistake about that, is there?

A. No mistake.

Q. A broom hit the box and you saw money?

A. Yes.

Q. When was that? When was that? What date, what month? You don't know, do you?

A. It was in the middle of August.

Q. 1933?

A. 1933. It was on a Sunday—

Q. Middle of August?

A. Yes.

Q. Was your wife home?

A. My wife, she was home, yes.

Q. Yes.

A. She was home.

Q. And you went to the closet?

A. I went to the closet.

Q. And you took the broom?

A. Yes.

Q. You were going to take it out, were you?

A. I took it out to clean something.

Q. You went to the closet to take a broom out, isn't that it?

A. Yes.

Q. And you were going out with it, isn't that right?

A. That is right.

Q. And when you did that, walking out of the closet with the broom, you hit that box?

A. No, walking that way I couldn't, I couldn't hit the box.

Q. Well, how did it happen then? That is what I want to know.

A. Probably the broom was mixed up or there was another broom and stuff laying in the closet.

Q. What shelf on the closet was it?

A. The upper shelf.

Q. Upper shelf, top shelf?

A. Top shelf.

Q. I want you to take a look at this picture of the kitchen and tell me whether that is a correct picture of the kitchen and the closet, that part of it shown by the photograph?

A. Yes, that's right.

Q. That shows your closet and shows your kitchen, does it?

A. Yes.

MR. WILENTZ: All right, I offer it in evidence.

...

Q. You met Mr. Fisch at the Henckle's home, didn't you?

A. I met Mr. Fisch at Hunters Island.

Q. Weren't you introduced to Mr. Fisch by the Henckles?

A. We knowed each other before.

Q. You knew who before?

A. Fisch and I.

Q. Fisch and you?

A. Yes.

Q. Fisch lived with the Henckles, didn't he?

A. He lived in the same house.

Q. The same house?

A. Yes.

Q. And you met Mrs. Henckle in the summer time at Hunters Island, 19—

A. About June, yes.

Q. June, 1932?

A. Yes.

Q. While your wife was away?

A. Yes.

Q. And you met Fisch at Hunters Island?

A. Before, yes.

Q. Not with Mrs. Henckle?

A. Not with Mrs. Henckle.

Q. Not through Mrs. Henckle?

A. Not through Mrs. Henckle.

Q. Now, Hauptmann, isn't it a fact that you are saying that you met Fisch before June because you are attempting to account in that way for the monies that you deposited before June?

A. Positively not.

Q. Didn't you tell to the police in your explanation of how you met Fisch that when you went to the Henckle home to meet Mr. Henckle, Mr. Fisch came into the house, and they introduced you?

A. But we knowed each other before.

Q. Didn't you say to the police at the Bronx, when they asked you, "How did you come to meet him?" meaning Mr. Henckle, "Who introduced him?" Didn't you answer as follows: "I was sitting with the family named Henckle; he was boarding in the same house. Mr. Fisch used to be upstairs and he often came downstairs for company." Didn't you say that?

A. Probably I said that, yes.

Q. And they asked you where did you meet him, didn't you say 127th Street?

A. Yes.

Q. Isn't 127th Street the Henckle home?

A. Yes.

Q. Isn't that where you met him?

A. Yes.

Q. Isn't that where you were introduced to him?

A. But it doesn't mean first.

Q. Oh, you forgot to put first in. Didn't they ask you who introduced you to him and didn't you say at the Henckle home that you were sitting with a family named Henckle, that is when you were introduced to him?

A. Well, I say we know each other long before.

Q. You didn't tell that to the police though, did you?

A. Well, this came too sudden.

Q. It can't be certain?

A. Came too sudden.

Q. Came too sudden.

A. Yes.

Q. When they asked you where you met Fisch, you told them you met him at Henckle's home, didn't you?

A. Yes.

Q. All right. Let's stay there for a minute. There you were in the police station, you told them that you had gotten this Lindbergh ransom money from a man by the name of Fisch.

A. Yes.

Q. You were trying to clear yourself of this story.

A. No, sir.

Q. They asked you then about Fisch, didn't they?

A. I can't remember.

Q. And they said to you, "Who introduced you to Fisch?" and you told them, "at the Henckle home."

A. I practically can't remember any question he put at me at this time.

Q. Well, you know that this business of Mr. Fisch—that was your story at the time and they were getting from you the explanation as to how you met him and when you met him, and all about it, and you told them you met him at Henckle's, isn't that so?

A. I really can't remember what I said.

Q. And didn't you say to them that you met him in July 1932?

A. Can't remember what I said.

Q. Will you say that you didn't tell the police, when you were first asked, that you met him in July 1932?

A. Well, to tell the truth, I really can't remember the questions the police put at me this time.

Q. When did you meet Fisch?

A. First part of March or first part of April.

Q. After March the 1st?

A. After March the 1st.

Q. No question about that?

A. I guess I am sure about it; it was after.

Q. You are sure about that. Now, take a look at these ransom notes. You have seen them all anyway, haven't you? You have seen all these notes, haven't you?

A. Yes.

Q. You saw them in the Bronx and you saw them here?

A. Yes.

Q. And you have listened to the testimony about them for days?

A. Yes.

Q. You have seen large reproductions of them here?

A. I did.

Q. Does it look as if somebody copied your handwriting? That is the way it looks, doesn't it?

A. Well, I am not familiar mit handwriting experts and so on.

Q. Well, you are familiar with your handwriting, aren't you?

A. Yes, I am.

Q. It looks as if somebody copied it, doesn't it, imitated your handwriting, doesn't it; some of these, anyway?

A. That is possible, yes.

Q. Well, does it look that way to you, that some of them were imitated, somebody copied them? That is the way it looks, doesn't it?

A. That is the way it looks.

Q. That is the way it looks. Now just stay there for a minute. Some of these notes, as you saw them, and as you have seen them, it looks as if somebody copied your handwriting, isn't that the way it looks?

A. (Nodding head.)

Q. You are shaking your head and the stenographer doesn't get it.

A. There are some figures in the handwriting looks like mine.

Q. It looks like somebody copied it, isn't that right?

A. Yes.

Q. All right. Now, before March 1, 1932, Isidor Fisch didn't know you and you didn't know him, did you?

A. I didn't know him, but I don't know if he didn't know me.

Q. You didn't send him any letters, did you, before March 1, 1932? Did you?

A. No, I did not.

Q. He wasn't in your home before March 1, 1932, was he?

A. No.

Q. So Isidor Fisch didn't write the ransom notes, did he?

A. I never said that.

Q. I know you didn't, but you know Isidor Fisch didn't copy your handwriting, don't you?

A. I don't know.

Q. He didn't know you then or you didn't know him?

A. I didn't know him.

Q. You had no business with him?

A. No.

Q. You don't say now that Fisch wrote those notes, do you?

Richard Hauptmann

A. I don't—I can't say anything about them notes.

Q. Can't say anything. All right, sir. But it looks like your handwriting, doesn't it, Mr. Hauptmann?

A. Some of them figures look like my handwriting.

Q. Yes. Now we will get back to Mrs. Henckle for a minute. You visited at the Henckle home quite frequently, didn't you?

A. Yes.

Q. What business was Mr. Henckle in?

A. Painter.

Q. And in 1933 you were there quite frequently, weren't you?

A. You mean 1932?

Q. 1932, 1933 and 1934.

A. Well, not so very often.

Q. You used to stop in in the mornings, didn't you?

A. Sometimes.

Q. Stopped in to see Mrs. Henckle in the morning, didn't you?

A. To see Mr. and Mrs. Henckle.

Q. Well, Mr. Henckle wasn't there when you got there, was he?

A. Well, he didn't work steady.

Q. When he was working he wasn't there, was he?

A. Of course he couldn't be there.

Q. Certainly not. But you stopped in just the same, didn't you?

A. Yes, I did.

Q. Visiting Mrs. Henckle in the mornings on your way to the stock market: is that it?

A. Yes.

Q. Now, you gave her a Christmas present too, in 1933, didn't you?

A. I don't think so, in 1933.

Q. Well, what year did you give her a Christmas present?

A. I guess 1932.

Q. 1932?

A. Yes.

Q. Henckle used to go to work at six o'clock in the morning, didn't he?

A. I don't know.

Q. Well, you know when you got there he wasn't there, you know that?

A. Sometimes he was, sometimes he was not.

Q. Did you have your coffee there in the morning?

A. Sometimes.

Q. Have breakfast there in the morning?

A. No, sir.

Q. Well, when you would have coffee in the morning with Mrs. Henckle, what would that be, the second cup of coffee, or was it the first?

A. Well, sometimes I am came in, came in, said "Do you want a cup of coffee?" I took a cup of coffee.

Q. Sure. You would have the coffee. About what time in the morning would that be that you would have the coffee?

A. Nine.

Q. Nine o'clock?

A. Nine o'clock, quarter after nine.

Q. Well, that would be the second cup that you would have, wouldn't that be, that day?

A. That is right.

Q. You always had the first cup in the morning with your wife?

A. Yes.

Q. You always took her to work in the morning, didn't you?

A. Now, listen: my wife worked only till '32.

Q. Well, while she was working, you would take her to work and have a cup of coffee with her in the morning; wouldn't you have breakfast?

A. Sometimes, sometimes not.

Q. Well, after 1932 you were no longer a carpenter, you no longer were working regular hours, so you had time, didn't you?

A. I still was a carpenter.

Q. Well, you weren't working at it, though?

A. Once in a while, but not steady.

Q. 1933, you continued to call at the Henckle home in the morning, didn't you, at nine o'clock about, or ten o'clock?

A. I sometimes went in between nine and ten on my way down.

Q. And when Mr. Henckle was there you were surprised, weren't you?

A. No, sir.

Q. No?

A. (Shakes head.)

Q. Did you go to visit Henckle or did you go to visit his wife?

A. I go to visit Mr. Henckle and—

Q. But—

A. —and Mr. Kloeppenburg.

Q. Kloeppenburg?

A. Yes.

Q. You would go to visit Mr. Henckle, but sometimes you would have hard luck and only Mrs. Henckle was there: is that it, is that what you mean?

A. No, I only stayed for five minutes, ten minutes; I made out appointment for playing cards or something.

Q. Would you make the appointment for playing cards with Mrs. Henckle?

A. If there was nobody there, yes.

Q. You met her at Hunters Island, didn't you, while your wife was in Europe?

A. Yes.

Q. And nobody introduced you to her, did they?

A. (No answer.)

Q. And nobody introduced you to her, did they? Oh, I think you said you don't need any introduction in Hunters Island.

A. Her family was there camping right next to us.

Q. Mrs. Hauptmann, when she came home, didn't like the new friendship, did she? She complained about it, didn't she?

A. Not—she didn't like it so well much.

Q. She didn't like it so well. That didn't make any difference to you, you still continued the friendship with the Henckles?

A. Well, she didn't say for me to stop it, not to go down there.

Q. No. Did you take Mr. Henckle out on hunting trips, gunning trips?

A. Well, he invited me.

Q. He invited you?

A. Yes, sir.

Q. Did you go along with him?

A. Yes.

Q. You used to stay there late at night at the Henckle home?

A. Well, sometimes we was playing cards.

Q. Late at night until the early hours of the morning?

A. Oh, usually one o'clock.

Q. Mrs. Hauptmann didn't like that, did she, your staying out away from her, did she, at the Henckle home.

A. Oh, sometimes she was along.

Q. Yes, but she didn't like your being at the Henckle home away from her, did she?

A. Well, I say she sometimes came along with me. We was together down there. Sometimes the Henckle family was in our house.

Q. Didn't Mrs. Hauptmann tell you not to bring Mrs. Henckle to your home?

A. I can't remember that.

Q. Will you say that she didn't tell you?

A. I can't remember my wife ever said anything to me like that.

Q. Didn't you have a fight with her about it, and she said, "I don't want that woman in my home?"

A. No.

Q. Didn't she say to you, "Richard, you are acting awfully funny since I came back from Europe; what's happened to you?"

A. No, sir.

Q. Didn't you pay all the expenses for Mr. Henckle when you went up on this trip?

Richard Hauptmann

A. I paid only for the gade—guide.

Q. For the guide?

A. Yes.

Q. What expenses didn't you pay?

A. Other expenses we split half and half.

Q. Didn't you buy a gun for the hunting trip?

A. Yes, I did.

Q. Did you pay for that?

A. I paid for it.

Q. Where did you buy that gun?

A. I don't know where I bought it.

Q. What gun was that?

A. It was a rifle.

Q. A rifle?

A. That is right. I paid it for him because in the summer time I got many times my supper by family of Henckle and I didn't pay anything at all, and so I paid him the rifle for it.

Q. You used to leave your car parked pretty near all day in front of the Henckle home, didn't you?

A. No, sir.

Q. You didn't?

A. Didn't.

Q. Where did you have your meals, Mr. Hauptmann, during 1932, March to April to May, etc.?

A. My meals?

Q. Yes.

A. Hardly can remember.

Q. Hard thing to remember?

A. Yes.

Q. Why? It was just you and your wife?

A. You probably mean when my wife was away, don't you?

Q. No, I don't mean when your wife was away. I mean when your wife was not away, March, 1932. Was she away then?

A. March, '32?

A. Yes.

A. I—

Q. Up in Jamaica?

A. No.

Q. Kingston?

A. No, sir. This time my wife was working and I was working.

Q. Then she was home?

A. Yes.

Q. That is the time I mean. Where did you have your meals?

A. At home.

Q. At home?

A. Yes.

Q. Breakfast?

A. When I was working I took breakfast along.

Q. When there wasn't work where did you have breakfast?

A. In a restaurant.

Q. In the restaurant?

A. Yes.

Q. What restaurant?

A. When I was around Sixth Avenue.

Q. Not the restaurant Mrs. Hauptmann worked at? You don't mean that, do you?

A. This restaurant was up in the Bronx. I can't travel 50 miles for breakfast.

Q. No, I am not talking about the time when you were working. When you were not working, where did you have breakfast?

A. When I was not working?

Q. When you were not working?

A. I got breakfast in the bakery from my wife.

Q. Where did you have your lunch?

A. Lunch? Whenever I was home I cooked myself something, when I was out, in a restaurant.

Q. What restaurant?

A. Just depends, where I was.

Q. Which place did you frequent, where did you go often, I don't want every restaurant, where you usually went, I mean. You see, we want to find out what you were doing around March 1st, that is why I am asking you the question.

A. This time I didn't have any usual restaurant at all.

Q. How about dinner time? Supper time, at night?

A. In the bakery or at home.

Q. Either bakery or at home.

A. Yes.

Q. If there was any restaurant you ate regularly, you have forgotten about it?

A. There is no restaurant I ate regularly.

Q. How about Hahn's, Fritz Hahn's restaurant?

A. That was not regularly.

Q. Didn't you go there with your friend Kloeppenburg?

A. Sometimes.

Q. Didn't you bring your wife there?

A. Yes.

Q. Didn't you have Mrs. Hahn visit you at your home?

A. Yes.

Q. Didn't you have Mr. Hahn visit you at your home?

A. I don't know about Mr. Hahn.

Q. You were customers there?

A. Yes.

Q. So you say you don't know whether he visited—

A. I am not quite sure.

Q. You used to be in his place very often?

A. I was.

Q. You used to talk about the Lindbergh case in there?

A. I can't remember.

Q. You listened to the radio the night that the word came over the radio that the Lindbergh child was found: you were there, weren't you?

Classics of the Courtroom

A. I don't know.

Q. And you rushed right out, didn't you, that night?

A. I?

Q. Yes, you. You, Hauptmann: didn't you?

A. No, sir. I can't remember when I hear it the first time even.

Q. You can't remember?

A. I don't know when I hear it the first time.

Q. But you were a customer of the Hahns, weren't you?

A. Yes.

Q. Why didn't you tell us so a minute ago? Are you afraid about the Hahns?

A. No. I told you there are so many restaurants that I really don't know.

Q. Did you have any other restaurant keeper come to your house like you had Mrs. Hahn?

A. (No answer.)

Q. You don't remember?

A. No, I don't think so.

Q. Did you ever have any other restaurant keeper come up and show her the clothes that you bought for your wife, the dresses, on her way to Europe, after the ransom money was paid?

A. You mean I bought my wife dresses since?

Q. Did you have any other restaurant keeper up at your house to show your wife's dresses to her, when your wife was leaving for Europe in May 1932?

MR. POPE: Now, we object to the question because there isn't a particle of evidence in the case that he ever had any restaurant keeper or anybody else up at the house and showed his wife's clothes. In other words, the question assumes something which is not in evidence, and which has no basis in fact.

THE COURT: I do not see its materiality at the moment.

MR. WILENTZ: All right, if your Honor please.

THE WITNESS: I will answer the question, your Honor.

MR. WILENTZ: Well, I think that—

THE COURT: Well, if you want to answer the question you may

answer it.

A. I never pay a dress for my wife; she always pays it herself.

BY MR. WILENTZ:

Q. The question was, was there any other restaurant keeper or proprietor, outside of the Hahns, with whom you were friendly enough to have come to your house? Now, that question was objected to; the Court sustains it. Do you still want to answer it?

MR. POPE: That wasn't the question that was objected to.

A. My brother-in-law.

A. My brother-in-law, he got a restaurant, he came in my house.

Q. Your brother-in-law?

A. Yes.

Q. So you did eat at Hahn's, once in a while.

A. Yes.

Q. Did you not?

A. Yes, I did.

Q. You remember around March 1st you went in the restaurant the first, or the second, the third or the fourth, at night, in the night time?

A. Well, which year do you mean?

Q. 1932.

A. That is one thing I can't remember.

Q. Do you remember some time around the first week of March or the middle of March when you came into that restaurant Mr. Fritz Hahn hollered to you, "Richard, how is your leg?" right across the restaurant; do you remember that?

A. No, sir.

Q. And you said absolutely nothing, do you remember that?

A. Will you fix a date, set the time?

Q. About the middle of March, maybe the first week of March, after the first of March?

A. I really can't remember in dis time, I was in his restaurant at all, I don't tink so.

Q. You don't think so?

A. No, sir. I guess I am positively sure I was not.

Classics of the Courtroom

Q. Well, were you in there in March at all, 1932?

A. Give me a chance to think a little bit.

Q. Yes. You can have a chance.

A. I can't remember, but I hardly tink I was in.

Q. I see.

Q. Do you know what this is, Mr. Defendant? (Exhibiting the plank S-204 to the witness). You do, don't you?

A. A piece of board, yes.

Q. From your house? What is the number of this board, do you know? It is S-204.

A. I really don't know if it is from my house. That is a piece of trimming and a piece of trimming from every house looks the same.

Q. That is from your closet, isn't it?

A. I am not quite sure.

Q. You are not quite sure?

A. No.

Q. That is your handwriting on there, isn't it?

A. No.

Q. What?

A. No, sir.

Q. That is not your handwriting?

A. (Shaking his head.)

Q. You take a look at that. You have seen it many times before. I will take the paper off for you so it will be easier. (Counsel removed the cellophane wrapper on the board.) Take your time about it now. First, tell me, are the numbers your handwriting?

A. The numbers look familiar upwards. I can't remember for putting it on.

Q. Just keep looking at those numbers and tell me whether or not they are in your handwriting and that you wrote them, the numbers?

A. I can't remember putting them numbers on.

Q. Did you remember better when you were talking to District Attorney Foley?

A. At that time I was quite excited.

Q. Were you excited when you got before a Supreme Court Justice in the State of New York in your extradition proceedings?

A. I say yes.

Q. You didn't tell the truth there, you mean?

A. Well, I was quite excited then.

Q. Do you remember that you had a hearing before a Supreme Court Justice by the name of Mr. Justice Hammer in the Bronx court house in New York?

A. I remember that, yes.

Q. Do you remember why you had the hearing, that you did not want to come to New Jersey to face the charge that you are now facing? Do you remember that?

A. I don't know what is the reason for this.

Q. Well, you were fighting extradition proceedings, weren't you?

A. I don't know what it, what it means.

Q. And you were asked this question with reference to Exhibit 204—

MR. REILLY: Page, please.

MR. WILENTZ: 83.

Q. Finally, you were asked this question: "Finally, one day thereafter you were brought in and questioned by District Attorney Foley, were you not?" And your answer was "Yes." "And District Attorney Foley asked you if you recognized a certain piece of wood or lumber, do you remember that?" And your answer was "Yes." Is that correct?

A. I will—let's explain before you read further.

Q. No. Wait a minute. I am going to let you explain when I find out what your answer is. Did District Attorney Foley ask you—No. Withdraw that. Isn't this the question that was asked of you in the Bronx County Court before a Supreme Court Justice while you were under oath?

A. I can't remember the, what the question was.

Q. "And District Attorney Foley asked you if you recognized a certain piece of wood or lumber, do you remember that?" And your answer is "Yes." Is that correct?

A. Well, I really can't remember what—all the questions.

Q. Now, the next question, "And you said yes, that was your handwriting, is that so, yes." Is that correct?

MR. REILLY: Just a moment. That isn't his answer.

MR. WILENTZ: That is the question.

MR. REILLY: That is the question, but that is not his answer.

MR. WILENTZ: Well, we are getting to that.

Q. Isn't that the question "And you said, 'Yes,' that was your handwriting, is that so, yes." Was that question put to you?

A. I really can't remember this question.

Q. Then the Court says—

MR. REILLY: He can't remember the question.

Q. —then the Court says: "You better mark this Exhibit A." You see this Exhibit A—Ex. A, referring to the board.

A. I see it.

Q. You see it?

A. All right.

Q. And then the next question that I asked you in the Bronx,

So that when you looked at Exhibit A, which was presented to you by the District Attorney of Bronx County, and you looked at the handwriting thereon, you said that was your handwriting, isn't that so, and your answer there was, "I said that is my lumber; I could not make out the handwriting." Do you remember that?

A. I can't remember them questions.

Q. Did you say that was your lumber, but that you couldn't remember the handwriting in the Bronx court?

A. I guess I did.

Q. You guess you did?

A. But you see if anybody shows me a piece of lumber, that is, a piece of trimming—

Q. Yes.

A. —you will find the piece of trimming in every house.

Q. Why didn't you say so in The Bronx instead of saying this was your lumber?

A. Well, I didn't think at all.

Q. You didn't think at all. All right, then, we will come to the next.

Richard Hauptmann

Your answer was, "I said that is my lumber, I could not make out the handwriting." Now, the next question, "You said the number on there is your handwriting," do you remember that question?

A. No, I don't.

Q. You mean to tell me that you don't remember being asked the question about the number on the lumber?

A. There was so many questions that I can't separate it.

Q. And didn't you answer "Yes" to that question? You said the number on there is your handwriting, "yes," in the Bronx Court, before Supreme Court Justice Hammer—didn't you say yes?

A. I can't remember this.

Q. Will you say that you didn't say "Yes"?

A. No, I said nothing about it.

Q. You said nothing about it?

A. No.

Q. Why, didn't we spend a half hour on that lumber in that court?

A. I don't know how much you spend on it.

Q. Well, you remember, do you—you were there, weren't you?

A. I suppose I was there.

Q. Sitting on the stand?

A. Yes.

Q. You suppose you were there?

A. (The witness nods.)

Q. You suppose you were in the Bronx, in the Court House?

A. Yes.

Q. You know what the hearing was about, don't you?

A. No, I really don't know what the hearing was about.

Q. You don't know about it? You don't know about it?

A. No.

Q. And then you were asked this question: "What about the Decatur"—and you were shown the word on the board—"What about the Decatur?" And your answer was, was it not? "A. I could not make out whether that was my handwriting and numbers." Do you remember that?

A. (No answer.)

Q. "I could not make out whether that is my handwriting or numbers."

A. There was many questions about it.

Q. You answered the question; was that your answer, in the Bronx Court House?

A. I can't remember my answer.

Q. You can't remember your answer. Now let me give you the next one: "The numbers are in your handwriting, are they not?" You remember being asked that again; and you said "They are." Do you remember that?

A. That's what I said, I can't remember what I said of it.

Q. Didn't you swear in the Bronx County Court House before Supreme Court Justice Hammer, swear unto God, that it was?

A. I did.

Q. You did.

Q. And the numbers you talked about were 2974, isn't that so? It is a little blurred now, isn't it?

A. Looks like it.

Q. It looks like 2974, and the numbers down here, 3-7154, isn't that right? Take a look at it. You don't wear glasses, do you?

A. No, I don't.

Q. You can see pretty well, can't you?

A. Not so very well.

Q. Not so very well?

A. No.

Q. All right then. Do you want it closer?

A. No, that is all right.

Q. Do you see it, 3-7154?

A. Yes.

Q. And between those two numbers are some words, it looks like "Decatur" first and "Sedgwick" second, you see that, don't you?

A. I can't make it out.

Q. You can't make it out. All right. Now, I was just talking to you about your testimony before the Supreme Court of the State of New

Richard Hauptmann

York in the extradition proceedings of the State of New Jersey against you, and you have just told us about it. Now, were you before that time, however, before Mr. Foley, the District Attorney of the Bronx, and he spoke to you about this piece of lumber, which is Exhibit S-204. You remember him talking to you about that?

A. Yes, I remember that I never could quite make out right if this was my writing or not.

Q. We will come to that. I want to see what you told him.

Q. (Continuing) "Hauptmann, I want to ask you some questions about this board. You know it is from the closet in your own house, don't you?" And your answer was, "It must be." Is that correct, do you remember that?

A. I can't remember every single question he put at me.

Q. No, I know you can't remember every single question, but you ought to remember something about that number. You know what that means, don't you, that number and that address on there?

A. Not exactly.

Q. Well, you know it is Dr. Condon's address and telephone number, don't you?

A. I know it now.

Q. You know it now. All right. You knew when Foley was talking to you about it, didn't you, that he was talking about Condon's telephone number and address on this board?

A. No, I did not.

Q. You didn't? All right, we will come to it then. The next question he asked you: "It is the same kind of wood, your handwriting is on it?" Do you remember that question?

A. I told you I can't make out any single question he put at me, there was so many questions.

Q. Well, you could remember your answer, if you had such a question, couldn't you?

A. I hardly think so.

Q. You hardly think so.

A. Because there was hundreds, hundreds of questions.

Q. Didn't you know that the State was charging that you got $50,000 from Dr. John Condon? You knew that was part of the charge, didn't you?

Classics of the Courtroom

A. Yes.

Q. Didn't you know that Dr. Condon was an important figure in this case, didn't you know that?

A. I learn it after.

Q. Didn't you know that if you had Dr. Condon's telephone number and address on the inside of your closet, that that was a serious thing so far as you were concerned?

A. I never was thinking about it.

Q. Didn't Mr. Foley ask you about it?

A. I can't remember that.

Q. You can't remember? Well, if Foley showed you this board and asked you whether that is your handwriting, Condon's address and telephone number, and if it wasn't you would know it, wouldn't you?

A. Well, he showed me dis piece of board.

Q. Yes.

A. And about the numbers and the handwriting—

Q. Yes.

A. —but right from the beginning I said I—

Q. You don't know?

A. —can't remember ever putting—

Q. You can't remember it?

A. —putting this on.

Q. Right from the beginning you said it?

A. Yes.

Q. Just listen to this answer then, and tell me whether or not you made it: "It is the same kind of wood your handwriting is on it? A. Yes, all over it." Did you make that answer?

A. No, I don't think so.

Q. You don't think so?

A. No.

Q. You couldn't be mistaken about something as important as this, could you? Did you say it wasn't?

A. I—

Q. Pardon me.

A. I can't remember I ever said something like that, "all over it."

Q. Well, let me then—

A. I don't think so.

Q. You think maybe you didn't say "Yes, all over it"?

A. (Witness shakes head) No, sir.

Q. Well, let me see, we are coming to another part of it. Do you remember the next question: "What did you write on that board, read it to the stenographer?" And you answered, did you not, "I can't read it any more." Do you remember that?

A. No.

Q. And do you remember the next question: "Who rubbed it out? Can you read the address on it?" And your answer was, "2974, I can't make out the first. I read the number down below, 37154." Do you remember reading the numbers just as I have given it to you?

A. Yes, he give me a big glass.

Q. A glass, a magnifying glass?

A. A magnifying glass, and that is how I could make out the numbers.

Q. And so you gave him the numbers when you got the magnifying glass, is that it?

A. Yes.

Q. And Mr. Foley asked you "What else can you read on that board that you wrote yourself?" And you kept the magnifying glass and you answered as follows, did you not, "I can't read, that is 'A', 'T', 'U', 'R', another one I can't make out." Do you remember that?

A. I guess this was like that.

Q. Yes. You looked at this board and out of the "Decatur"—D-e-c-a-t-u-r—all you could read was a-t-u-r, and you said "Another one I can't make out."

MR. POPE: We object to that question, because the witness has never said that he ever read "Decatur" on there.

MR. WILENTZ: He never said what?

(Pending objection read by the reporter.)

MR. WILENTZ: I said out of the Decatur he was only able to read those—

MR. POPE: That is merely the conclusion of the Attorney

General, that the word is intended to be "Decatur." It is for the jury to determine what the word is intended for.

MR. WILENTZ: That is the fact.

THE COURT: Well, of course, but the Attorney General is cross examining this witness, a fact that it seems to me you are inclined to overlook. I think the question is proper.

MR. POPE: He is examining him upon something which is not based upon any direct premise.

THE COURT: Well, that is your notion about the thing; I have a different notion.

MR. POPE: May we have an exception?

THE COURT: You may have your exception.

(Exception allowed, and the same is signed and sealed accordingly. Judge.)

Q. So you did read those letters that I have just read, did you not, the "a" and "t" and "u" and "r"?

A. No.

Q. You didn't read that?

A. No.

Q. You didn't answer "I can't read," you didn't answer that?

A. I read it through the glass.

Q. The magnifying glass. Did you read some of the letters, "a," "t," "u," and "r," and say "The others I can't make out"?

A. I guess I did; I am not quite sure.

Q. Then Mr. Foley said to you "That is Dr. Condon's address, isn't it?" And you answered, "I don't know." Do you remember that?

A. I can't remember whether I said, "I don't know."

Q. Don't you remember him saying to you, "That is Dr. Condon's address," and you saying, "I don't know"?

A. Well, I guess I was right, because I didn't know it.

Q. You guess you were right: is that your answer?

A. I said—

Q. You didn't know?

A. I didn't know it.

Q. What I want to know is whether Mr. Foley asked that question

Richard Hauptmann

and whether or not you answered it in the way I have just read it. Did Foley ask you this question: "That is Dr. Condon's address, isn't it?" And did you answer it, "I don't know"?

A. I can't remember this particular question.

Q. You can't remember it. Did he say anything to you about Condon, that this was Condon's address and telephone number?

A. I guess he said something, but I can't remember what he said.

Q. Well, he was talking to you about the Lindbergh case, wasn't he?

A. Yes, sir.

Q. And he was talking to you about the telephone number of somebody, and address of Condon: isn't that what he was talking to you about?

A. That is what he told me after.

Q. And he was talking to you about this board, wasn't he, this piece here, S-204, wasn't he?

A. I guess it was this one.

Q. You guess it was? You are doing a lot of guessing this afternoon about this board, aren't you?

A. Oh, no.

Q. You're not, hey? All right. Then listen to the next question. Do you remember him asking you, "Why did you write it on the board?" Do you remember that? Do you remember the question?

A. I can't make out them single questions.

Q. Now, do you remember this answer to that question: "I must have read it in the paper about the story. I was a little bit interest and keep a little bit of a record of it and maybe I was just in the closet and was reading the paper and put down the address;"—do you remember that?

A. Not exactly; I—

Q. Will you say that you didn't?

A. I don't want say that, I didn't—

Q. You don't want to say you didn't answer Mr. Foley that, do you?

A. I really can't say yes or no about it.

Q. You can't say yes or no. All right; we will let it go at that for

Classics of the Courtroom

the minute.

A. Yes.

Q. You don't want to say yes and you don't want to say no?

A. (Nods head.)

Q. That is to say you don't want to say yes or no to this: that you told Foley that you must have read it in the paper, the telephone and the address of Dr. Condon, you were a little bit interested, and you kept a little bit of a record, and maybe you were in the closet and were reading the paper and you put down the address. You won't say yes or no, that that was what you told him?

A. I guess I told him something about it.

Q. What do you think you told him?

A. I—

Q. Now, we will give you a chance to tell just what you think you did tell him.

A. Yes.

Q. Tell us, please.

A. That is a habit, when I read something in the paper or something in a book—

Q. Yes.

A. —that I make a notice on a, mostly I put it in the kitchen. When you look through my kitchen I guess you find plenty of notice like that.

Q. Well, why didn't you say so in the first place, instead of stalling with me and fighting with me: you have a habit of writing down telephone numbers, isn't that it?

MR. POPE: Now, this—

MR. WILENTZ: Please.

MR. POPE: There is no evidence of stalling. The witness has answered the question.

MR. WILENTZ: I think there is evidence that he has been stalling for a half hour with me on this thing.

MR. POPE: May we ask that the Attorney General be admonished for those remarks?

THE COURT: I decline to admonish the Attorney General.

MR. POPE: And that the jury be instructed to disregard them?

THE COURT: I decline to make any such instruction.

MR. POPE: May we have an exception?

THE COURT: Yes, sir.

(Exception allowed and the same is signed and sealed accordingly. Judge.)

Q. Now, Mr. Hauptmann, what you mean then is this, that you have got a habit of writing down telephone numbers and addresses of things that are interesting; isn't that right?

A. Yes.

Q. From the paper.

A. From the paper or—

Q. Or from anything else?

A. From books.

Q. Yes. And you must have read this in the paper, and you were near the closet, so you wrote it down; that is what you mean, isn't it?

A. There is a possibility, but I can't remember—you took this piece of wood, you said you took this piece of wood from the closet, and it is impossible to stay inside in the closet and to write or read.

Q. That is—

A. That is, I guess that is what you said, or Mr. Pope meant, and so I said it is impossible that I would ever put this on this board.

Q. Well, you know you wrote some of it; you know that, don't you? You remember that.

A. But I am positively sure I wouldn't write anything in the inside of a closet.

Q. You know that part of it, part of the numbers are your handwriting; you know that, don't you?

A. It looks like it.

Q. Yes. Well, you know it is; you have said so many times, in the Bronx.

A. I don't say it is.

Q. Well, didn't' you say in the Bronx many times that you wrote the numbers on?

A. I said it looks like.

Classics of the Courtroom

Q. You told Mr. Foley that it was, and you told me in court that it was, in the Bronx, didn't you?

A. (No answer.)

Q. And didn't you say at that time that the reason you wrote it in there was just like you said a minute ago, that you had a habit of writing those things.

A. Yes, I said so, but that doesn't—

Q. And that is why—sir?

A. That doesn't include this board. I wouldn't make any notice on the inside of a closet where you have no chance to stand to write or read, it is impossible.

Q. In the closet, no chance to stand to write or read in the closet, that is why you put it in the closet, you didn't think anybody could find it, isn't that why you put it there?

A. No, I make notice sometimes when a person is born that means his birthday, I want it in a place where I can see it.

Q. That is why—

A. No, that is why I always put it in the kitchen.

Q. Now let met get back to your question and answer and don't get me off the track again. Did you tell Mr. Foley that that was your handwriting? We will start all over again.

A. Yes, all over again. I don't know, sir, that I did.

Q. You think you did?

A. I think I did not.

Q. Did you say to Mr. Foley when he asked you why did you write it on the board, do you remember that question, and you said to him substantially what you have just told us here, "I must have read it in the paper about the story. I was a little bit interest and keep a little bit record of it and maybe I was just on the closet and was reading the paper and put down the address." Did you say that?

A. I say I don't know if it is exactly what I said to him.

Q. It sounds all right?

A. I said something to him, I know.

Q. Something like that?

A. Something like it, yes.

Q. Substantially that?

Richard Hauptmann

A. What does "substantially" mean?

Q. It means practically that, that is what it means, the same thing.

A. I said to him something about my habit of writing numbers.

Q. You had a habit of writing numbers?

A. No, not numbers—for instance, I am interested in a book and for instance there is a person, when this person was born or that person, and that was why I was interested to remember this in history, I am much interested in history and so I couldn't forget. I always put it on the place. It was usually the place underneath the mirror in the kitchen.

Q. In other words, you were interested in historical events and dates?

A. Yes, sir.

Q. And you had the habit of marking down in the kitchen on the wood, is that what you mean?

A. Yes.

Q. Were you interested in historical events relating to aviation?

A. No.

Q. You were interested in that?

A. No.

Q. Do you know who was the greatest aviator for Germany during the World War?

A. Yes, I know.

Q. What was his name?

A. Richtofen.

Q. What was his first name?

A. Manfred.

Q. Mnafred Richtofen?

A. Manfred Richtofen, yes. Besides I was just reading the book in the jail, and that brings my memory back.

Q. You are reading a book about the greatest aviator in the German Army in the jail?

A. About four weeks ago I read it in the jail here.

Q. Tell me what his name is again?

A. Manfred Richtofen.

Classics of the Courtroom

Q. Manfred Richtofen?

A. Yes.

Q. Now, we will get back to this board again and the telephone number or the words written on that board. So that you say now that when Mr. Foley asked you why did you write it on the board you said something to him that you had a habit of writing dates and other things about historical events.

A. I told him something, yes, about that.

Q. Well, Mr. Foley wasn't satisfied with that, was he, he asked the next question, "How did you come to put the telephone number on there?" And your answer was, was it not, "I can't give you any explanation about the telephone number." Do you remember that?

A. No, I can't.

Q. You can't remember that?

A. I can't remember all, in dem days—

Q. I want to know whether you can remember that question and answer and whether or not you gave that to Mr. Foley.

A. I can't remember.

Q. You were then talking to the District Attorney of Bronx County, you were incarcerated, you were kept in custody and you were charged, you knew you were being charged with murder by the State of New Jersey.

A. No, I didn't know that.

Q. You didn't know that?

A. No.

Q. You knew you were arrested in the Lindbergh case.

A. Yes.

Q. Yes, sir. You knew the Lindbergh child had been dead, you knew that, didn't you?

A. Yes.

Q. You knew somebody had gotten $50,000 or so they said, from Dr. Condon, you knew that?

A. That is what I read in the paper.

Q. And you were asked about Dr. Condon's telephone number and home address in your closet on a board which was then right before you, you remember that.

A. Yes.

Q. And today you don't remember what you said to Mr. Foley about that.

A. I said I can't remember all them single questions, because there was so many questions at this time.

Q. Can you remember any of them?

MR. POPE: Let him answer.

MR. WILENTZ: Yes, I think possibly I have interrupted him.

THE COURT: You may answer.

MR. WILENTZ: Mr. Reporter, before you go out, will you let us have the question and the answer. If he wants to add to it, he may do so.

(Question and answer read by the reporter as follows:

"Q. And today you don't remember what you said to Mr. Foley about that? A. I said I can't remember all them single questions, because there was so many questions at this time.")

Q. You have answered the question then, haven't you?

A. (No answer.)

Q. You have finished that answer, haven't you?

A. I have finished this answer.

Q. You wanted to tell Mr. Foley the truth, didn't you?

A. Yes.

Q. Mr. Foley treated you well, didn't he?

A. Very well.

Q. He is a very delightful man, isn't he?

A. Yes.

Q. A very fine man?

A. Yes.

Q. Yes. And you were sitting in there in his office and he was asking you about it, wasn't he?

A. Yes.

Q. And you were answering him?

A. Yes.

Q. And there was a stenographer there, isn't that right?

Classics of the Courtroom

A. Well, there were quite a few people in the room.

Q. Yes, but there was a man writing, wasn't there?

A. I can't remember seeing anyone writing.

Q. Did you tell the District Attorney at that time the truth when he was talking to you about this board, S-204?

A. Well—

Q. You don't know whether you told him the truth? Why don't you answer the question, Mr. Defendant?

A. For the first time he brought this piece of wood and he said that's from my closet. Well, anybody can show me a piece of wood like that; you find it in every house. I didn't even think of it, what I said.

Q. Oh, you didn't even think of it. Did you tell District Attorney Foley the truth when he spoke to you about this board, S-204? You might just as well answer it because I am going to stay here until you do.

A. The truth? Well, I told him—

Q. Did you tell him the truth?

A. I told him the truth, yes.

Q. You told him the truth?

A. Yes.

Q. Did you tell the truth about this board in the Supreme Court in New York?

A. I—

Q. Why do you hesitate?

A. I am not.

Q. Well, then, why don't you answer? Either you did or you didn't.

A. You have to give me a chance.

Q. I will give you all day, but you ought to know whether you told the truth in court.

A. No, I have to trans—I am thinking in German and I have to translate it in American language, and it needs quite a bit of time; so excuse me.

Q. Yes, sir. But just the simple question of whether you told the truth in The Bronx courthouse about this board—

A. When I told Mr. Foley—

Q. No, please. I am going to ask you the question again. When you were examined in the Bronx County courthouse specifically about 204, did you tell the truth there?

A. I was.

Q. Please will you—

A. I was not willing—

Q. Pardon me. Will you please answer the question? Can't you answer it Yes or No, you either told the truth or you didn't? Then you can give the explanation.

MR. POPE: We think that the witness is trying to answer it and that he should be given an opportunity to do so.

THE COURT: Yes, he ought to be given an opportunity and I think he is being given an opportunity. The question was as to whether or not he told the truth there. He may answer that and then he may add to it anything he desires to add to it by way of explanation. That I think the witness is entitled to.

Proceed, Mr. Attorney General.

Q. Did you tell the truth in the Bronx Court house, Yes or No? And then if you want to explain it you may explain it as far as I am concerned.

A. Well, I guess I explain it first.

Q. Will you please do us the kindness of abiding by the rules of the court and answer first Yes or No did you tell the truth about this board when you were being examined in the Bronx County Court House under oath about this board?

A. Then I say No.

Q. You didn't tell the truth there?

A. No.

Q. All right. Now, just stay there for one minute.

MR. POPE: Wait a minute, now.

A. You want to give me a chance to explain?

Q. Yes, sir.

THE COURT: He may have it.

A. When I saw Mr. Foley the first time speak about this particular board here I never said Yes and I never said No, because I never could make out and I never could remember ever putting it out, and when it came up in the court room I only simple said Yes, mitout thinking of it.

Q. You simply said Yes, what?

A. When he asked me if I put it out.

Q. You simply said Yes, in the court room without thinking about it?

A. Yes, without thinking about it.

Q. You mean that you just paid no attention, you have no interest in the case?

A. No, interest—Of course I got to have interest in it, but really is to get over it, first place, I didn't know what to say, so I said Yes. Just as well I could say No.

Q. When was that, before Foley or in the court?

A. In the courtroom.

Q. Go on, tell us. You want to explain. Go on and explain.

A. I guess I am finished with the explanation.

Q. You are finished with the explanation?

A. Yes.

Q. What do you mean by explanation? Do you mean that you said No, it didn't make any difference to you or rather you mean you said Yes, and that wasn't the truth? That is the first thing you mean, isn't it?

A. Yes.

Q. That is in the court house when you said Yes you wrote that on the board, you really meant No?

A. This came—

Q. Is that what you mean? Is that what you mean, Mr. Hauptmann?

A. Will you—

Q. In the court house you say you didn't tell the truth because when you said Yes that you wrote this, you didn't mean it?

A. I didn't mean it, that is right.

Q. That is right. So you did say in the court Yes you wrote it, in the Bronx County court, but that was not the truth?

A. This was not the true.

Q. Not the truth?

A. After I was thinking of it, this board, special from the pl where they took them, and it is impossible I ever put it on.

Q. Now, you were examined by District Attorney Foley on S tember the 25th, 1934, you remember that, about a week after y were arrested.

A. That is about.

Q. And after you were examined by District Attorney Foley, hearing in the Bronx, October 17th, 22 days after you made the st ment to Mr. Foley, you came into the Bronx County Court Hous oppose the efforts of the State of New Jersey to bring you here trial, so you had some time to think about the board, didn't you?

A. I really—I never was thinking about it.

Q. You had a lawyer in court, didn't you, in the Bronx Cou Court?

A. I did, yes.

Q. Yes, sir, and you were represented by a lawyer when this h ing was on?

A. Yes.

Q. You were in the courtroom where they were taking your tures every day, weren't they?

A. Yes.

Q. You knew how important it was?

A. Well, I don't know exactly how important it was.

Q. You don't know how important it was?

A. No.

Q. Your wife was in there saying to you, "Richard, please tell truth," every day, wasn't she?

A. Yes, she was.

Q. And with all of that, with a charge of murder against you the State of New Jersey and your wife pleading with you to tell truth, you walked in before a Supreme Court Justice in New Y State and you lied, and when you lied you knew you lied, didn't y

A. No, that is not lying, I give this answer mitout thinking a thing, I could just as well say no or yes.

Q. Well, it wasn't one question and one answer, Mr. Defend

Classics of the Courtroom

as it?

A. My physical condition wasn't so well at this time.

Q. At that time?

A. No.

Q. October 17th?

A. No.

Q. It was just as good as it is now?

A. No, sir.

Q. It wasn't?

A. No.

Q. Let's see. Did you say anything to the Judge at the time about your physical condition, that you couldn't answer or didn't want to answer?

A. I can't remember to make any complaints.

Q. Did you say anything in court at the time that you would like to have the hearing postponed?

A. I don't think I did.

Q. Your physical condition was good enough to deny that you were in the State of New Jersey on March 1st, wasn't it?

A. That is one thing I am positively sure of.

Q. Sure. Your physical condition was good enough to deny that you murdered the Lindbergh child, wasn't it?

A. I never saw the Lindbergh child.

Q. You jumped out of your chair when I asked you about that, didn't you, in the Bronx courthouse?

A. In the Bronx courthouse I jumping out of my chair?

Q. Yes.

A. I said No.

Q. Your physical condition was good enough for that?

A. That is one thing that is so absurd that you can sleep when you are up against that.

Q. That is one thing you are sure of?

A. Yes.

Q. You were never in that Lindbergh house, were you?

A. No, sir.

Q. Certainly not?

A. Certainly not.

Q. You never went in there and took that child out of that room, did you?

A. No.

Q. You never took that chisel into that bedroom, did you?

A. I never was.

Q. You never took that ladder up there, did you?

A. I even didn't build that ladder.

Q. You didn't even take that ladder out of your attic, did you?

A. No, sir.

Q. You didn't collect the $50,000 either?

A. No.

Q. You got part of it, didn't you? Who got the rest of it?

A. The—

Q. Who got the rest of it?

A. I don't know anything about it.

Q. You don't know anything about it but you wrote Condon's name and address on this board, and that is what we are back to now.

A. No, positively not.

Q. Positively not?

A. Positively not.

Q. Let me read you some of your answers then:

"How did you come to put the telephone number on there?" And your answer was, "I can't give you any explanation about the telephone number." Then your next question—I read that to you a minute ago. "Your only explanation for writing Dr. Condon's address on this board and telephone number is that you were probably reading the paper in the closet and you marked it down, is that correct?" And wasn't your answer as follows: "It is possible that a shelf or two shelves in the closet and after a while I put new papers always on the closet and we just got the paper where this case was in, and I followed the story of course, and I put the address on there."

Did you say that to Foley?

A. Yes.

Q. All right.

A. I say that.

Q. You said that to Foley. It is possible you were reading a paper and you were in the closet and you were interested in the case, so you marked it down on the closet?

A. But it is impossible to mark it down in the closet.

Q. And then the next question: "That's why you marked it on the door?" You had something on the door, too, didn't you? Some numbers of some bills, some big bills?

A. On the panel.

Q. On the panel?

A. Door panel.

Q. You had on the door panel, that same door, some numbers of big bills, didn't you?

A. Yes.

Q. What were the size of those bills, $500 and $1,000, weren't they?

A. It was a thousand, I guess.

Q. Thousand dollar bills?

A. Thousand dollar bills.

Q. How many thousand dollar bills did you have?

A. I can't remember now. When I put it on, it was Summer time '32.

Q. Yes, sure, Summer time '32; after April the 2nd, 1932?

A. No; Summer time '33; I wish to correct.

A. Oh, I see.

A. I got $2,000 I should put in the stock market and I didn't put it in the stock market, I brought it to the bank, and I kept it home for a few days.

Q. Two one thousand dollar bills?

A. Yes.

Q. Tell me, where do you get those one thousand dollar bills?

A. That is Mr. Fisch brought it in my house, to put it in the margin.

Q. Oh, Mr. Fisch brought it?

A. Yes, sir.

Q. We are going to come to Mr. Fisch in a little while.

A. Yes.

Q. Now let's get back to the board again.

A. Yes.

Q. The next question—oh, I just asked you about that; that is, the next question was why you marked it on the door and you said, "That is the only explanation I can give."

Q. And then you were asked by Mr. Foley, "Your answers to my questions are made of your own free will: is that correct?" And you answered, "Yes." Isn't that right? That is, you made the answer to questions, Mr. Foley asked you if you made the answers of your own free will, and you said Yes, isn't that right?

A. Yes; I guess I said to everybody, everything Yes at this time.

Q. Now, do you remember being asked this, "Is there anything more you want to say about it or add to it," you were asked that, and your answer was this: "No. About them two numbers, I am sure it was five hundred or thousand dollar bills." Do you remember saying that?

A. I guess I did say so.

Q. You didn't even know whether it was a $500 or a $1000 bill, isn't that right, it was one or the other?

A. Yes, one or another.

Q. You mean to tell me that you sat in The Bronx courtroom, talking to Foley about $500 bills and $1000 bills, and didn't know whether it was five hundreds you had or thousands?

A. That is true, I don't know if it was a five—

Q. You didn't know?

A. —hundred dollar bill or a thousand dollar bill.

Q. A man that had, the greatest amount of money you ever had in Europe was a hundred dollars, and you couldn't remember in 1932 whether the bills laying around the house were thousand dollar bills or five hundreds?

A. This time, '33, I get quite a lot of money to put in the market, put in force, so I really, I couldn't remember if it was 500 or 1,000.

Classics of the Courtroom

Q. And that is what you told Mr. Foley?

A. Yes.

Q. All right. As you remember, then, you were asked, "When you say those two numbers you don't refer to anything on this board, when you talk about the two numbers you don't mean anything written on this board, but other numbers written on the door," and your answer was, "Yes, on the door." That is true, isn't it? That is, you told Foley that you didn't mean anything on that board, you meant the numbers on the sash or the door?

A. On the door pillar?

Q. Yes.

MR. PEACOCK: Panel of the door.

Q. On the panel of the door?

A. Panel of the door.

Q. And then you were asked, "Is there anything else that you would like to add," and you answered "No," isn't that correct?

A. Well, I can't—that is what I say; I can't remember.

Q. All right then, weren't you asked then, "Do you remember the day that you wrote this memorandum on the board," the memorandum, referring to the memorandum on Exhibit S-204, you were asked that question, weren't you: "Do you remember the day that you wrote it?" and your answer was "No." You remember that, don't you?

A. That is what I said, I can't remember them questions and the answers.

Q. Then you were asked again, "You remember that you did write it?" And your answer was, "I must write it, the figures, that is my writing." Do you remember saying that to Mr. Foley?

A. I guess I said it must be, it looks like my writing.

Q. Do you remember saying that to Mr. Foley?

A. No, I can't.

Q. "I must write it, the figures, that is my writing"?

A. I guess I said it looks like my writing.

Q. You guess you said it looks like your writing?

A. I guess; I can't exactly remember, but I said—

Q. You say you didn't say that, "I must write it, the figures, that is my writing"?

Richard Hauptmann

A. That is what I said, I can't remember that what I said.

Q. Well, at any rate, you had talked to Foley, all these questions, September, 1932, you knew when you were coming into the courthouse to answer the complaint of the State of New Jersey, you knew you were going to be asked about it, again, didn't you?

A. Well, I didn't know if I was going to ask again about it.

Q. What did you think they were going to ask you about, your hunting trip up in Maine?

A. No. I really don't know.

Q. You didn't know?

A. I know there is a lot of things to put on the particular board.

Q. This is funny to you, isn't it? You are having a lot of—

A. No, absolutely not.

Q. You are having a lot of fun with me, aren't you?

A. No.

Q. Well, you are doing very well, you are smiling at me every five minutes?

A. No.

Q. You think you are a big shot, don't you?

A. No. Should I cry?

Q. No, certainly you shouldn't. You think you are bigger than everybody, don't you?

A. No, but I know I am innocent.

Q. Yes. You are the man that has the will power, that is what you know, isn't it?

A. No.

Q. You wouldn't tell if they murdered you, would you?

A. No.

Q. No. Will power is everything with you, isn't it?

A. No, it is—I feel innocent and I am innocent and that keeps me the power to stand up.

Q. Lying when you swear to God that you will tell the truth. Telling lies doesn't mean anything.

A. Stop that!

Q. Didn't you swear to untruths in the Bronx Court house?

A. Stop that!

Q. Didn't you swear to untruths in the court house? Didn't you lie under oath time and time again? Didn't you?

A. I did not!

Q. You did not?

A. No.

Q. All right, sir. When you were arrested with this Lindbergh ransom money and you had a twenty dollar bill, Lindbergh ransom money, did they ask you where you got it? Did they ask you?

A. They did.

Q. Did you lie to them or did you tell them the truth? Did you lie to them or did you tell them the truth?

A. I said not the truth.

Q. You lied, didn't you?

A. I did, yes.

Q. Yes. Lies, lies, lies, about Lindbergh ransom money, isn't that right?

A. Well, you lied to me, too.

Q. Yes, where and when?

A. Right in this courtroom here.

Q. We will let the jury decide about that. In this courtroom. Did I ever ask you a question outside of this courtroom? Did I ever come into that jail to ask you a thing?

A. No.

Q. Did I ever ask you to sign a paper?

A. No.

Q. Did I ever ask you to make a statement?

A. No.

Q. I asked you if you wanted a cigar or cigarettes when I brought you here from the Bronx, didn't I?

A. I don't remember.

Q. I asked you if you would like to stay in the corridor or if you would like to go up to the cell, I asked you that, didn't I? Isn't that right?

A. I can't remember those things.

Q. You can't remember that. Now let's get back to the Lindbergh ransom money. You were arrested by the police?

A. Yes.

Q. You see you are not smiling any more, are you?

A. Smiling?

Q. It has gotten a little more serious, hasn't it?

A. I guess it isn't any place to smile here.

Q. "I am a carpenter."

A. I am.

Q. That was funny, wasn't it?

A. No, sir, there is nothing funny about it.

Q. There is nothing funny about it? You had a good laugh, didn't you? Did you plan that in the jail there, did somebody tell you to give that answer when I asked you about the ladder, to stand in front of the jury and say "I am a carpenter"?

A. No, sir.

Q. You thought that out yourself?

A. No, I didn't think a thing about it.

Q. Let me ask you something: You have got a peculiar notion about will power, haven't you?

MR. POPE: Well, I think this has gone just about far enough.

MR. WILENTZ: I will withdraw the question. If it has, may we have a recess, if your Honor please?

MR. POPE: I think we ought to come back into a court room and see if we can't get down—

MR. WILENTZ: Now, I object to that. I think it is a reflection on the Court.

THE COURT: What do you mean by that, Mr. Pope?

MR. POPE: Well, I mean this patent abuse of the witness. It seems to me it is about time we protested against it. It has been going on for quite a while.

THE COURT: Whenever you have any occasion to protest, you make your protest to the Court while the thing is going on, and the Court will deal with it; it always has and will continue to do so. We will now take a recess for five minutes.

.....

Q. Now, Mr. Defendant, when you were up in the Bronx County Courthouse, and you say you were a little excited—you said you were a little excited when you were with Mr. Foley—were you excited because that was the first time you were in court? Hadn't you had experience?

A. No.

Q. You had had experience in court, hadn't you?

A. No, I did not. That is from the treatment I get in New York from police.

Q. But you knew what it was to be on the stand and to tell the truth or not to tell the truth, didn't you?

A. I know it.

Q. Sure. You had 17 days in jail there before they called you to the hearing and you had talked to your wife about the whole case, and you talked to your lawyer and to investigators about it before you took the stand?

A. I talked very little to my wife, mostly about the child we was talking.

Q. Who told you to change your story today?

A. Nobody told me anything about it.

Q. Who told you in New Jersey, since you have been in jail, to change your story about this board?

A. Nobody.

Q. No investigators?

A. I guess I didn't even see investigators.

Q. Who did you talk to about this board and about Dr. Condon?

A. Is nobody.

Q. Nobody at all?

A. No.

Q. You remember these chisels?

A. Yes.

Q. You had them in a cigar box, didn't you?

A. No.

Q. You didn't have them in a cigar box?

A. Laying on the shelf.

Q. Where?

A. South wall of the garage inside.

Q. Didn't you have those chisels in the closet of your home?

A. Closet?

Q. Yes, in the closet of your home in a cigar box?

A. Oh, I guess there was one chisel laying over there. You mean in the apartment?

Q. Yes, in your apartment.

A. Yes, I guess one chisel was laying there.

MR. WILENTZ: Oh, this is in evidence already?

MR. PEACOCK: Yes.

Q. Now, will you just take a look at this? Do you recognize this as being part of your attic (referring to Exhibit S-215)?

A. Yes.

Q. Well, you have been up to your attic, haven't you?

A. Yes.

Q. And when you get up to your attic, you can only get there through your linen closet, isn't that right?

A. It used to be a linen closet, but we never use it for linen.

Q. What did you use it for?

A. To put in the—well, most the wash, my wife put the washing in there.

Q. The closet was your closet.

A. Yes.

Q. Yours and your wife's?

A. Yes.

Q. Mr. Reilly was asking you the other day about the families that lived in the house and you said there were three families, I think.

A. Yes.

Q. You meant your family was one family.

Q. Yes.

Q. And your family is the only family occupying the upstairs, second floor?

A. Yes.

Q. The other families were downstairs?

A. Downstairs.

Q. And they had nothing to do with that closet.

A. Nothing.

Q. And they had nothing to do with the attic.

A. Nothing.

Q. You have been up to that attic, haven't you?

A. Yes.

Q. So that you were familiar with the attic, you knew about the attic.

A. I knew about our attic.

Q. And, of course, being a carpenter, you looked at the floor where the joists had no boards on it on either side and in the middle they had these boards across.

A. I noticed that there.

Q. Now, when you looked at the attic, that board was right across, wasn't it (indicating)?

A. I can't remember that.

Q. You can't remember whether or not this board here was right across?

A. No.

Q. You can't remember?

A. I know when I moved in I put away a whole lot of stuff I couldn't use; I put it in the attic and I never bothered with it.

Q. You never bothered with it?

A. No.

Q. And you don't remember whether or not there was a piece of board missing there?

A. No, I can't.

Q. Well, do you know who left the sawdust up there, when it was sawed off?

A. No.

Q. Do you recognize this as being a part of the floor, the part that is shown there, S-226?

A. No, I can't.

Q. You can't recognize it. What kind of wood is it?

A. That is what we call roofing boards.

Q. Roofing boards? Well, what kind of wood?

A. It is North Carolina pine.

Q. Well, they call it all North Carolina pine, don't they?

A. No, that's pine.

Q. Well, it is North Carolina pine, whether it comes from South Carolina, or North Carolina; they call it the same thing, don't they?

A. NC pine.

Q. You wouldn't want me, a lawyer, to be telling you about pine, would you? It is NC pine?

A. NC pine.

Q. Yes. And it is flooring, isn't it?

A. Roofing.

Q. Roofing. You don't know whether this comes from your attic or not?

A. I don't know.

Q. And you don't know whether that was all the way across or not?

A. I never noticed that.

Q. You never noticed that?

A. If that piece is missing or not.

Q. I see. Do you know the dimensions of that closet?

A. Well, about 14 inch deep, a little bit more—16.

Q. In order to get up to the attic—

A. Oh, this one.

Q. When you were using it as a closet, you first had to remove the shelves, didn't you?

A. It wasn't necessary.

Q. You didn't have any shelves there?

A. No, I mean to go to the attic it wasn't necessary to remove the shelves.

Q. How did you get up there then?

A. There was still room enough to get up.

Q. How would you go up with the shelves in there?

A. You use the cleats from the shelves.

Q. You would have to climb up on the shelves?

A. Yes.

Q. Is that it?

A. Yes.

Q. Well, of course, Mrs. Hauptmann couldn't get up there, could she?

A. I guess she was up there one time.

Q. You think she was. Did she use a chair?

A. Well, me put a chair, the corner from the chair, inside of the closet.

Q. Yes. You had to put something in in order to get up, except, of course, an athlete like you. You could get up there, you could climb that easily, couldn't you?

A. Well, I say not easily. It was quite a job to get up there.

Q. It was quite a job to get up there, wasn't it?

A. Yes.

Q. That is the place you made the ladder, wasn't it, up in the attic? That is where you did your work, wasn't it?

A. No, I got a garage.

Q. You got a garage where you built the ladder, is that what you mean?

A. I never built the ladder.

Q. You never built one in your life, did you?

A. No, sir.

Q. How many years did you say you were a carpenter?

A. Nine or ten years.

Q. Of course not nine or ten years at the job, you don't mean that.

A. No, I mean all together.

Q. All together?

A. Yes.

Q. Does that include the time that you have been a stock market operator?

A. Well, I have been a carpenter one year in Germany—

Q. Let's get back to the time you were arrested and they found this twenty dollar bill on you, the ransom money bill, and the police asked you where you got it. Isn't that right?

A. Yes.

Q. And you said to the police, "This twenty dollar bill, yes, I had three hundred dollars worth. I saved it, got it from my friends and got it from the banks and this is the last of the three hundred dollars of gold bills." Isn't that what you told them?

A. Yes, I told them that.

Q. And when you told the police that you knew at the very time that you told them that you were not telling the truth, isn't that right?

A. That is right.

Q. You see now we are getting along fine. A little bit later they asked you whether you had any more money and you said No, is that right?

A. That is right.

Q. But that wasn't the truth, either, was it?

A. It was not.

Q. No. Well, they finally find a lot of gold in the house, didn't they?

A. I told them about it, later.

Q. Later you told them about it.

A. Before they found it.

Q. You told that to General O'Ryan, you say?

A. Yes.

Q. You say you told them before they found it.

A. Yes.

Q. But up to the time you told them about that—they brought the money there, they told you they found it, you told them where to find it and they told you they got it, is that right?

A. I told them first, fourteen thousand dollars, south wall of the garage.

Q. They found that money, is that right?

A. Yes, sir.

Q. They came to you and said, "Mr. Hauptmann, we found the money," and they said to you, "is there any more money, ransom money?" Is that right?

A. Yes.

Q. What did you say? You said No.

A. I said No.

Q. And when you said No, you knew you were not telling the truth, isn't that right?

A. Yes.

Q. So when they found the first bill, you didn't tell them the truth, and you knew you weren't telling them the truth, and afterwards when they found the other money, you told them again you had no more money, and when you told them that you knew then what you were telling to them, you were not telling the truth: that is right, isn't it?

A. That is right.

Q. So they brought some more money to you and they said, "What about this" and Mr. Foley said to you, did he not, "This is Lindbergh money?" And you said, "Yes," isn't that right?

A. I don't know about that, sir.

Q. Well, let me refresh your recollection, not as to what Mr. Foley said but as to what happened in the Bronx Supreme Court.

MR. WILENTZ: What page is it on?

Q. You don't mind waiting just a minute, please.

A. No objection.

MR. WILENTZ: Page 112, gentlemen.

Q. The next question—this is the next question that Mr. Foley is supposed to have asked you, and I am asking you in the courtroom in the Bronx, the question, "Do you remember that you wrote that on the board? A. Yes." Do you remember that? That board there, that is that board there.

A. The trimming?

Q. The trimming, yes.

Richard Hauptmann

....

Q. That was your broom closet in the kitchen, wasn't it?

A. Broom closet in the kitchen.

Q. Your wife used to go there every day?

A. Yes.

Q. She never found that box, did she?

A. Well, all her stuff was usually on the first and second shelf.

Q. Just answer the question, please. She never found or saw that box so far as you know, did she?

A. No.

Q. And you never told her about it, did you?

A. No.

Q. Well anyway, one day you took that broom and what? You were going to sweep something up, weren't you?

A. Yes.

Q. And you hit the box somehow?

A. Yes.

Q. And that showed it was money?

A. Yes.

Q. I think you said that you weren't glad, you weren't sad, but you were excited?

A. Yes.

Q. Well, you were really glad, weren't you, when you saw all this money?

A. No, I can't say I was glad. I was excited. I didn't know what to think of it at all, first.

Q. You didn't want to go out and celebrate about finding all this gold?

A. Oh, no.

Q. You had never been married in your life before, had you?

A. No.

Q. No. You had only had one wife all during the time, hadn't you?

A. Yes.

Q. And as I said before, you and your wife had been sort of

partners, hadn't you?

A. Yes.

Q. You didn't declare her in on this partnership, did you?

A. No.

Q. Why not, Mr. Hauptmann?

A. In the finances, in my whole financial transactions, even the stock market, I guess my wife didn't know yet what is going on in the stock market.

Q. Certainly not. You told her you were making money, didn't you?

A. I guess—

Q. We will stop here. You told her you were making money, didn't you?

A. I did.

Q. And you weren't telling her the truth.

A. I told her the truth, I made money.

Q. You actually lost money in the market, didn't you?

A. No, I made money.

Q. In the end did you make money?

A. Yes, I made it.

Q. Well, up to April 2nd, you lost about three thousand dollars, isn't that right?

A. Yes.

Q. And from April 2nd to 1934, when you were arrested, you lost about five or six thousand, didn't you?

A. No, no.

Q. What was the situation?

A. My account was standing actual money $9,500.

Q. Well, what do you mean, it was standing $9,500?

A. Dis date, 19—which date you prefer?

Q. September, 1934.

A. September, 1934?

Q. When you were arrested.

A. Yes, I—up to this time my gain was around $2,000.

Q. Up to that time your gain was—

A. Yes.

Q. —$2,000?

A. That is when I figured this time the stock was worth about around $6,000.

Q. Yes.

A. But, mitout figuring the stock market from Carleton-Mott, I— I forgot it; I only counted from April, from '32. I made still around three to four thousand dollars.

Q. You made three to four?

A. Yes.

Q. Did you hear Mr. Frank of the Intelligence Unit of the United States Government testify about your figures?

A. Yes, I heard it.

Q. Did you hear him say that that account lost $5,800 from April 2nd, 1932, till the date of your arrest?

A. Yes, which account?

Q. The brokerage account in your name.

A. In the brokerage account, yes.

Q. In the name of your wife?

A. Yes.

Q. That account did lose, didn't it?

A. That account did lose, yes.

Q. But you mean the loss was Fisch's, not yours, is that what you mean?

A. Some of them was Fisch, some of them was mine.

Q. I see.

A. But—

Q. Well, the loss altogether was $5,800, Mr. Hauptmann. Now which part was Fisch's and which part was yours?

A. Well, I can't say it mitout my books or anything else.

Q. Well, you went over them over the weekend. You sat on this witness stand for pretty nearly three hours answering questions for Mr. Reilly from your figures about the brokerage accounts?

A. Ja.

Q. You lost $1,240.65 in 1933 and $4,263.24 in 1934, do you remember that?

A. Didn't figure out I don't know 1934.

Q. Well, take the whole account before 1932, from 1929, and your whole loss including Carlton & Mott was $9,132, yours and Fisch's together. How much of it was Fisch's and how much was yours?

A. Fisch stepped in the market 1932.

Q. Yes. Well, how much?

A. And he lost in the market I figured out it was around $15,000.

Q. $15,000?

A. $15,000.

Q. $15,000. You know that is not the truth.

A. I know it is the truth.

Q. And you know we can prove it is not the truth, don't you?

A. It is the true.

Q. You know that you have books with those stock accounts, don't you?

A. Yes.

Q. And you know the books won't show those figures. You know that, don't you?

A. My books shows only partly.

Q. Oh, only partly?

A. Yes.

Q. Who were you hiding that from in your books?

A. When I bought for Fisch I give in the slip when I bought it, marked the slip "Fisch"; when I sold his stock always at Fisch request.

Q. Yes.

A. I got a paying and selling.

Q. Yes.

A. Only there is a difference.

Q. But you kept an account with every stock that you bought, didn't you?

A. Every stock what I bought, yes.

Q. And you kept an account of the stocks you bought for Fisch?

A. No, sir.

Q. Well, you have them in your book, haven't you?

A. I know. I kept one time account of Fisch. I told him to give me $2,000 and I will keep care of that.

Q. Did Fisch own an automobile?

A. No.

Q. Did Fisch drive an automobile?

A. I don't know.

Q. Well, you never saw him drive one?

A. I never saw him.

Q. You know he didn't own an automobile, you know that, don't you?

A. Yes.

Q. You loaned Fisch $5,500, didn't you, in cash?

A. No.

Q. Now, Hauptmann, you tell the truth. Didn't you loan him $5,500 in cash?

A. No.

Q. Out of your private bank account?

A. No.

Q. Didn't you write to Fisch's family, after Fisch died, after he died, didn't you write them, "I gave him $5500 out of my private bank account"?

A. Yes, to make it clearly I wrote him this way—

Q. You wrote him that, didn't you?

A. Yes.

Q. Wait a minute now. My God, don't you tell anybody the truth?

MR. FISHER: That is objected to, your Honor.

THE COURT: Yes, that is objectionable. I sustain the objection.

Q. Did you write to the Fisch family after your friend died and explain your accounts with Fisch? Didn't you write to them that you loaned him $5,500 in cash out of your private bank account?

A. Yes, I did.

Q. Didn't you tell the police that when you were arrested?

A. I don't know if I did.

Q. Well, you wouldn't say you didn't, will you?

A. Before you go farther, may I explain?

Q. Yes, sir.

A. The 5,500—

Q. Yes, sir.

A. In November, '33—

Q. Yes.

A. When I make clear what I said—

Q. Go ahead.

A. Because nobody knowed how we was standing, profit from furs, and there was some from the stock account. In other words, I got to get $5,500 for Mr. Fisch.

Q. He owed you $5,500?

A. Yes.

Q. Yes.

A. But he said he hasn't got any money, he has got all invested in furs.

Q. Yes.

A. And I said, "All right, leave it this way, I leave them $5,500 in your account."

Q. Yes.

A. I make it short in explaining, I go to his brother, I give him $5,500.

Q. Now Hauptmann, he owed you $5,500, didn't he?

A. Yes.

Q. And two thousand more you gave him in November before he sailed to Germany?

A. Yes.

Q. Seventy-five hundred?

A. Yes.

Q. When you knew that he was dead, your friend, your partner, and you got a letter from his brother or from his family, telling you about it—

A. Yes.

Q. You answered that letter, didn't you?

A. I did.

Q. You told them how sorry you were?

A. I did.

Q. You told them he was your best friend?

A. I did.

Q. And you told them all about your account?

A. Yes.

Q. And you told them that you gave him $5,500, didn't you?

A. Yes, I explain it this way.

Q. Yes, sir. But you told them in the letter that you got, $5,500 that you gave to him came from your private bank account, isn't that the fact?

A. That's the fact.

Q. You knew it wasn't the truth?

A. That's the truth.

Q. Did you get it out of your private bank account?

A. This $5,000—

Q. Did you get it out of your private bank account, please? You can explain it later. Did you get it out of your private bank account?

A. I didn't have any private bank account.

Q. Then you didn't get it out of any private bank account, did you?

A. No.

Q. Then you didn't tell them the truth in the letter, did you?

A. That is the truth.

Q. Well, where did you get it then?

A. The $5,000 is still $5,000, if I take it from the bank or if he owes me.

Q. Why did you put in the letter then, "private bank account"?

A. To make it short, not to make a big explanation about $5,500, I put it in these words.

Classics of the Courtroom

Q. Now, let's see about this explanation. You wrote him a long letter because you wanted to get your money back, didn't you?

A. Yes, I wanted them $5,500 and $2,000.

Q. Yes. You wanted to get your money back and you wanted to find out whether Fisch had any furs some place. He left some furs with you, didn't he?

A. 400 skins.

Q. 400 skins. And you wanted to find out if he had furs some other place?

A. Yes.

Q. You wanted to be the administrator; you asked his brother to trust you, just like Isidor trusted you?

A. I did.

Q. Sure. You were going to take care of him?

A. I made this suggestion to take—

Q. You told him not to trust the lawyer; you told him that, didn't you?

A. I told him that, yes. There wouldn't be much left.

Q. Because there wouldn't be much left. That is right. And all the time you were trying to get him to trust you, to make you the administrator, all the time you were writing him that you gave him $5,500 in cash from your private bank account, and that wasn't the truth at all, was it?

A. You are all wrong.

Q. All right. You tell me where we are wrong then.

A. My strongest suggestion was to Mr. Fisch—

Q. Fisch, yes.

A. —I mean his partner—

Q. Yes.

A. —to come over here hisself and settle the whole affair.

Q. Yes, but if he didn't come to make you the administrator?

A. To make me the administrator or take a lawyer.

Q. And that was—take a lawyer?

A. Yes.

Q. You never suggested that, you told them not to take a lawyer, didn't you?

A. I suggested it, but I said it wouldn't be advisable to take one.

Q. You suggested it?

A. Yes.

Q. It is a sort of backhanded invitation—

A. I don't know about that.

Q. You suggested it, but you suggested not to do it?

A. Yes, that is right.

Q. You told them not to take a lawyer because there wouldn't be much left?

A. Yes.

Q. At any rate, in that letter, there couldn't be any mistake, because you wrote it in German, didn't you? The letter was written in German?

A. No, I don't think there was any mistake.

Q. Certainly not, and if you put in there "5,500 from my private bank account," you mean $5,500 from your private bank account, don't you?

A. That is only to—I figured out probably if his brother knows Fisch lost so much in the stock market—

Q. You didn't want to tell his brother?

A. I wouldn't tell him.

Q. That is it, so you put that in there because you didn't want his brother to know about it.

A. Yes.

Q. Why didn't you say so in the first place?

A. You didn't give me much chance to explain it.

Q. Oh, I thought I gave you a chance to explain it for five minutes, at least, that is what it seemed to me. Well, at any rate, the rest, your books are right, aren't they, if you got 5500 in your books, that must be right, you weren't trying to fool Fisch's brother through your books.

A. Oh, no, that is perfectly all right.

Q. That is right, isn't it?

A. That is right.

Q. Now, when you wrote to Fisch's brother you told him that you and Fisch had a little business together, didn't you?

A. Yes.

Q. And you told him when you started it, you told him November 1st, 1933, didn't you?

A. Ja, that is when we settled.

Q. When you settled?

A. Yes.

Q. And you told him that you put up $1,200 in stocks?

A. Yes.

Q. And that he put of $2,100 in furs.

A. Yes, I guess $20,000.

Q. About $21,000?

A. Yes.

Q. If it is—I am not going to hold you to a thousand or two. At that time you were dealing in thousands, so if we are making a little mistake, don't you take advantage of my mistakes and I won't of yours. Somewhere around 12,000 stocks and twenty or twenty one thousand dollars in furs.

A. Yes.

Q. In order to make it even, you put in your account, you gave Fisch 5,500 in cash, so that made your investment 17,500, isn't that right?

A. No, that is not right.

Q. That is what you said, wasn't it?

A. No.

Q. In the letter?

A. That is not right.

Q. That is what you have got in the book, your book, isn't it?

A. Maybe I put it in the letter this way to make it shorter, but Fisch, he put—

MR. WILENTZ: Where is the book?

A. —Mr. Fisch bought too much furs.

Q. Yes, you told us about that.

Richard Hauptmann

A. Over 21,000.

Q. What I want to know is whether or not you put those figures in your book and in the letter to the Fisch family, $17,500 as your share on account of the $12,000 stocks and on account of the $5,000 cash you gave Fisch. Did you put $12,000 in stocks into that account?

A. No.

Q. You didn't?

A. No. I never did have $12,000.

Q. Well, why did you put it in the book then, your book?

A. Yeah, that was my, what I made in the market.

Q. Is this your handwriting?

A. It is.

Q. Especially the bottom part; take a look at it, because that is where this business is, that bottom part. Is that your handwriting?

A. Let me see.

Q. Yes, sir, you may see it. Take a look at it and if policemen wrote it in there, say so.

A. No, that is my handwriting.

Q. Well, all right. Now—

A. I put there—

Q. We will get to that. I am going to let you explain everything if you will let me do the examining. Now this is in English, isn't it?

A. In English.

Q. But some of the little words, they were in German, weren't they?

A. Yes, mixed up.

Q. So in the last eight years you learned something about the English language, but there were some things you didn't learn, is that it?

A. Yes.

Q. All right. Now, "im 21/10/1933", that is your German way of saying October 21, 1933, isn't it?

A. Yes.

Q. Then after that you say you put in stock $12,000, in furs $5,500?

A. Yes.

Classics of the Courtroom

Q. All right, sir. Now you see that, don't you?

A. Yeah.

Q. That is the $12,000 plus the $5,500—that makes up your share of $17,500, isn't that right?

A. That is correct.

Q. All right, sir. This is your book, by the way, isn't it?

A. Yes.

Q. Referring to page 102 of a book which will be marked, please, for identification, what number?

THE REPORTER: S-267.

(The book was marked State's Exhibit S-267 for identification.)

Q. This is your book, isn't it?

A. Yes, you—now may I explain?

Q. Do you want to explain this?

A. Yes.

Q. Yes, sir, go ahead and explain it.

A. We made a clean table. We didn't know, then we were standing, my account, all the money, I got in the market, I made in the market was $12,000, and there was $5,500 coming to me from Mr. Fisch from fur profit and there was some in the market he lost. I—

Q. $5,500 fur profit?

A. I don't know how much it was, three thousand something fur profit.

Q. You know after you get off the stand we can't change this testimony. Was it $3,000 or $5,500 in fur profit? Just think it over now. I don't want you to make any mistake about that. I want you to tell us about your records.

A. I can't exactly say if it was three thousand a couple of hundred, or $4,000.

Q. Tell me what the $5,500 represents.

A. It represents some fur profit—

Q. Yes.

A. —and $12,000 Mr. Fisch was keeping hundred shares—no, thousand shares, Eitingdon-Schild's.

Q. He has it E-i-t-i-n-g S-c-h-i-l-d.

A. He said he wanted this private.

Q. Let's get back to the $5,500. Don't take me away from it. What does that $5,500 represent?

A. Partly fur profit and probably what is coming from the stock market.

Q. But that is money that Fisch owes you?

A. Yes.

Q. And that you added t the $12,000 in stocks in order to make up your $17,500: is that right?

A. That is correct.

Q. So that your investment was 17,500.

A. Yes.

Q. 12,000 stocks, $5,500 that you had coming to you?

A. Yes.

Q. Fisch had furs up, $21,000.

A. Yes.

Q. All right. That is the partnership.

A. Yes.

Q. Fisch with furs, you with stocks, and 5,500.

A. Yes.

Q. Now you are saying Yes.

A. Wait a minute.

Q. Do you understand what you are talking about?

A. In stock—that means only 9,500.

Q. Well, 9,500, all right—not 12,000 stock?

A. No.

Q. 9,500?

A. 9,500.

Q. But you understand what you are talking about now, don't you?

A. Oh, yes.

Q. I don't want to take advantage of you.

A. No, I understand.

Q. I think you did say before—No, I will withdraw that. Instead of the 12,000 you mean you only had 9,500 in stock?

A. 9,500.

Q. Why did you write the Fisch family in 1934, May, June, July—you wrote them that you put up 1,200 in stock.

A. Maybe I forgot it.

Q. Well, you really did have 12,000 in stock, didn't you?

A. I wrote Mr. Fisch a letter about Eitingdon-Schild—I sold it for him. I don't know if he still got the letter yet or not.

Q. Let's forget the Eitingdon-Schild. Your books show that you put up $12,000 in addition to 5,500 as your share of this partnership; isn't that right?

A. Yes.

Q. And that was in 1923 you put that up. Now in 1934, after Fisch died, you wrote to Fisch's family that you put up $12,000 in stock and $5,500 in cash; isn't that right?

A. The $12,000—

Q. Now, please, won't you answer the question?

A. —Was standing, was standing in stock.

Q. Won't you please answer the question? Isn't that what you wrote to the Fisch family?

A. Yes, that is right.

Q. Was it the truth?

A. Yes.

Q. And does the book show the truth?

A. Yes.

Q. So that Fisch put no money up; he put furs up?

A. He put—

Q. Isn't that right?

A. Yes. There is only one thing on those $12,000, only $2,500 belong to Fisch.

Q. Now, as a matter of fact, so there is no mistake about it, early in the game, when you and Fisch first started, you and Fisch did put up a few thousand for stock, didn't he, $2,000, didn't he?

A. Well, the first, I don't know; it was only I guess around $700, $800.

Richard Hauptmann

MR. WILENTZ: Will you mark this book for identification.

THE REPORTER: State Exhibit S-267 for Identification.

MR. WILENTZ: What number is it?

THE REPORTER: S-267 for Identification.

Q. The book is your book, isn't it?

A. It is.

Q. You were quite a bookkeeper, weren't you?

A. I don't think so.

Q. You were very careful, I mean about your monies and about your stocks and about your furs?

A. Well, I have to keep kind of a record.

Q. Yes. So that in this partnership you did put up $12,000 in stock and $5,500 in—

A. Not extra money.

Q. In something else, because that is what you just said is the truth. Well, you put up $17,500 worth of equities of some kind, didn't you?

A. That is the most money I made in the market.

Q. Well, yes, all right, I don't care where you made it, but November 1st, 1933, you put up $17,500 somehow, whether it is profits or what it was?

A. Yes.

Q. $17,500?

A. Yes.

Q. $17,500 and you didn't take a dollar of that from that money that Fisch left in the garage for you in the box?

A. No, sir.

Q. November 1st, 1933, you had $17,500 worth of assets there that you put into this partnership?

A. Yes.

Q. You see, I am asking you the same question?

A. Yes. But later on I find out it isn't true.

Q. Wait a minute. Now, in addition—what part of it wasn't true? When did you find it out?

A. When, after Fisch—

Q. Died?

A. —Fisch died.

Q. Well, he—

A. Then I started investigating.

Q. Well, Fisch died in November 1933, didn't he? Oh, no—he died in March or April, 1934?

A. Yes.

Q. And then you found out that that wasn't true, that the furs weren't worth as much money, you mean?

A. Yes.

Q. But the 12,000, your investment, the part you put up, your assets, you didn't fake anybody, you actually put up 17,500, didn't you?

A. No.

Q. You put 12,000 dollars worth of stocks you say you made it in profits or something like that.

A. The 5,500, I never saw it, that is only a matter of bookkeeping.

Q. So when you say it is only a matter of bookkeeping, you weren't telling the truth when you wrote to Fisch's family in June or July, 1934, a month or two before you were arrested.

A. That is perfectly true.

Q. Perfectly true.

A. Yes.

Q. When you found out that there was Fisch's money, $14,000 in gold, did you write to Fisch's family and tell them about it?

A. Well, it was a short time before I got arrested when I found it.

Q. You found it when?

A. Middle of August.

Q. Middle of August?

A. Yes.

Q. And you were arrested on the 19th of September?

A. Yes.

Q. You were spending the money already, weren't you?

A. Yes. I guess I am entitled to it.

Q. We will get to that in a minute.

Richard Hauptmann

A. Yes.

Q. You were spending some of it, weren't you?

A. Yes.

Q. You had from August 15th until about September 19th that you had this money.

A. Yes.

Q. Did you write to the family of your best friend and say "I found this money"?

A. No, I did not.

Q. You wrote them a couple of months before that that all you had was a couple of trunks worth nothing, didn't you?

A. Yes.

Q. You wouldn't tell them about the money when you found some, would you?

A. I knew Mr. Fisch was coming over anyway.

Q. You wouldn't tell them that, would you?

A. I would.

Q. You wanted to cheat your best friend in death, didn't you?

A. No, sir.

Q. You cheated his family, didn't you?

A. No.

Q. You never sent them a dollar, did you?

A. No, I did not.

Q. Don't you know that you have got in your books how much money you got from Fisch in all your business transactions?

A. From Fisch?

Q. Yes. You know you kept a record of it?

A. Yes. It is close to $16,000.

Q. You know very well that you have got in your handwriting that you only got a couple of thousand dollars from him. You know that, don't you?

A. I got $16,000. That's what we put in the stock market.

Q. $16,000. Can you show us a paper, can you show us a writing, can you show us anything except what you say, that fisch ever gave you 16,000 cents?

A. No, I can't.

Q. Fisch had a bank account, didn't he?

A. Yes, he did.

Q. Fisch had a safety deposit box, didn't he?

A. Yes.

Q. Did you ever get a check from Fisch?

A. No.

Q. Certainly not. Why didn't you say to him, "Mr. Fisch, this is a funny thing. You are a business man, dealing in furs. You are giving me thousands of dollars in cash. Why don't you give me a check?" You were a business man then. Why didn't you ask him?

A. Well, the same thing, when he was asking for money, especially the last time, the $2,000 he said he don't want any check, he want it in cash. I got a check and cashed it then.

....

Q. Now, Mr. Defendant, you said the other day that on April 2nd, 1932, being the night that it was testified to that $50,000 was paid, that that was the day you left your job.

A. Yes.

Q. You resigned; and you testified that you resigned not because you got $50,000 but because you found out they were only going to pay you $80 a month instead of $100?

A. Yes.

....

Q. Now, Exhibit Number S-268, which is the check for $36.67, that check you cashed at the National Lumber & Millwork Company, isn't that a fact?

A. Yes.

Q. That is the lumber yard where you used to work.

A. Yes.

Q. That is in the Bronx?

A. Yes.

Q. That is a company owned and operated at the time, in 1932, by Mr. Hirsch and Mr. Miller who were here, isn't that right?

A. Excuse me, let me look on that date when I cashed it.

Q. Yes, certainly.

A. Yes, I cashed it on the 5th of April.

Q. 5th of April?

A. Yes.

Q. 1932?

A. Yes.

Q. Well, that was a few days after March the 31st, wasn't it, five days?

A. Yes.

Q. But you cashed it at the National Lumber & Millwork Company?

A. Yes.

Q. That is the lumber company at which you worked?

A. Yes.

Q. That is the lumber company owned and operated by the two men who were in court the other day?

A. Yes.

Q. Who testified you purchased some lumber from them?

A. Yes.

Q. You did not know Violet Sharpe, did you?

A. No.

Q. You didn't know anybody who did know her, did you?

A. No.

Q. You never heard of Violet Sharpe, did you?

A. Well, I read the stories in the paper.

Q. I mean prior to March the 1st, 1932.

A. No.

Q. You didn't know anybody connected with the Lindbergh household prior to March the 1st, 1932, did you?

A. No.

.....

Q. In May 1932 you bought a radio, didn't you?

A. Yes.

Q. How much did you pay for the radio?

A. $400.

Q. $400?

A. Yes.

Q. In cash?

A. Yes.

Q. What date in May, do you know?

A. No, I can't remember which day.

Q. After April the 2nd, 1932, you bought some field glasses too, didn't you?

A. I guess was in July.

Q. 1932?

A. Yes, July, I guess.

Q. How much did you pay for the field glasses?

A. Well, $126.

Q. $126?

A. Yes.

Q. Before March the 1st, 1932, did you own field glasses?

A. Yes; yes.

Q. You did own field glasses?

A. Yes.

Q. But after March the 1st, 1932, and particularly in July, I think you said, you spent $125 for a new pair of field glasses?

A. Yes.

Q. Now, before you bought that radio you already had a Victrola in your home, hadn't you?

A. Yes.

Q. And where did you keep that?

A. In the front room.

Q. Did you ever put any money in that Victrola for safekeeping?

A. No.

Q. Particularly in the months of April, May, June or July of 1932, did you keep any money in that Victrola?

A. There is a possibility I keep the rent in it.

Q. I don't mean the rent, I mean money, lots of money?

A. No, never.

Q. Packages of money?

A. Never, never got packages of money.

Q. Well, you had packages of money from Mr. Fisch, didn't you?

A. Well, 1934.

Q. Yes. Well, in 1932, too, didn't you?

A. No.

Q. 1933, too, didn't you?

A. No.

Q. Didn't you get $6500 from Fisch in July, 1933?

A. Well, I always—

Q. Didn't you? Please answer the question.

A. Yes, but not at home.

Q. Well, you got it anyway in cash?

A. Yes.

Q. Yes, always in the broker.

A. Yes.

Q. Anybody ever see him give it to you in the brokerage office that you know of?

A. No, I don't think so.

Q. You don't know. Anybody ever help you count it, the broker's man, the customer's man, the margin man, the bookkeepers, the cashier, anybody count it for you while Fisch was there?

A. Well, I can't remember if somebody saw us.

Q. You can't remember?

A. But I suppose.

Q. At any rate, during the months that I have indicated, early in 1932, during any months in 1932, you did not have any packages or bundles of money in that Victrola?

A. No.

Q. Is it not a fact that during some of those months, particularly after April the 2nd, 1932, that you opened that Victrola and when you opened it in the presence of Fritz Hahn, the restaurant man I spoke to you about yesterday—

A. Yes.

Q. —that there were in that Victrola right on top two envelopes about 11 inches long, maybe 14 inches long, a few inches thick of money, two packages, two envelopes? Is it not a fact?

A. No, absolutely not.

Q. Absolutely not?

A. No.

Q. Absolutely not?

A. No.

Q. And didn't Mr. Hahn ask you about the money?

A. No, I really can't remember Mr. Hahn was ever in our house, but I will not say no, but I really can't remember he was in my house.

Q. Let me ask you just to refresh your recollection you don't ever remember him being in your house?

A. No.

Q. You remember when you took him to Rye Beach?

A. That is I remember.

Q. On your way home did you stop at your house with Mr. Hahn?

A. I know it was Mr. Hahn, Mrs. Hahn and a little boy.

Q. Yes.

A. But I really can't remember if we stopped in our house, because my wife wasn't home this time.

Q. No.

A. She was in Europe.

Q. She was in Europe then?

A. Yes.

Q. But you had taken Mr. Hahn and Mrs. Hahn to Rye Beach, hadn't you?

A. That is right.

Q. They were friends of yours?

A. Yes.

Q. They are still friends of yours, aren't they?

A. Well, I wasn't in the lunchroom practically a year and a half, two years.

Q. Yes, but there is no trouble between you and the Hahns?

A. No, no.

Q. The Hahns don't owe you any money that they didn't pay you, do they?

A. No.

Q. You have had no trouble with them at all?

A. No trouble.

Q. And you say now that when Mr. Hahn was in your home in 1932, after April the 2nd, 1932, that you did not open the Victrola and there in his presence he saw these two bundles and called to your attention bundles of money?

A. Well, you said envelopes before.

Q. Yes, that's right, envelopes, bundles, bundled up with money.

A. No.

Q. No?

A. No.

Q. All right. Did you open the Victrola while Mr. Hahn was there?

A. Well, I didn't know if Mr. Hahn was ever in our house.

Q. Don't you remember when you got to the bedroom you said, "This room you cannot go in"?

A. No.

Q. You don't remember that?

A. No, I didn't say that.

Q. You didn't say that?

A. No.

Q. Don't you remember when you were in your parlor with Mr. and Mrs. Hahn on an occasion that you were looking in one direction, you said to him, "If you only turn around like this—" and then you stopped—does that refresh your recollection about his visit?

A. No.

Q. You won't say Mr. Hahn was not in your house, will you?

A. That's what I say. I can't remember he was at our house.

Q. You won't say he was not at the house.

A. No, I can't say that either.

Q. How many times was Mrs. Hahn in the house?

A. I don't know—This—

Q. Was she—Pardon me—

A. I guess she was visiting my wife.

Q. Was she in the house before your wife—immediately prior to your wife's departure for Germany?

A. I cannot tell.

Q. You cannot tell. Don't you remember her asking you how much money you are giving your wife for this trip to Germany and you said about a thousand dollars I guess will be all right?

A. No.

Q. You didn't say that?

A. No.

Q. Well, do you remember whether she was there talking to you?

A. No.

Q. Will you say that Mrs. Hahn wasn't there?

A. That's what I say.

Q. You don't remember that at all?

A. I cannot remember Mrs. Hahn was in my house. Maybe she was there and I wasn't home, my wife was home.

Q. No, when you were home.

A. I can't remember.

Q. Do you remember your wife showing her the dresses and everything she had before she went to Europe?

A. No.

Q. You don't remember?

A. No.

Q. Did you invite Mr. and Mrs. Hahn to your home early in 1932?

A. It is possible we invite the family of Hahn.

Q. I don't want to know whether it is possible, please. I want to know whether you did or did not invite them, if you know; or can't you remember that?

A. I can't remember that.

Q. After you got the new $400 radio, didn't you tell Mr. Hahn you would like to have him down and see your new radio?

A. I even really don't know if he knows I got a new radio.

Q. Didn't you say on your way back from Rye Beach, "Come on, I want to show you my new radio"?

A. No.

Q. Didn't he say to you, when you got in the house, "My, this is a swell radio; it must have cost a lot of money;" don't you remember that?

A. I got the impression you are making up a big story here.

Q. Well, we will see about that.

(Confusion in the courtroom.)

Q. Will you please answer the question now?

A. Will you repeat it again?

Q. Who told you to say that, about your impression?

A. That's my impression.

Q. One of your advisors?

A. No, that's—

Q. Weren't you told last night to say that?

A. No, sir.

Q. You weren't?

A. No, sir.

Q. Weren't you told in this court room to signal your wife when a witness was on the stand, to holler at her?

A. That is ridiculous.

Q. It is ridiculous, eh?

A. Yes.

Q. Were you told to change your story about the board yesterday?

A. Never was spoken about it.

Q. Were you told to change your story about the dog?

A. What dog?

Q. Did you ever testify about any dog in the Bronx proceedings when you were on trial with reference to extradition proceedings, particularly about March the 1st, 1932?

A. I never was asked.

Q. And you never told about it, did you?

A. Because I wasn't asked.

Q. Because you weren't asked?

A. No.

Q. Weren't you asked where you were March the 1st, 1932?

A. Yes.

Q. Weren't you asked what you did that night?

A. Yes.

Q. Didn't you tell your whole story about March the 1st, 1932?

A. Oh, they are so many little things you can't remember the first time.

Q. But March the 1st, 1932, was the entire story in the Bronx Court, wasn't it? The question was where you were March the 1st, 1932, wasn't that the case?

A. Yes.

Q. And you took the stand about that and your wife took the stand about that. Did you or anybody else talk about a dog or your being out with a dog that night, when you were in the Bronx court?

A. No, I don't think so. Anybody—

Q. You never mentioned it, did you?

A. No.

Q. You never said a word about walking the street with a dog and meeting anybody or walking the street with a dog and not meeting anybody: you never said that, did you?

A. No, but I remember afterwards I was out mit a dog.

Q. So that you didn't remember that night—No, I withdraw that.— So that on the day you were in the Bronx court you didn't talk about the dog on March 1st, because you didn't remember it at that time?

A. Well, I guess I know it but I never thought it was important.

Q. You didn't think it was important?

A. No.

Q. Well, the only thing that was important was the question

whether or not you were in New Jersey, as the State of New Jersey claimed, and that was the issue in that court: isn't that it?

A. Yes.

Q. So it was important as to where you were every minute of the night of March 1st, 1932, isn't that a fact?

A. Yes.

Q. And you testified in that courtroom, did you not, that you went down to your wife's restaurant?

A. Yes.

Q. That you had supper with her, and from there you went home and you stayed home all night?

A. Yes.

Q. You never said a word about going out with any dog, did you?

A. I did not.

Q. No. Now, who told you to change the story and put the dog in the case?

A. Well, nobody told me about that, but I—

Q. Nobody?

A. —I find out about the dog myself.

Q. You found out about it?

A. Yes.

Q. Who did you find it out from?

A. From nobody.

Q. Who told you about it?

A. From my own recollection.

Q. Who reminded you of it?

A. Nobody.

Q. Who told you it would be a good thing to give the story about the dog?

A. Nobody.

Q. Now, let's get this straight about this Victrola and the money. You say now again that you never opened that Victrola in the presence of Fritz Hahn, your friend, early in 1932, and that when it was opened there was revealed two packages or two envelopes, or two bundles of money?

A. I even can't remember Mr. Hahn was in our house.

Q. Now please answer the question. You don't remember him seeing any bundles there or envelopes or packages of money in the Victrola?

A. No, because there wasn't any there.

....

Q. Well, you heard the gentleman from the Federal Government testify about your deposit slips?

A. I didn't check up with this, might have been, too.

Q. Here is another one $10 in silver, is that right?

A. Yes. Well, $115 bills.

Q. $115 bills, $10 in silver?

A. $6.77 checks.

Q. April 16th, 1932, where did you get that money?

A. Some of the money—my wife was a little disgusted there was no more money in the bank, I put something from the $4300 in the bank.

Q. Your wife was a little bit disgusted because there was no money in the bank?

A. Yes.

Q. So you took out of the $4300 that you were hiding away from her in the trunk and you put that money in there?

A. Some of them, yes.

Q. Well, that part. Here is another one, Central Savings Bank, $74 bills, $10 in silver?

A. 1933, is it?

Q. I don't see the date, where is the date?

A. Makes no difference.

Q. All right, that is $10 in silver?

A. Yes. Well, there are sometimes slips where the Trust Company has marked $200 in silver and now you compare them slips, I guess the highest is $12 in silver.

Q. Well, these are just three slips and that is $10, $12 and $10, that is $32 in silver?

A. For all them slips.

Q. Takes a lot of nickels to make $32 in silver?

A. I never got a nickel job.

Q. You talked about depositing $750 in gold or exchanging it?

A. Yeah.

Q. That day you exchanged $500 more in gold, didn't you?

A. What?

Q. The day you took $750 in gold to the Central Savings Bank?

A. Yes.

Q. You took $500 more in gold, didn't you, that day?

A. No; I got $500 in gold currency laying in the strongbox in the Central Savings Bank.

Q. I see. And you deposited that?

A. I deposited it.

Q. The $750 that Mr. Reilly asked you about the other day, and he said to you you went down and took this gold and deposited it in your name: do you remember that?

A. With Central Savings Bank.

Q. Remember him asking you that?

A. No, I can't remember exactly the question.

Q. Do you remember testifying the other day that you took $750 in gold down to the Central Savings Bank, a bank which you dealt with, deposited it in your name, where they had your address?

A. Yes.

Q. You didn't deposit it, did you, the gold?

A. Yes.

Q. You exchanged it, didn't you?

A. (Shakes head.)

Q. And then deposited the bills?

A. Now, the gold, the gold currency—

Q. Not the gold coins, the gold bills.

A. I don't know what is operation, but I didn't take any money out, I left the money in the bank.

Q. I know. But you told here the other day that $750 in gold bills you took to your bank, the Central Savings Bank, where you had an account for years, under your name, and you deposited that $750 in gold; you deposited it, you say. Did you make a mistake the other day? If you did, you correct it.

A. Let me—I explain it from the beginning.

Q. Yes, sir.

A. I went down to the Central Savings Bank and went down to the strongbox where I got the gold coins and even certificates was laying in the strongbox.

Q. Yes, sir.

A. I dug it out, went upstairs and put it in for deposit.

Q. For deposit?

A. Yes.

Q. You didn't exchange them, did you?

A. Well, I don't know what is, was operation, you have to exchange it first and then deposit it, or I really can't remember.

Q. Well, you testified, that is the reason I want to give you a chance to correct it.

You testified that you took that gold, particularly with reference to the gold bills, and you deposited it in your regular account, the gold. Now, what I want to know is this: isn't it a fact that what you did was you took the $750 in gold bills to some place and exchanged it for other bills and took the $750 of non-gold bills and deposited it in the Central Savings Bank?

A. No.

Q. All right. That was March, 1933, you said, wasn't it?

A. Well, I—about the time of the—

Q. About the time of the bank holiday?

A. No, the time Mr. Roosevelt called the gold in.

Q. That is the time Mr. Roosevelt called in the gold?

A. Yes.

Q. Well, now, take a look at this.

MR. WILENTZ: Will you get me the $750 slip?

MR. PEACOCK: Mr. Attorney General, wait until the jury see those slips, they are examining them carefully.

MR. WILENTZ: Would your Honor mind while the jury is inspecting those slips, that I take a moment while they are inspecting those slips.

THE COURT: Why, as you wish, Mr. Attorney General.

BY MR. WILENTZ:

Q. While the jury is looking at that, will you please look through this book? Those papers in there have nothing to do with the book except to help me, but you can look at those too.

MR. REILLY: While he is looking at the book, General, may I speak to you a minute?

MR. WILENTZ: Yes, certainly.

(Mr. Wilentz and Mr. Reilly confer out of the hearing of the jury.)

A. Do you want to have this (indicating S-258)?

Q. As soon as you are through, to see if it is your handwriting and everything. That I showed you yesterday.

A. I can't remember everything you showed me.

Q. All right.

A. (The witness examines the exhibit page by page.)

Q. That is your book, isn't it?

A. It is.

Q. Showing you book S-258. It is a book in which you kept accounts of stocks and furs, is it not?

A. Yes.

Q. It is a book in which you kept account of your dealings with Fisch?

A. Yes.

Q. And it is a book in which you kept account of your own stock?

A. Yes.

Q. You kept the book for yourself, did you not, for your own information?

A. No, that's the book, yes.

Q. Yes. But you kept this book, you kept this record, S-258, for your own information?

A. Yes.

Q. You didn't keep it to fool anybody, did you?

Classics of the Courtroom

A. No, no.

Q. You didn't keep it to hide anything from anybody?

A. No.

Q. It is a true and accurate and correct statement of what is in here?

A. Yes, but it is not all in.

Q. It is not all in?

A. No.

Q. During the time that it covers is it correct or incorrect?

A. It is incorrect.

Q. It is incorrect?

A. Yes.

Q. Why did you keep it incorrectly?

A. Because I didn't put everything in it what should be in.

Q. Why didn't you?

A. Well, some of them was not my business.

Q. Well, whatever is in here is correct, isn't that so?

A. Yes.

Q. And the only part that is not correct is that you left out some things?

A. Yes.

Q. But if it says you put up $17,500 in the books that is correct, isn't it?

A. That is not actual money, seven thousand; it is only—

Q. But if the book says so, is it correct?

A. Well, let me explain it, please. Them $75 means securities bought $12,000—

Q. Stocks, you mean?

A. Yes.

Q. Your stocks?

A. My stocks, $9,500 mine.

Q. Well, your book says 12. Is that a mistake?

A. Yes. This was agreement between us, Mr. Fisch and me, that he wants to keep them hundred shares.

Q. But if your book says $12,000 of your stocks it is not correct, it should be $9,500, is that right?

A. Yes, it should be nine—

Q. And if you wrote to the Fisch family in 1934 and said $12,000 in stocks, that was not correct?

A. Well, I wrote Mr. Fisch—

Q. No. Please answer the question. If you wrote them that you put up $12,000 worth of stocks then you were mistaken in the letter too, is that so?

A. No, I can't say so.

Q. Well, was it correct, the $12,000, when you wrote it to Mr. Fisch, Mr. Fisch's brother in Germany, that you put up $12,000 worth of stock? Was that correct when you wrote that in 1934, or was that a mistake?

A. No, that is correct.

Q. It is correct?

A. It is correct.

Q. So you did put up $12,000 in securities?

A. Yes.

Q. All right. Not $9,500?

A. No. But I was pretty near sure when I sold Isidor's stock, I wrote in a letter, I am going to sell your stock, it was one thousand Eitingon-Schild.

Q. Who did you write that to?

A. To Isidor.

Q. When?

A. I guess this was in January or February, one, either of them month.

Q. When you wrote to Isidor's family, after his death, did you say anything about the stock you sold for him in January or February?

A. No, I did not.

Q. He only had a 20 per cent interest in the stocks, didn't he?

A. Oh, no.

Q. Did he have a 20 per cent interest in anything?

A. Let's explain it. When I said to Mr. Fisch, I said to him, "Give me $2,000, I will keep care of it," we start only for a very short period and then he changed it again, it was, he didn't make enough money in it, that is really the most money, and I said, "Now listen, we will make it this way, we will give them $2,000 over und I give you 20 per cent for all my stocks from the profit or from the loss."

Q. Yes?

A. And he said, "All right, that is O.K."

Q. Well, that is right.

A. And one or two days after, he changed his mind and he said, "I don't like it this way, I pay for myself again." All right, so I leave it this way.

Q. When did you and he start up this account where you were to put up $17,500 and he was to put up $17,500?

A. In October, end of October 1933.

Q. You didn't start this partnership in stocks until October 1933?

A. From this date it was a fifty-fifty partner.

Q. From that date?

A. Yes.

Q. When did you start your partnership in stocks, fifty-fifty or otherwise?

A. Fifty-fifty was only in certain stocks.

Q. When did you start your partnership before October, 1933, the 20 per cent partnership?

A. The 20 per cent partnership in stocks really didn't get into effect.

Q. Never got into effect?

A. No.

Q. So then you started dealing in stocks before October 1933 with Mr. Fisch, didn't you?

A. Oh, yes; he was in—he bought stock in '32.

Q. Everything that was bought was bought in your name or Anna's name, Anna Schoeffler, isn't that right?

A. Yes.

Q. By you for him?

A. Yes.

Q. But by you?

A. By me for him.

Q. He never gave an order to the broker, did he?

A. No. But he usually used to call me up if he wants something.

Q. So that you were his broker?

A. Yes.

Q. You were the man that handled his money.

Q. Yes.

Q. After April the 2nd, 1932, you told us you bought—you told us about the radio and you told us about the field glasses. Did you buy a canoe?

A. Yes.

Q. Did you take a hunting trip, several hunting trips?

A. Well, I really can say only one.

Q. Did you take a trip to Florida?

A. Yes.

Q. And your wife went to Germany?

A. Yes.

Q. And during all that time neither you nor your wife worked?

A. I was working—Well, I made enough money on the market and on the fur.

Q. Now please answer the question. During that time you didn't work, did you?

A. I did work.

Q. In the market?

A. Yes. In the market and as carpenter.

Q. Well, about how much would you say you earned as a carpenter, from 1932, April 1932, until September, 1934?

A. Couple hundred dollars.

Q. A couple of hundred dollars?

A. Yes.

Q. Your wife quit work too, when she went to Germany, didn't she?

A. Yes.

Q. So that from June, or from April, 1932, April the 2nd, 1932, to September, 1934, when you were arrested, you made $200 as a carpenter and your wife did no work at all either, she quit work?

A. Yes, she quit work.

Q. In June, 1932?

A. June, 1932.

Q. You put this money into the bank because your wife was disgusted on account of the condition of the bank account, isn't that right?

A. Yes.

Q. She was also disgusted because you quit your job, wasn't she?

A. No.

Q. Didn't she say to you, "Richard, why are you quitting your job, we have only got a few dollars in the bank?" And isn't that why you then went and put some money in the bank?

A. She wasn't hollering at me when I quit the job.

Q. When was she hollering at you?

A. I say she was not hollering at me when I quit the job.

Q. You say she didn't holler at you when you quit the job. Did she holler at you some other time?

A. No, I really can't remember.

Q. You can't remember?

A. No.

Q. On the day that you were arrested and this $20 was found in your possession and you told this story, you told the authorities that you had started to circulate these gold ransom bills for a few weeks: isn't that right?

A. I can't remember what I said to them.

Q. Well, you did, you had been circulating them for a few weeks, hadn't you?

A. Yes.

Q. Why?

A. Why?

Q. Because you needed the money?

A. Oh, no, I didn't need the money really—

Richard Hauptmann

Q. Didn't you say—

A. There is practically no particular reason why I put it in circulation. I just keep as well put it in the box and leave it there. I don't see really any particular reason for put it in circulation.

Q. Why did you circulate it then?

A. Well, I thought I don't, I wouldn't take any check for stock account, and so I spent it.

Q. So that you took it because you didn't want to take money out of your stock account and you had to have money for living expenses, so as you needed money for living expenses you took, if you needed money for gasoline you took a ten dollar bill, or a five dollar bill, whatever it was, and you went down and you got gas and you got change: is that right?

A. Yes, that is right.

Q. In other words, you and your wife went in to buy a pair of shoes.

A. Yes.

Q. You had to have money, of course, to buy shoes with.

A. Yes.

Q. So you didn't want to take the money from the broker, so you took a ten, a twenty dollar bill or a ten dollar bill out of this money, isn't that right?

A. That is right.

Q. And you needed money from time to time to buy groceries, or whatever it was, if you needed the money you would go down and get one of these bills and you would go out and cash it, isn't that right?

A. Well, I never went down simply for one bill, that is what I say; the first time I took a couple out; when I count the second one I took a couple out. So I figure altogether I put in circular twelve to fifteen bills.

Q. Now you see you are getting away from the point. The point is you took them out two or three at a time as you needed them to buy various things; you didn't want to take the money from the brokerage account.

A. Yes.

Q. Before that time when you needed living expenses, you took it from the brokerage account, isn't that right?

A. Well, or check out of the bank.

Classics of the Courtroom

Q. Or out of the bank, yes, before that; after that, if you needed money to buy some things to run your household, or whatever it was, during those few weeks you took those—what did you say about twenty of them?

A. About twelve or fifteen.

Q. About 12 or 15 of them. As you needed it you would go into that gold heap and take out one or two at a time, is that right?

A. Four or five at a time.

Q. Well, four or five at a time. That was only when you got through with four or five and you needed more money to buy either food or shoes or something else, then you would go in for the other four or five, is that right?

A. Oh, I really didn't go except—I took the money out when I count it.

Q. But you took the money out because you needed it for your household expenses and you needed it for necessary things and you didn't want to take it from the brokerage account; that's right?

A. Yes, that's right.

Q. There is no question about that? You are sure about that?

A. (No answer)

Q. You didn't take this money out just to cash it, in other words, did you? You took it out for things you needed, is that right?

A. Took it out for living.

Q. Yes, you didn't take the bills out to cash, just to get rid of the gold and get others?

A. No.

Q. You took it because you needed it for groceries, for shoes, for other things, for living expenses, isn't that right?

A. Yes.

Q. And you didn't want to take the money out of the brokerage account?

A. That is right.

Q. Well, if you needed that money so badly while you were doing that in August and September, 1934—

A. Yeah.

Q. —you didn't want to take money out of the brokerage accounts?

A. Well, this money was laying there and was just handy.

Q. Why did you deposit a couple of hundred dollars during August and September if you needed the money and didn't want to take it out of the brokerage accounts?

A. There was—I took out from one bank, there was close to about—

Q. Pardon me. Mr. Fisch was dead at that time, wasn't he?

A. Yes.

Q. You didn't get that from Fisch, did you?

A. Yes—

Q. Why did you make deposits in August and September at the very time that you were taking out gold from this money because you needed it for your living expenses and didn't want to take it out of your brokerage account?

A. The one bank I opened—it was from the Mount Vernon bank, Mount Vernon Trust Company. This bank was closed, und—and I opened a new bank in 86th Street, I took out $109 from Mount Vernon and the rest—in the meantime I spent the money, them gold certificates, I still took out a check from my brokerage account, and even from the bank account we took out the money.

....

Q. Do you remember the excuse you gave yesterday in this court room for not having written to Fisch, Fisch's brother?

A. What was my answer?

Q. Do you know the answer?

A. Well, that is my answer.

Q. Do you remember it?

A. I said Mr. Fisch was coming over here anyway.

Q. That's it. That's what you said yesterday?

A. Yes.

Q. Now, today you say that you didn't write to Fisch because you didn't get an answer to your letter; you had written him and you didn't get an answer, and so you didn't tell him.

A. No, you are mixed up again.

Classics of the Courtroom

Q. I am mixed up? Well, then you straighten it out. Didn't you just a moment ago say that?

A. Yes.

Q. I ask you why you didn't write to Fisch during the months prior to your arrest, and you said you wrote to him and you didn't get an answer.

A. In the meantime I found—

Q. And then you said in the meantime, then you were arrested. Now you say you remember that yesterday you stated that you didn't write to Fisch about this gold because he was coming to the United States anyway: isn't that right?

A. Yes.

Q. As a matter of fact, you knew that you were planning to go to Germany right at that time, weren't you?

A. Oh, that is planned for over a year already.

Q. Certainly. For over a year you had planned to go to Germany?

A. Yes.

Q. And you had written to your mother about it and she had written to you about it, isn't that so?

A. I wrote to Mr. Fisch even about it.

Q. And she had gone to the police to straighten out whatever difficulties there were, isn't that right?

A. There wasn't any difficulty.

Q. She wrote you back that the Statute of Limitations—or the thing was automatically expired?

A. Yes.

Q. Isn't that right?

A. Yes.

Q. And that you could come back?

A. Yes.

Q. That was right about that time in 1934, isn't that right?

A. Yes.

Q. Yes. So you were planning all the time to go to Germany about that time anyway, weren't you?

A. Yes; and if I remember right I was telling Mr. Fisch in the letter if he wants me to bring all his stuff over there, them two satchels.

Q. When did you plan this trip to Germany? You said it was planned a year already.

A. About a year.

Q. A year before September, 1934?

A. I mean a year from the date, about.

Q. From what date?

A. From today.

Q. From today?

A. Yes.

Q. You hadn't planned it a year at the time of your arrest, you don't mean that?

A. No. We spoke a couple of times about going to Germany, but the date was set for 1935, because my mother is seventy years old.

Q. Now in January, 1934 then, you planned to go to Europe, is that right?

A. (No answer.)

Q. That is when you started your plan, January, 1934—this is January, 1935, you said about a year ago?

A. Yes, but this is in our mind to go over to Germany for years and years, but there wasn't any date, final date set.

Q. You wanted to go over because your mother was seventy years old?

A. Yes.

Q. You sent her $50 a year, didn't you?

A. Oh, I really don't know how much I sent her.

Q. Well, about $50 a year?

A. Yes.

Q. That is about how much you sent her each year?

A. One year a little bit more, one year less.

Q. One year a little bit more, one year a little bit less?

A. Yes, and if I wrote my mother, if she needs any money she should write.

Q. Yes, you sent her about $50 a year?

A. I can't remember how much I sent.

Q. Now you had $4,300 in a trunk?

A. Yes.

Q. And you always kept money home, didn't you? That is why you had the $4,300, you always took off some money to hide away?

A. Yes.

....

Q. You remember yesterday you read one of the ransom notes for me, starting off as follows: "The baby would be back long ago. You would not get any result form the police, because this kidnaping—" Now the next part is the part I want to direct your particular attention to—"because this kidnaping was planned for a year already." Do you remember that? Now, let me read another one to you—what number was that—S-23—Then in S-55, "This kidnaping was prepared for a year already," do you hear that: "Was prepared for a year already" in S-23. You have heard those two expressions in those notes: "Was planned for a year already." "Was prepared for a year already," and your statement a while ago about your trip to Germany, "Oh, that is planned for a year already."

A. Yes.

Q. That is your method of speech, isn't it?

A. Well, I guess it is correct.

Q. Yes.

A. How can I say it otherwise?

Q. Well, you can say "Planned for more than a year," "Planned already for a year," "Planned a year ago."

A. How you would say.

MR. REILLY: May I suggest there is a statement by you, you have read from two portions of kidnaping letters and then you read from a portion of a statement of testimony of the witness yesterday and today that he intended to go to Europe and that that trip to Europe was planned and then the Attorney General sits down without him asking any questions about it.

He wants to leave the inference with the jury, unjustly and improperly, that because a man said he was going to Germany a year before he was arrested, that that fits in and gibes with what is in two kidnaping notes, so that the jury might receive the inference as a circumstantial fact that from those three this defendant is guilty of a crime.

THE COURT: Well, what is there improper in the examination?

MR. REILLY: There wasn't any question asked. He says, "Did you read me the part of this yesterday?" And "Did you read me part of that yesterday?" And "Did you say that yesterday?"

Then he sits down, doesn't ask the witness any question about it—

MR. WILENTZ: I think counsel has forgotten it.

MR. REILLY: No, I haven't forgotten it.

THE COURT: He asked three questions; he asked three questions.

MR. REILLY: Then I submit, sir, he should be permitted and asked to follow it up with a question to the witness as to whether or not there is any connections between the two kidnap notes and his statement that he was going to Europe, and not suddenly drop this hot, in the lap of the jury, with the idea that because a man said he was going to Germany that fits in with the kidnap note.

THE COURT: Well, you see, the cross examiner must put his questions. They can't be put according to the idea of his adversary.

MR. REILLY: But—

THE COURT: Now he has asked three questions. I don't recall whether they were answered.

MR. WILENTZ: I think so. I asked him whether or not did he notice the similarity, was that his style of expressing himself, and he then asked me in answer to that, "How would you say it?" And I attempted to tell him how I would say it.

MR. REILLY: Now, I say that that is no answer to the question. I recall very definitely as to the suggestion whether or not counsel should ask the question that in my examination of a certain witness the Attorney General arose and asked whether or not the Court would not direct me to incorporate into a certain question his idea so that we would keep on the subject and I did it. Now I say here when the witness is asked by the Attorney General a question about an inference that he is seeking now to leave in the lap of the jury, that it should be followed by a question which would clear the matter up while we are on the subject.

MR. WILENTZ: May we read the record if it is of some import?

Classics of the Courtroom

THE COURT: I think that the record had better be read.

MR. WILENTZ: May I proceed while we are waiting and we will come back to that and read the question?

Q. Mr. Witness, when you were arrested and you were asked why it was that you had not turned in this gold to the Federal Reserve Bank did you say "I was afraid they would hook me up if I turned it in"?

A. I can't remember that.

Q. Will you say that you didn't say it?

A. I said I cannot remember that.

Q. You won't say that you didn't say it, will you?

A. I answered my question.

Q. You just don't remember?

A. (No answer.)

Q. Well, you weren't afraid they would hook you up, were you?

A. (No answer.)

Q. You weren't afraid they would hook you up, were you?

A. No.

Q. That is not the reason you didn't turn them into the Federal Reserve Bank?

A. Well, the big amount, there was so many questions and I am illegal in this country and I probably would have trouble and beside it wasn't my money so that was the reason I didn't want it in any bank.

Q. You didn't want to take it down because it wasn't your money?

A. It wasn't my money and besides there was so many questions, would be so many questions and I am illegal in this country.

Q. You are in this country illegally?

A. Yes.

Q. And you were afraid of it?

A. Yes.

Q. That is the excuse you gave to the police for—That is the reason you attributed to the police for having changed the accounts into your wife's name because you were illegally in this country?

A. That is not the reason.

Q. Didn't you tell the authorities when you were first arrested that you didn't take the money to the Federal Reserve Bank because you didn't know where there was a Federal Reserve Bank?

A. I couldn't remember right away—I know a Federal Reserve Bank.

Q. Oh, you couldn't remember at the time so you told them the reason you didn't take the money to the Federal Reserve Bank was because you didn't know where there was a Federal Reserve Bank.

A. I know there is a Federal Reserve Bank, but I couldn't think so fast.

Q. And you couldn't think so fast, so you told the authorities that you didn't know where there was a Federal Reserve Bank, isn't that right?

A. I don't know if I said it like that.

Q. Didn't you tell the authorities when you were arrested that you did not know where there was a Federal Reserve Bank?

A. I can't remember my answer I give.

Q. Will you say that you didn't say it to the authorities?

A. I guess I answered my question.

Q. Will you say that you didn't say it to the authorities?

A. I said something about it, but I can't remember what I said.

Q. Yes, you said something about not knowing where there was a Federal Reserve Bank?

A. Yes.

Q. And all the time when you were saying that, you knew very well that you had been into a Federal Reserve Bank and had deposited gold?

A. Later on, I was thinking about Federal Reserve Bank, must be on Wall Street, and I remember I was in.

Q. You remember then you were in?

A. Yes.

Q. So you made a mistake the first time you told them that you didn't know where there was a Federal Reserve Bank?

A. Well, I know there is.

Q. Then you corrected it?

A. I know there is a Federal Reserve Bank, but I couldn't remember first the location.

Classics of the Courtroom

Q. But you made a mistake first when you told them that you didn't know where there was a Federal Reserve Bank, then you remembered that you did know, is that it?

A. Yes.

Q. Your answer is yes, isn't it?

A. Yes.

MR. WILENTZ: The testimony is here.

THE COURT: The secretary will read it, the reporter will read it.

(The reporter read as follows:

"Q. You remember yesterday you read one of the ransom notes for me starting off as follows: 'The baby would be back long ago. You would not get any result from the police, because this kidnaping—' Now, the next part is the part I want to direct your particular attention to—'because this kidnaping was planned for a year already.' Do you remember that? Now, let me read another one to you—what number was that—S-23—

"Q. Then in S-55, 'This kidnaping was prepared for a year already,' do you hear that: 'Was prepared for a year already,' in S-55 and 'was planned for a year already,' in S-23. You have heard those two expressions in those notes: 'Was planned for a year already;' 'Was prepared for a year already,' and your statement a while ago about your trip to Germany, 'Oh, that is planned for a year already.'

A. Yes.

"Q. That is your method of speech, isn't it?

A. Well, I guess it is correct.")

THE COURT: Now, what is wrong about that?

MR. REILLY: There is more of it.

MR. WILENTZ: That was the question.

MR. REILLY: Nowhere is the question from the witness to the Attorney General.

THE REPORTER (reading):

"Q. Yes.

A. How can I say it otherwise?

"Q. Well, you can say 'Planned for more than a year,' 'Planned already for a year,' 'Planned a year ago.'

A. How you would say."

Then Mr. Reilly objects.

MR. REILLY: Yes. Now that is what I object to. It is rather confused.

THE COURT: Well, if this matter is left, as you seem to think, in a state of confusion, you can clear it up on your redirect examination.

MR. REILLY: I wanted, if possible—of course it is past now, the moment is past, but at that particular minute if it was possible to clear it up so that the mind of the jury would be focussed upon it, it would have been better, rather than to take it up on redirect. Of course, then the effect may be lost.

However, I will take it up.

MR. WILENTZ: Not if Mr. Reilly takes it up, the effect won't be lost.

MR. REILLY: General, you are always so kind.

....

Q. How much did Fisch lose in the stock accounts?

A. Stock account, Fisch lose, I figure out close to $15,000.

Q. How much did he put in?

A. About the same amount.

Q. So that he put in about $15,000 and he lost about the same amount?

A. Yes, 1933 in November he was even.

Q. So that—

A. He lost—

Q. So he was finally even too?

A. He was.

Q. He put in about fifteen and he lost about fifteen?

A. Yes; it was different, I can't remember any more if it was a little bit less or a little bit more.

Q. How much did you put in?

A. Very little.

Q. How much?

A. 50 shares was—

Q. How much cash did you put in, please?

Classics of the Courtroom

A. For which day?

Q. Then your brokerage accounts from April 2nd, 1932?

A. I guess around 2,000.

Q. Two thousand dollars?

A. 2,000 or 1,500.

Q. 2,000 or 1,500?

A. Yes.

Q. And how much profit do you say that you earned from April 2nd, 1932, until the date of your arrest?

A. It was $9,500.

Q. Profit?

A. Yes. I never took any money out from my stock account for living, I took out money from the fur account, and if you follow closely my books you will find—

Q. You didn't take money out of your—

MR. REILLY: May he answer it, General? You shut him off.

MR. WILENTZ: Go ahead. I thought he did answer it.

MR. REILLY: No.

A. (continued) If you will follow my books, the time Mr. Fisch left for Europe, I always took, since dis time, my living expenses from the stock account, because there wasn't any more money coming in from fur account. He was away, and I guess you find it in the book too.

Q. You took some part of your living account from the ransom money, didn't you?

A. I never got any ransom money in my possession; I didn't know it—

Q. You spent some of the ransom money for your living expenses in September and in August 1934, didn't you?

A. I didn't know that was ransom money.

Q. I didn't ask you if you knew it, but you spent some of that money, you know it now, don't you?

A. I spent twelve to fifteen in bills, yes.

Q. Yes, so you did take some?

A. Yes, I did.

Q. You didn't take any living expenses out prior to that time, before 1933, you say?

MR. REILLY: From what, General? From what do you mean?

Q. From your brokerage account, you said you took no money out for your living expenses, I think, since October 1933?

A. I took very little. Sometimes there wasn't—Fisch didn't have any money, so I took some, a check, but very little.

Q. Then you did take some money out of your brokerage accounts for a living before November 1933?

A. Amounts practical for nothing.

Q. Well, whatever it is, you are satisfied to stand by the books, aren't you, your books?

A. Well, I can't remember so, right from the air.

Q. You asked me to follow the books. Are you willing to follow the books?

A. Yes.

Q. Your books?

A. Yes.

Q. Will you stand on the accounts in your books?

A. I stay on it, yes.

Q. Will you stand on the fur accounts between you and Fisch in the books?

A. No.

Q. Will you stand on the brokerage accounts in the books of you and Fisch?

A. Yes.

Q. Will you stand on $2,000 as being the only money that Fisch gave you up to July 1933, for brokerage?

A. No.

Q. That is not true, is it?

A. That is not.

Q. Not correct?

A. That is not correct.

Q. So you won't stand on your books, will you?

A. To a certain extent, yes.

Q. Yes, to a certain extent the testimony in the Bronx, is that right—is that correct?

A. That's correct.

Q. To a certain extent the testimony before Sam Foley, is that correct?

A. (No answer.)

Q. Is that correct?

MR. REILLY: That wasn't testimony, General; it wasn't under oath, it was just questions.

Q. Questions and answers before Sam Foley; your answer is you only want to stand on them to a certain extent, is that right?

A. Some of them I said I remember afterwards was a little bit different.

Q. Didn't you testify the other day that you only wanted to stand on the answers you gave to Mr. Foley to a certain extent, didn't you say so?

A. Well, I correct my answer.

Q. Do you want to correct it now?

A. No.

Q. No. But you so testified the other day, isn't that right?

A. Yes.

Q. So that to a certain extent the testimony in the Bronx before Mr. Foley and now to a certain extent your own books—

A. My own books doesn't show anything. I told you before, didn't I?

Q. The book shows $2,000 as being invested by Fisch up to July, 1933, isn't that right?

A. And I explained them $2,000, didn't I?

Q. Yes, sir.

A. Well—

Q. But is that correct, that is all he put up until July, 1933?

A. No.

Q. Then why did you put it in there, $2,000, on account of Fisch and Hauptmann?

Richard Hauptmann

A. I told you before. I said I will keep care of them $2,000 special.

Q. Not what you told me, by the book, you asked me to follow the book, didn't you?

A. And that is standing in the book.

MR. WILENTZ: Where is that book?

Q. You want the jury to follow the book, don't you, your book?

A. It can.

Q. Sir?

A. It can. There is no objection to it.

Q. All right, sir. Now your book says that Fisch put in $2,000 on account of Hauptmann and Fisch in July, 1933. Isn't that right (showing book to the witness)? What page is it, Mr. Frank? Do you know? "Isidor Fisch put over to account of Isidor and Richard $2,103 July the 10th, 1933 to a 20 per cent basis"?

A. Yes, and that—

Q. And that includes the $2,000 on these stocks which you have outlined here, which you bought for Fisch, isn't that right?

A. You know my book better than I do, I guess. Listen. This date Mr. Fisch, I said to Mr. Fisch, "Give me $2,000 and I keep care of it, I pay stock and I sell stock how I think." And that's what I did.

Q. Yes, sir.

A. When I get—

Q. You were his manager about the purchase and sale of stock, is that right?

A. Please let me finish my explanation.

Q. I thought you did finish.

A. No, sir, I did not.

Q. Yes, sir, you may finish.

A. And then I keep care of them stock I bought for him what I thought is best.

Q. Yes.

A. Now I made $103 on it and he wasn't satisfied, it was too little—

Q. Now please—

Classics of the Courtroom

MR. REILLY: Let him finish, please.

MR. WILENTZ: Just a minute. I am interested now in an answer about the book and the account.

MR. REILLY: Well, he is trying to explain.

MR. WILENTZ: No, he is talking about a conversation with him.

THE WITNESS: I am coming to it.

MR. WILENTZ: Now I think I have permitted the conversation and it is not responsive, and I think I have the right under those circumstances either to stop him or move to strike it out.

MR. REILLY: He is explaining the items in the book.

THE COURT: Well, he was doing something more than that, I think.

MR. REILLY: Of course he might have been putting in a few more words, but he was explaining that item.

MR. WILENTZ: If your Honor please, if your Honor will permit, when I am through with the account of the book, I am willing to sit here for an hour and listen to his explanation and I won't object; but I want to find out about the entry in the book.

THE COURT: You may proceed.

Q. Will you find me in the book where you have an account of Fisch giving you anything like $15,000?

A. It is not special marked.

Q. Will you show me anything in your book in which Fisch is shown as putting in anything outside of that $2,000; show me any notation in which you have Fisch putting up money.

A. You wouldn't find it in this book.

Q. Will you find it in any one of these books?

A. No, but I guess in Fisch, Fisch kept a book.

Q. I am talking about your books now.

A. No, you wouldn't find it.

Q. All right. Let me have the book for a minute. So that you have got the stocks here that you purchased and sold, haven't you, all this reference being to S-258 so you have your book here of the stocks that you bought and sold in this book, have you not?

A. In Fisch account includes only $2,000.

Q. Will you please answer the question? Does this book include the brokerage accounts including the stocks bought and sold?

A. Yes.

Q. Does it include Fisch's brokerage account, bought and sold?

A. It includes Fisch account but it isn't separate from my account.

Q. That is right. But it includes them.

A. Includes them in my name.

Q. That's right. But the stocks purchased and the stocks sold are in this book S-258, aren't they?

A. Yes.

Q. And you have got an entry here of $2,103, Isidor Fisch, put over to the account of Isidor and Richard, July 10, 1923, to 20 percent basis. You have got that in there?

A. Yes.

Q. But you haven't got another piece of evidence in this book or a writing that shows that Fisch put in another dollar, have you?

A. No, I have not.

Q. And it is your book?

A. Yes, it is my book.

Q. And it is your book?

A. It is my book.

Q. The police didn't write it, did they?

A. No.

Q. And I didn't write it?

A. No, I did.

....

Q. Fisch's stocks and your stocks are all mixed together?

A. All mixed together.

Q. Is there one line in your records that shows that Fisch gave you one dollar outside of $2,000?

A. No, dare is not.

Q. There isn't. Did you ever get a certificate of stock in the name of Isidor Fisch?

A. All the certificates are of my name.

Q. Yes. Were you interested in the fur business at all?

A. Well, I didn't understand it.

Q. No.

A. I left—

Q. Do you know any legitimate fur dealer that you did business with?

A. Yes, the address in here.

Q. You don't know of any of your own knowledge?

A. No.

Q. Now, what did you say about Woodlawn Cemetery; did you say that you knew where the cemetery was before March, 1932?

A. Yes, I did.

Q. Were you familiar with it?

A. No.

Q. You were not familiar with it?

A. No.

Q. How about St. Raymond's?

A. St. Raymond's, I hear the name St. Raymond's, I guess, when I get arrested, in the courtroom.

Q. That is the first you heard it?

A. Yes.

Q. When you went to the Mt. Vernon Bank to make your deposits, didn't you have to pass Woodlawn Cemetery?

A. No, that is only about two blocks from my house.

Q. What is two blocks from your house?

A. Two miles from my house, an entirely different direction.

Q. Did you work at the National Lumber Company which is near one of these cemeteries, at their branch?

A. I get the contracts for the National Lumber Corporation.

Q. Sir?

A. I get the contracts from National Lumber Corporation.

Q. Did you work at a lumber company whose plant was near that cemetery?

A. Yes.

Q. Near what cemetery was it?

A. Woodlawn.

Q. So you were familiar with Woodlawn Cemetery, were you not?

A. Nothing at all.

Q. How close to the cemetery did you work?

A. I will say it is about a mile away from it.

Q. A mile away?

A. Yes. You can see Woodlawn Cemetery from quite a distance.

Q. You can or can't?

A. You can.

Q. You can?

A. Yes.

Q. So that you knew where it was, generally?

A. Oh, yes. I guess everybody knows.

Q. Did you work at Marble Hill Avenue in February 1928, in the Bronx?

A. What is that again?

Q. Did you work at Marble Hill Avenue in the Bronx in February 1928?

A. '28?

Q. Yes.

A. Oh, I have worked so many places it is impossible for me to remember.

Q. Well, didn't you have to pass the cemetery, the Woodlawn Cemetery, every day when you went to work at the Marble Hill Avenue house?

A. No. Now, let me think where Marble Hill Avenue are located.

Q. If you can't remember it, why, we will pass to something else.

A. No, I never passed Woodlawn Cemetery on my way to work; never.

Q. You worked at 204th Street and Bainbridge Avenue once, didn't you, Bainbridge Avenue and 204th Street?

A. Yes.

Q. Let me see if I can find it on this map: Bainbridge. Do you know where it is, sir?

A. Bainbridge? I have to look myself. The name is familiar, but I have worked so many places it is hard to remember.

Q. Here is Bainbridge Avenue and 204th Street.

A. Yes.

Q. Now, how did you go from there to your home?

A. Which year?

Q. Whenever you worked there.

A. That depends when I got a car, when I use the car.

Q. Did you go up to Gun Hill Road and then over?

A. No.

Q. How would you?

A. Webster Avenue.

Q. Webster Avenue?

A. Yes.

Q. And then up to Gun Hill Road?

A. Gun Hill Road, yes.

Q. Well, doesn't Gun Hill Road on Webster Avenue—isn't that right at the edge of Woodlawn Cemetery?

A. I guess you can't even see Woodlawn Cemetery from Gun Hill Road.

Q. Just about a block away, isn't it?

A. More than a block.

Q. More than a block?

A. I guess you cannot see it.

Q. What did you say about St. Raymond's, didn't know anything about that, did you?

A. I know that there is a cemetery in this direction, but I didn't know the name.

Q. Do you know there was a cemetery there, did you see it there on occasions?

A. I passed this cemetery one time.

Q. Just one time?

A. Yes.

Q. Did you work on Haviland Avenue job with Mr. Grizzle, Haviland Avenue job with Mr. Grizzle?

A. Haviland Avenue?

Q. Yes. Do you remember it or don't you remember it?

A. No, I remember it.

Q. You do?

A. I guess that is right, Haviland Avenue.

Q. Is that right near St. Raymond's Cemetery?

A. No, that is a far distance.

Q. It is a far distance?

A. Yes.

Q. How far away is it?

A. I don't know.

Q. From St. Raymond's.

A. I don't know how far.

Q. You can't see St. Raymond's from there?

A. No.

Q. Can't you look right across Westchester Creek into St. Raymond's Cemetery from the Haviland Avenue job that you worked on?

A. I didn't see any cemetery at all over there.

Q. Did you visit Fred Brandt's place in 1927 when you were employed as a carpenter by Mr. Breslin?

A. Yes. That is the time I passed, one time the cemetery, that is what I remember.

Q. Yes. That was in the vicinity of his home?

A. And I have to pass by.

Q. Did you go to Yonkers often?

A. Yonkers?

Q. Yes.

A. I was working in Yonkers.

Q. And when you were working in Yonkers, did you go from your home at 222nd Street?

A. No. When I was working Yonkers I left on Needham Avenue—

Classics of the Courtroom

well, it is not far from there.

Q. Not far from there. And did you pass St. Raymond's cemetery on your way to Yonkers?

A. No. You are mixing up with Woodlawn.

Q. What, sir?

A. You are mixed up with Woodlawn Cemetery.

Q. Then you passed Woodlawn Cemetery?

A. No, not Woodlawn Cemetery either.

Q. Now, you say I am mixed up in my cemeteries. When you went to Yonkers I said you passed St. Raymond's Cemetery and you told me I am mixed up with my cemeteries. Do you mean by that you didn't pass St. Raymond's but that you passed Woodlawn?

A. I didn't pass any cemeteries.

Q. What did you mean when you said I was mixed up?

A. This cemetery of St. Raymond's Cemetery, this location is entirely different direction.

Q. That is right. The Woodlawn Cemetery, that you pass when you go to Yonkers, isn't it?

A. No, I didn't pass it.

Q. You didn't pass it?

A. No.

Q. Whenever you got away from Yonkers you got away from that cemetery?

A. I don't have to go to that.

Q. How did you go? Tell us the course that you took.

A. To Yonkers, well, I worked, I guess it was in '29—that is the time I worked over there.

Q. Well, how did you get from your home?

A. Well, mostly I was driving mit the car mit friends.

Q. How? What road would you start on? You were living on 222nd Street?

A. Yes.

Q. All right, which way would you go?

A. We went up White Plains Road.

Q. Yes.

A. I don't know how far.

Q. Yes.

A. You wouldn't mind to give me the stick?

Q. No, go ahead (handing pointer to the witness).

A. That's White Plains Road here (indicating).

Q. Yes, sir.

A. And that's my house (indicating).

Q. Yes, sir. You would drive along East 222nd Street in a westerly direction until you got to White Plains Road?

A. Yes. Over here the carpenter was living (indicating).

Q. Yes.

A. I went to his house, took out his car.

Q. And you—

A. And I go over here and follow all this, White Plains Avenue, all the way up, about as far as that (indicating); then we went over to Yonkers.

Q. And all the time you did that, once you left White Plains Road, all the time you did that you were a couple of blocks away from Woodlawn Cemetery; first on the side and then on—

A. That's quite a distance over there.

Q. But I mean White Plains Road that is about—well, a few blocks away from Woodlawn Cemetery, isn't it?

A. Yes, but there is no connecting road between.

Q. You never really drove along Woodlawn Cemetery did you, in front of it?

A. Oh, I passed by, sure.

Q. Did you ever ride in front of it on Jerome Avenue?

A. No, I can't remember.

Q. You don't ever remember driving in front of Woodlawn Cemetery along Jerome Avenue?

A. No.

Q. You never drove along Woodlawn Cemetery on East 233rd Street, did you?

Classics of the Courtroom

A. It is possible.

Q. But you don't remember.

A. I can't remember now, but it is possible I was driving over there.

Q. And St. Raymond's Cemetery you never remember driving along East Tremont Street, did you?

A. No, I always used Eastern Boulevard.

Q. And not—well, Eastern Boulevard is in the vicinity of the cemetery, it is near there, isn't it?

A. I didn't see any cemetery at all.

Q. Well, you see Eastern Boulevard is right here, don't you (indicating)?

A. No.

Q. Isn't that Eastern Boulevard?

A. You won't mind giving me this stick?

(Mr. Wilentz lets witness take pointer.)

Q. It says so on there.

A. I mean Southern Boulevard here.

Q. Southern Boulevard?

A. No.

Q. Well, it is Eastern Boulevard, but it is way up there, you mean that part of it?

A. That part of it here.

Q. A good distance away?

A. And follow over here.

Q. Yes, sir.

A. There was always follow from this corner the shore line from Throgg's Neck, but never came in this neighborhood.

Q. All right, sir. So that when you did come down Eastern Boulevard you always drove away from St. Raymond's Cemetery and never passed down past it?

A. I—no, I never passed it.

Q. Never passed it?

A. No.

Q. When you would get at this corner here—can I mark it "Y", is

Richard Hauptmann

that all right, any objection?

A. It is all right with me.

Q. When you got to the point "Y", why, that is when you drove away, is that it? You drive off Eastern Parkway and onto that road that leads some other place?

A. Yes, because I have got nothing to do down there.

Q. Yes, certainly. So you never drove past St. Raymond's Cemetery either on East Tremont Avenue or on Eastern Boulevard, on the end near—

A. No.

Q. Never did?

A. No, I am positively sure about it.

Q. How did you drive to Mueller's house from your house?

A. To Mueller's?

Q. Yes.

A. I was, there is two ways, you mean Marian Avenue; I guess sometimes I went through the Bronx Park, Mosholu Parkway.

Q. Which parkway?

A. Mosholu Parkway, and there is a cut right through Marion Avenue.

Q. Yes. What would be the other way?

A. And another way, one block downtown from the house where Mr. Mueller lives, I cut through the Webster Avenue and follow Webster Avenue to Gun Hill Road, and sometimes Gun Hill Road and White Plains Avenue, and sometimes Boston Road—that is just how I feel.

Q. How far away from Dr. Condon's home did Mr. Mueller live at any time since 1932?

A. I don't know where Mr. Condon lives.

Q. What street did Mueller live on?

A. Marion Avenue.

Q. How far is Marion Avenue from Decatur Avenue?

A. That is only one block, but Mr. Mueller moved in, I guess, about only one year ago.

Q. Yes.

A. Yes.

Q. That is about a year ago, a year ago Mr. Mueller lived about a block on the first block paralleling Decatur Avenue, is that right?

A. He is still living over there yet.

Q. He is still living there?

A. Yes.

Q. And Dr. Condon lived then and still lives at Decatur Avenue, so far as you know?

A. Yes.

Q. Were you familiar at all with the section of the Bronx where Dr. Condon lived at that time?

A. Well—

Q. March and April, 1932.

A. Not particularly around there.

Q. Well, you knew the section, didn't you?

A. I probably knew in the Bronx—

Q. You knew East Fordham Road, didn't you?

A. Fordham Road, oh, yes.

Q. You knew Webster Avenue?

A. Webster Avenue everybody knew.

Q. You knew Gun Hill Road?

A. Yes.

Q. Webster Avenue paralleled Decatur Avenue that is one block away from each other, isn't that so?

A. I find that out later.

Q. Yes, of course you didn't know it in March or April, 1932?

A. I did not.

Q. But you found out later that you had been traveling about a block away from Decatur Avenue every time you drove down Webster Avenue?

A. Yes.

Q. Yes.

A. But I never have to cross Decatur Avenue.

Q. You never were on Decatur Avenue, were you?

A. No, sir; no, sir, not in this time.

Q. Well, at any time.

A. When I finish the house for Mr. Miller—

Q. But before that time, before March the 1st, 1932, you had never been on Decatur Avenue in the Bronx?

A. No.

Q. And you had never been in St. Raymond's Cemetery?

A. Oh—

Q. You had never been in the front or on the side of St. Raymond's Cemetery?

A. I passed by.

Q. Just on one of those roads, off roads, isn't that so?

A. I passed by mit the streetcar in 1927 or sometimes.

Q. Right in front of the cemetery?

A. That is in front of the cemetery.

Q. St. Raymond's?

A. Saint—well, I didn't know the name.

Q. You didn't know the name?

A. I know now the name.

Q. And how about Woodlawn? Did you ever pass in front of Woodlawn Cemetery?

A. Well, I say yes, passed by. It is not far from my home.

Q. Now, you recognize this board again that we talked about yesterday, do you not?

A. Yes, I do.

Q. You know now, don't you, that the address on this board and the telephone number are the address and telephone number of Dr. Condon as of March and April and May, 1932?

A. Yes, you told me so.

Q. Yes. You have heard it in court, haven't you?

A. Yes.

Q. You heard the telephone man talk about it too, didn't you?

A. Well, I was here when telephone man was here.

Q. You heard Inspector Bruckman and the carpenters from New

York testify that they took this board from your home?

A. That is what they said.

Q. Yes. Can you now give this Court and jury any explanation why this number of Dr. Condon and why this address of Dr. Condon was on this board, 206—204, which came from your rooms?

A. I give you the answer yesterday already.

Q. You have no better answer?

A. No.

....

Q. You made a mistake about the board with Dr. Condon's name and telephone number on it, didn't you?

A. What you mean, mistaken?

Q. When you said Yes you meant No?

A. No, I never said correct, yes.

Q. Well, you said Yes—

A. In the beginning I was—it is funny, what I got in my mind; I know sometimes I was writing address and numbers in books and so—let me finish, please.

Q. Yes, sir. You have been doing a lot of explaining today.

A. Yes. So I thought it is possible I wrote it on some piece of wood, but now, after thinking, this inside of the closet it was impossible to write, there is no question.

Q. You thought it was possible for you that maybe you wrote Dr. Condon's number and address some place, but when you thought about the closet and how impossible it was to write in there, then you decided you didn't write it?

A. I didn't write it; I really can't remember ever writing on it.

Q. You can't remember ever writing it?

A. No.

Q. But you just said, did you not, that you thought maybe you would write it somewhere, but when you thought about writing it in the closet you knew you couldn't get in there, so you didn't write it: is that what you mean?

A. That's not exactly what I mean.

Q. To what other extent was it that you were mistaken in your sworn testimony in the Bronx?

A. I never got interest in Dr. Condon.

Q. When you said that this is Lindbergh money in answer to Foley's question, when you answered the same question before Supreme Court Justice Hammer and the Court said to you, "Do you understand the question," and you said "Yes," what did you mean?

A. What was the question?

Q. "Is this Lindbergh money?" The extra money, the last money that was found.

A. I said Yes.

Q. Why did you say yes, it was Lindbergh money?

A. Because them eight hundred dollar came from the same shoe box. If the $40,000 is ransom money, the rest from $800 would be the same—that's common sense.

Q. What else did you mean when you said that you only stand on your sworn testimony in the Bronx to a certain extent? Anything else besides the board?

A. I guess it is only the board.

Q. How about March the 1st? Didn't you testify there that you were working on March the 1st?

A. No.

Q. Didn't you?

A. I said—

Q. Did you say you were working on March the 1st?

MR. REILLY: Let him answer.

MR. WILENTZ: He has answered.

MR. REILLY: No, he hasn't answered enough.

THE COURT: Let him answer.

A. I said that it is just another question—I said first March I am not quite sure if I was working or not. If I was working I was working in the Majestic Apartments. If not, I was down in my employment agency because I couldn't remember this time where I have been.

Q. When you were arrested did you say you were working March 1st?

Classics of the Courtroom

A. My first impression was—

Q. That is what you said, wasn't it?

A. —was I was working.

Q. Didn't you say in the Bronx that you started to work March the 15th?

A. That is what I said here, 15th or 16th.

Q. Did you say in the Bronx court that you started working in the Majestic March 15th?

A. I can't remember if I said yes or no.

Q. Did you say anything about a conversation between you and the employment manager telling you on March 1st to come back the 15th: did you say anything in the Bronx about that?

A. I guess I said but I don't know what I said.

Q. Well, you didn't know then that the employment manager told you to come back the 15th, did you? You said nothing about it in the Bronx, did you?

A. Well, listen, when I came back from Majestic, right away I went to the employment agency to try to get them $10 back.

Q. When did you leave the tools there?

A. The tools?

Q. Yes.

A. I took it up next day.

Q. Before March the 1st?

A. After.

Q. Didn't you testify here that you took the tools up there before the 1st of March?

A. You said when I took it back.

Q. When you took the tools up.

A. Up? What you mean by up?

Q. Up to the Majestic.

A. Oh, that is a Monday.

Q. Before March the 1st?

A. Yes.

Q. You took them up on Monday, the day before the kidnapping?

301

A. The day before I was supposed to work.

Q. And you took the tools up there as the alibi for March the 1st, didn't you?

A. No, sir.

Q. You did take them up the day before the kidnapping?

A. Because I was supposed to start on the 1st of March and I—

Q. So you—

A. —and I couldn't take the car down there, because too much traffic, so I sharpened the tools in the morning of the last of February, 29th, took the tools down to the Majestic and went home again.

Q. Did you take them home with you?

A. Well, I left it down.

Q. You left it there until the 15th of March?

A. No, sir.

Q. Till when?

A. Wednesday, the day after.

Q. Wednesday?

A. Yes.

Q. The day after the kidnapping?

A. Because what is the use to lay, to have the tools down in the Majestic? I couldn't start 'fore the 15th, I know it.

Q. You quit your work the day the $50,000 was paid, didn't you, April the 2nd, 1932?

MR. REILLY: I object to the form of the question. Let's leave out "The day the 50,000 was paid," and put a date. He left his work on April 1st, 2nd, or 3rd, whatever he wants to ask, but I object to this "You left your work the day of the kidnapping," and "You took your job back on the day the ransom money was paid." It is improper.

MR. POPE: He has answered it seven times.

MR. REILLY: It has been answered at least twenty times here. I assume we are working up to a climax. I think the form is bad.

THE COURT: I think the form of the question is a little bit unnecessary.

MR. WILENTZ: I withdraw the question if that is your Honor's thought about it.

Classics of the Courtroom

Q. To what extent didn't you tell the truth to District Attorney Foley. You have testified here that you are willing to stand on your statements to District Attorney Foley to a certain extent. What do you mean by that?

MR. REILLY: I object to this. It has been answered three times.

MR. WILENTZ: No, sir, it has not, I respectfully submit.

MR. REILLY: It was answered yesterday afternoon, it was answered here this morning and it is answered here now.

THE COURT: My impression is the witness has already answered this question, but if the Attorney General has any doubt about it he may put the question again. Answer the question.

BY MR. WILENTZ:

Q. What did you mean when you testified here that you were willing to stand upon your statements to District Attorney Foley only to a certain extent?

A. With reference to this board here.

Q. Is that the only extent?

A. Yes.

Q. You told Mr. Foley, did you not, that you never were arrested in Germany?

MR. REILLY: I object to that.

Q. Didn't you?

A. No, sir.

MR. REILLY: Mr. Foley had no right to ask him any such question.

THE COURT: I will have to sustain that objection.

MR. WILENTZ: I understood counsel asked a question in that regard.

MR. REILLY: Oh, no.

THE COURT: I didn't hear counsel ask such a question.

MR. REILLY: I asked him the question was he convicted.

THE COURT: The question should be limited to conviction.

Q. You told District Attorney Foley that you had never been convicted in Europe, didn't you?

A. Yes.

303

Richard Hauptmann

Q. And that wasn't the truth either, was it?

MR. REILLY: I object to that. He was under no obligation to disclose any of his past record to District Attorney foley who did not have him under oath; he was under arrest. He didn't have to testify to anything, nor did he have to disclose any trouble that he had been in before in the form of a conviction.

MR. WILENTZ: It is rather a novel situation where a man can proceed and make statements that are not the truth when he is being interrogated and say that he didn't have to tell the truth.

MR. REILLY: No, all the states and the laws of the country say you do not have to testify—

MR. WILENTZ: I disagree with you.

THE COURT: Gentlemen, let us proceed in an orderly manner. I think we can get along without very much excitement. It is competent in this Court for the Attorney General to prove conviction in Germany.

MR. REILLY: That is true. But the question is whether Mr. Foley asked him—

THE COURT: That I have excluded.

MR. WILENTZ: The question I am asking is with reference to his statement here, that he told District Attorney Foley the truth to a certain extent and he limits that certain extent to testimony with reference to the board. Now I am asking him "Didn't you tell District Attorney Foley that you were not convicted in Germany?" his answer was "Yes." Now my question is to him, "And that wasn't the truth?"

THE COURT: You may ask him if in fact he was convicted in Germany. You may put it in that form.

Q. When you told District Attorney Foley that you had not been convicted in Germany, at that time in fact you had been convicted in Germany, isn't that the fact?

A. Yes, but—

Q. Never mind the but.

A. When I said—

MR. WILENTZ: I submit, if your Honor please, he has answered it. I don't think he has got to give an alibi with each answer.

THE WITNESS: This case was overruled in the record.

THE COURT: One moment.

MR. WILENTZ: He has answered Yes.

THE COURT: Did he answer Yes?

MR. WILENTZ: Yes. He wanted to put a but on there.

THE COURT: Let it stand.

THE WITNESS: It was fifteen years ago and overruled.

MR. WILENTZ: Just a minute now, just a minute.

THE COURT: One moment. Your counsel will give you a chance to talk, if you want to explain anything.

MR. WILENTZ: Take the witness.

(Confusion in the court room.)

THE COURT: The people will have to keep quiet. Otherwise we will have to clear out the courtroom. We have a half an hour yet to work and we can't work with people conversing among themselves in the audience. That ought to be perfectly plain to these people here. Now proceed.

....

REDIRECT EXAMINATION

BY MR. REILLY:

Q. You testified in the Bronx, didn't you, that during March 1932 you went down to the Hotel Majestic, to see if they had some work for you, or the Majestic Apartments, rather?

A. Yes.

Q. And did you for a week or two before the 1st of March go down to the Majestic Apartments to see if they had any work for you?

A. I went down to the agency, Sixth Avenue

Q. That was, what agency was it?

A. I guess Reliable, or Liable.

Q. Did the agency send you to the hotel, or to the apartments?

A. Yes, it was on February 27th, it was on a Saturday. That means I get a letter from the agency to start on March the 1st.

Q. Are you right-handed or left-handed?

A. Right handed.

Q. Now, there was something said here yesterday about that trunk that you kept the money in and you said at one time the trunk was broken: is that correct?

Richard Hauptmann

A. Yes.

Q. When was it broken?

A. Oh, this was '33. I didn't have any money in there any more then.

Q. Do you recall the month?

A. Please?

Q. Do you recall the month that you saw it was first broken?

A. No, I can't.

Q. Was there at any time anything improper between you and Mrs. Henckle?

A. Nothing.

MR. REILLY: Mr. Attorney General, have you the Fisch letters?

MR. WILENTZ: We only have one postcard. Captain Snook, will you give Mr. Reilly the postcard.

MR. REILLY: While the Captain is getting the postal card—

Q. The Attorney General asked you whether or not since you have been in jail you obtained the use of a German-American dictionary, is that correct?

A. That's correct.

Q. When did you get it?

A. When?

Q. When, yes.

A. About two months ago.

Q. For what purpose did you get it?

A. I only read English books in here and some of the books I can't understand, so that's the reason I was asking for a dictionary.

Q. Do you recall some of the books you have read since you have been in jail?

A. Yes.

Q. Give us the names of some of the books you have read?

A. *Life of Lincoln*, and ancient history.

Q. Ancient history?

A. Yes; and stories from Canada, and South and North Pole expedition. That's a few of them.

Classics of the Courtroom

Q. How many letters did you receive from Mr. Isidor Fisch after he sailed back to Germany?

A. Letters and postal cards I will say around six to eight.

Q. Well, how many letters?

A. About four letters.

Q. Were those letters in your house when you were arrested?

A. There was—When I say six to eight that means from Isidor Fisch.

Q. Yes. That is what I am talking about—Isidor.

A. Yes, I guess them letters was in our house, but them letters Isidor Fisch's brother sent me. They was in my house.

Q. Well, do you know where the letters from Isidor to you—where were they if you know, at the time of your arrest?

A. I don't know.

Q. You don't know whether they were in the house or not?

A. I don't know that. But I am sure about them other letters from his brother because I keep the record of it.

Q. Well, then you are not able to place in your mind, are you, just where the letters from Isidor Fisch to you are at the present time?

A. No, I don't know.

Q. Do you remember the contents of the letters?

A. Yes.

Q. Now, referring to the first letter that you received from Isidor after he went back to Europe in December, 1933, will you give us your best recollection of what he said in that first letter?

A. In his first letter he didn't say anything particular; it was only about his trip and that he is well, and only little things, nothing important.

Q. Did you write to him then?

A. Yes.

Q. Was that one of the letters—Well, there was no letter produced. What did you write to him in answer to his first letter?

A. I guess I only wrote on a card.

Q. Postal card?

A. Yes, the first letter.

Richard Hauptmann

Q. Do you recall the second communication you received from Isidor: was it a letter or was it a card?

A. It was a card, the second, then I guess there was another card before the first letter.

Q. I show you a card which is produced by the Attorney General and ask you whether or not that is in the handwriting of Isidor Fisch.

A. Oh, that is Fisch's handwriting.

Q. Was that card received by you?

A. Yes, it was.

Q. About when?

A. Oh, I can't remember that, the date was the same.

Q. Well, the stamp appears to be Leipzig and the 20th or 21st of January, doesn't it—1/20/21?

A. No, that means 8th of January, 1934. I figure probably I received this postal card around ten days later, around the 18th, 17th or 18th.

MR. REILLY: Any objection to my offering this in evidence?

MR. WILENTZ: No, certainly not.

MR. REILLY: I offer it in evidence. There is no objection from the Attorney General.

(The post-card was received in evidence and marked Defendant's Exhibit D-43.)

Q. Now, will you read this or translate this German for us into English?

A. "I received your card. Am very glad you got a nice Christmas time. I read about the weather in New York. The cold weather in Germany is—the cold in Germany is not so strong any more. In next time I write you a letter. Best regards to Annie and Baby. Isidor."

Q. Now the next communication, was it a card or a letter?

A. It was a letter.

Q. Do you remember what he wrote?

A. He wrote about his case—

MR. WILENTZ: Just a minute.

A. —he had laying over here and he said in this letter—

MR. WILENTZ: No, if your Honor please, I object to it as not being the best evidence. I think that it is hearsay, if your Honor please, and I object to his mere statement that there was a letter as being a basis for an excuse for present testimony.

MR. REILLY: I think we have established that the letters were received, he received them, they were in his house, he doesn't know what happened to them, they have disappeared, either through something he did or something that somebody did when they arrested him. I think it lays a foundation for the introduction of secondary evidence as to the letters inasmuch as the Attorney General on his cross examination directed his attention to letters that passed between Fisch and himself and letters that afterwards passed between the Fisch family and himself.

MR. WILENTZ: There is no testimony, there was no question directed to him as to letters between himself and Isidor Fisch while Fisch was in Europe, not a question. This is not proper redirect; it is an entirely new matter, if your Honor please, not touched upon at all by the State. The fact is we couldn't have touched upon it because we had no knowledge or information that there were any such letters; and that I wouldn't object to so much except, if your Honor please, while I urge it as a basis for my objection it seems to me to be an improper way of trying to take from the lips of a dead man statements that your Honor can very readily see are impossible of answer. He will now attempt to reveal something that he says was contained in a letter from a person who is now dead, a letter which is, if it existed at all, missing, and which, if your Honor please, opens the door wide to the statement of anything at all, without any ability at all or any possibility on the part of the State to meet it.

Now, it is entirely new matter; it is not proper redirect examination and, while ordinarily I should hate to make any objection on that score because defense counsel particularly has not interposed any technical objections, I only do it because of the very serious nature of the effort being made at this time.

THE COURT: I wish counsel would state to me what it is, here at the side bar.

(Counsel conferred with the Court out of the hearing of the jury.)

BY MR. REILLY:

Q. Now I shall only direct your attention in the letters you received from Fisch along two lines, and ask you whether in any of the letters Fisch sent to you he spoke about the skins, the furs: did he?

Richard Hauptmann

A. Yes. I guess in all of them.

Q. Well now, just tell us without picking out any particular letter, if you can, just what he said to you in his letters about the furs, everything he said about the furs until you learned he died.

A. The debts, I guess, from Mr. Fisch it was about the furs, he only wrote me he had advanced in price about 20 or 25 per cent. In coming back to the letter, I am not—

Q. No, we just want about the furs at the present time.

A. Yes.

Q. Now, so that there was a continuous correspondence between you and Fisch about the furs?

A. Yes.

Q. Is that correct? Now I direct your attention to another angle in the letters. Was there anything said by Fisch about any stock profits or anything like that that was remaining?

A. He was, in every letter he was asking me how were the stocks and in one letter I told him I got to sell his thousand Eitingon-Schild.

Q. So there was continuous correspondence about the furs and stocks while he was in Europe before his death, is that correct?

A. Yes.

THE WITNESS: May I speak about them two letters I received?

THE COURT: No, you may answer the questions which you are ordered to.

Q. I show you this item in your book, State's Exhibit 259, and ask you what that is, what that word is.

A. "Boat."

Q. How do you spell it?

A. B-o-a-t.

Q. Now, is it not a fact that the German "t" is not like the American "t" or the English "t"?

A. That is, that is different from the English "t."

Q. This word in here written by you is b-o-a-t, isn't it as you say?

A. Yes.

Q. Now will you tell us again, please, when was it that President Roosevelt, when was the last day of President Roosevelt's gold surrender, when you think it was, or when do you say it was: the last day people could surrender gold certificates under the order of the President?

A. My best recollection is March '33.

Q. And about that time you turned in that $750?

A. Yes.

Q. So that in August, 1934, when this box of money, gold money, was discovered by you it was many months after the President had called in gold, is that correct?

A. Yes.

Q. Did you know that if any Government questionnaire was handed you to be filled out concerning your residence in the United States or any particulars about your citizenship that you could be picked up as an alien improperly in the United States?

A. Will you say it again in—

Q. Did you know that if you had to fill out any questionnaire, question blank, about any gold or about anything else for the Government in which they inquired as to your citizenship or residence in the United States and you disclosed that you were here illegally you could be sent back to Germany? Did you know that?

A. I know that.

Q. Now, after you found this money in the shoe box and took it out in the garage to dry, you passed about ten or twelve bills: is that correct?

A. Twelve to fifteen.

Q. Twelve to fifteen. And during what period were you passing those bills?

A. From the day I found it till my arrest.

Q. A little over a month, is that right?

A. Yes.

Q. During that time you always had the same licence plate on your car, didn't you?

A. Always.

Q. You always lived in the same house, didn't you?

A. Yes.

Q. You didn't run away, did you?

Richard Hauptmann

A. No.

Q. You didn't change your license plate?

A. No.

Q. You didn't change your name?

A. No.

Q. You didn't wear a disguise when you tried to pass these bills, or did pass them?

A. No.

Q. You brought your wife into a shoe store, did you, and bought a pair of shoes for her?

A. Yes.

Q. So that everything you did with the ten or twelve bills that you had for a month you did openly, didn't you?

A. Yes.

MR. WILENTZ: I move that the word "openly" be stricken. I object to the question with the word "openly"; that is calling for a conclusion, if your Honor please.

MR. REILLY: I will—

THE COURT: Well, I don't think that I will exclude that.

MR. WILENTZ: All right, if your Honor please.

THE COURT: He seems to have testified to what he means by the word "openly."

Q. And when the man at the gas station asked you something about the bill, you didn't make any effort, did you, to hide your license plates?

A. No effort at all to hide anything.

Q. And again I ask you: did one dollar of the Lindbergh—what we now call the Lindbergh ransom money, to identify it, did one dollar of that money pass into your brokerage accounts?

A. Not one dollar. In the time I passed the money—

MR. WILENTZ: Just a minute now, you have answered the question.

Q. Did you know that Uhlig and Fisch had an apartment somewhere in another part of New York?

A. I did not.

Q. Now, when you wrote to Isidor's brother, I think it was, and you said the words "private bank account," will you explain just what you meant by that?

A. I only wrote private bank account, it was $5,500, to make it more short and clearly, so I used the word "private bank account."

Q. You didn't have any private bank account by savings bank or check account, did you?

A. No.

Q. You had a private bookkeeping account and you designated, did you, your transactions with Isidor and yourself by saying "private bank account"?

A. Yes, I got a little bank, but it amounts only to a few hundred dollars.

Q. Now, in your letter to Isidor's brother, I think you used the words as translated "we share the profits and the loss," is that correct?

A. Yes.

Q. But, you did not say in the letter did you, "we share the profits and the loss fifty-fifty," did you?

A. I didn't say that in a letter?

Q. You used the words, didn't you, "we share the profits and the loss"?

A. Yes.

Q. But you did not use the words "fifty-fifty" did you?

A. No, half and half I used.

Q. Did you use half and half before the contract, the new contract of which you spoke that you were going to enter into with Isidor when he came back to this country?

MR. WILENTZ: Just a minute, I object to the question because the letter speaks for itself as to what he used. I have no objection to reading the letter.

THE COURT: Of course, the letter does speak for itself.

MR. WILENTZ: Yes.

THE COURT: But, you see, counsel is now asking as to the facts.

MR. WILENTZ: Now, he is asking as to the letter.

THE COURT: Oh, as to the letter?

MR. WILENTZ: I have no objection to the question as to the fact. I have as to the letter.

THE COURT: Yes. Mr. Reilly, I was pointing out to the Attorney General that the letter does speak for itself.

MR. REILLY: Yes.

THE COURT: But as I conceive it at the moment, there is no objection to your examining him as to the actual facts regardless of what was in the letter.

Q. Well, I direct the question to you, Mr. Defendant, because at one time in your testimony you said that there was some arrangement concerning a 20 per cent?

A. Yes.

Q. Now, what transactions, if you can recall, covered a 20 per cent relation to Isidor?

A. 20 per cent in stock transactions didn't get in effect.

Q. Didn't get in effect?

A. No. It was proposed, but after one day or two days he changed it.

Q. Well, when was it proposed?

A. Summer time, '33. I can't recall the month.

Q. And then after two or three days Isidor said he didn't want it any more: is that what you testified to?

A. That's what he said.

Q. Now, they have brought into court here and exhibited, and made an exhibit, a large plane.

MR. REILLY: Do you know the number?

THE REPORTER: S-177.

Q. Is this your plane?

A. That's my plane.

Q. Now, before your arrest, how long before your arrest had you used this plane?

A. This plane was never used since '28.

Q. Had it ever been sharpened since 1928?

A. No.

Q. Where was it in the garage?

A. It was on the rear shelf, on a shelf on the rear wall of the garage.

Q. And had not been used?

A. May I see it, please?

Q. Surely.

A. (The witness removed the blade from the plane, examined it, and replaced it.)

Q. And you had not used it since 1928?

A. No. There are two other planes in here, iron planes. This one, because it isn't good at all—one I keep always on the job where I was working, and one iron plane I kept home, for home work.

Q. The two planes you refer to now are in this box?

A. Yes.

Q. 196?

A. Two iron planes like that.

Q. Will you come down, please, and show us those planes.

(Witness opens box.)

A. It doesn't seem in here at all they are big planes like that (indicating), he didn't get it in.

Q. And the planes you refer to are not in the box?

A. Not in the box, two iron planes, big planes as long as that (indicating).

Q. About the same size as 177?

A. Yes, 16, 18 inch long.

Q. All right, go back on the stand. (Witness closes the box and resumes the stand.) Now, when did you last see the planes you have spoken of?

A. Oh, I really can't remember when I saw it last.

Q. Well, this 177 is a very cheap plane, isn't it, that wooden one?

A. I guess the cheapest you can buy.

Q. About how much?

A. I can't remember what I paid. I figure around two dollars.

Q. The other planes were better planes, the iron planes?

A. Yes, standard.

Q. And you used one you say on the job and one you had home?

Richard Hauptmann

A. Yes.

Q. Are there any of your chisels missing from this box, do you know?

A. I have to look the tool box over.

Q. Do you want to look it over?

A. Yes. (Witness steps down off witness stand and examines tool box.) There are three Stanley chisels missing, them chisels they are no good at all, they were laying in the garage. That is the chisels I bought first when I started carpenter over here.

MR. WILENTZ: Is the question answered, Mr. Reilly?

MR. REILLY: He says there are three chisels missing. I will get him to put these back and he will go back on the stand.

MR. WILENTZ: All right.

MR. REILLY: I will hold these things then. You go back.

MR. WILENTZ: I think if he left the box open, if we needed it—

MR. REILLY: All right.

(Witness resumes the witness stand.)

Q. Now, you have indicated that you wanted to say something about these three chisels. What did you want to say about part of this exhibit, the tool box?

A. Them two chisels, this one and this one—

Q. The larger—

A. That is very old chisels. They are probably at least ten years old. There was another set of chisel, it was a standard, Stanley set, good chisels—was a half inch, three-quarter inch, and one inch, but I see it disappeared.

Q. When did you see them last in that box?

A. I would say a couple days before I get arrested.

MR. REILLY: Now, may I have the book that had the sketch in it?

Q. The Attorney General has offered in evidence a book, 261 for the State, and showed you a picture of something that bears an "x"; is that your drawing?

A. No, it is not my drawing.

MR. WILENTZ: Just a minute. All right, it is answered.

Q. And yesterday I think it was marked—did you mark it with an "x"?

MR. WILENTZ: He marked it with an "x."

MR. REILLY: So that, your Honor, if I may interrupt you, it will be fresh in the minds of the jury when this 261 goes to them, it bears some kind of a drawing with an "x" that was marked yesterday during the Attorney General's cross examination of the defendant, and it was then said by him that it was not his. And to indicate it was not his the Attorney General had him mark this page with an "x." That is not his.

MR. WILENTZ: That is true. Also as to any other pages he marked with that kind of an "x." That indicates that is not the product of his hand.

MR. REILLY: So that when they come to examine it they will undoubtedly remember that that marked with an X is not his drawing.

THE COURT: Yes, yes.

RECROSS EXAMINATION

BY MR. WILENTZ:

....

Q. I want to show you Exhibit 41; first, I think I had better show you the earlier one, which is Exhibit 42 for the defense, and that purports to be a photostatic copy of the payroll, and you see on top here painters, quite a number of painters.

A. Yes.

Q. Then paperhanger?

A. Yes.

Q. Then a great number of painters again.

A. Yes.

Q. The days, the hours, the days, the hours, the rate of pay, and the name of the man, and the amount of the pay, and other remarks.

A. Yes.

Q. You see that, don't you?

Q. Then the second page: superintendent on top, then carpenters?

A. Yes.

Q. Then handymen?

A. Yes.

Richard Hauptmann

Q. Then porters, then painters again. That seems to complete that payroll. Now that is the payroll as you see for the week ending March the 31st, 1932?

A. Yes.

Q. Now let's come to your name. There is a check there. Do you see your name?

A. Yes.

Q. Richard Hauptmann?

A. Yes.

Q. How many days does it say?

A. It says eleven days.

Q. How much does it say for the rate of pay?

A. It says hundred dollar.

Q. How much does it say you were paid?

A. Thirty-six sixty-seven.

Q. Now take a look at the carpenter above, James Davie. How much is that rate of pay?

A. 150.

Q. Lockhead, how much is that?

A. Hundred.

Q. Allen Wilkinson?

A. Hundred.

Q. Gustave Kassens?

A. Hundred.

Q. Joseph Burnsides?

A. Hundred.

Q. Richard Hauptmann?

A. Hundred.

Q. Now let me get the next one. Now let's take the payroll record of the period or the week ending April 15th, it says. Now, that's the same sort of a payroll record, isn't it? I mean, it is the same thing only it is for April 15th. It gives the superintendent, does it not, first?

A. Yes.

Q. Then the stenographer?

Classics of the Courtroom

A. Yes.

Q. Then the carpenters?

A. Yes.

Q. How many? One, two, three, four, five, six, seven, eight, nine, ten, eleven, twelve carpenters, isn't that right?

A. Yes, but I never saw that much.

Q. Well, that's what the payroll record shows that your counsel offered in evidence, doesn't it?

A. Yes.

Q. Then handymen.

A. Yes.

Q. Then porters.

A. Yes.

Q. Then handymen and porters again.

A. Yes.

Q. Painter foreman.

A. Yes.

Q. Time keeper?

A. Yes.

Q. Do you see the name of the time keeper?

A. Morton.

Q. Edward Morton?

A. Yes.

Q. Do you remember him being on the stand?

A. Well, I remember the time keeper was on the stand.

Q. Yes.

A. I can't remember the name.

Q. You can't remember the name. All right. Then painter deputy.

A. Yes.

Q. Then on the next page again painter deputy and painter and painters and paperhanger and grainer, and something like N.B.

A. Yes.

Q. Now we will come to the days. Now we come to Richard

Richard Hauptmann

Hauptmann.

A. Yes.

Q. Under days it says 2 days, doesn't it?

A. Two days.

Q. Yes, sir. Then the next—

A. Wait a minute.

Q. Take your time. Now you can have it.

A. Yes.

Q. Two days, is that right?

A. Yes.

Q. Then the next entry is the rate of pay, a hundred dollars.

A. Yes.

Q. The next is the name Richard Hauptmann.

A. Yes, misspelled.

Q. Misspelled?

A. Yes.

Q. How do you spell it? Another "n?"

A. Another "n".

Q. I see. And the amount is $6.67?

A. Yes.

Q. And then it says "resigned."

A. Yes.

Q. Is that right?

A. That is right.

Q. Now is there anything on here that shows you worked the 2nd of April?

A. Well, it shows 2 days that I figure the 1st and the 2nd.

Q. Yes, but—

A. And that is the day I was working.

Q. I know, but that's your testimony; but there is nothing on this record that shows it is the 1st and 2nd or whether it is the 1st and 4th, is there, on this record?

A. I don't know how they keep the record.

Q. Well, you see it. I mean you have seen it.

A. I see there are 2 days.

Q. Yes. But it doesn't say which days, does it on the record? Take a look at it.

A. Well, I—

Q. Take a look at it and when you are ready you answer the question.

A. When it says "days" then I am positively sure it says the 1st and the 2nd.

Q. I know you are positively sure that it is the 1st and the 2nd, but what I am asking you now is whether that record shows that you worked the 1st and the 2nd, or does it just show 2 days in April?

A. Well, I am not familiar with this record, how they keep it.

Q. I know you are not familiar with it, but you look at it, that's all you have got to do.

A. (No answer.)

Q. Maybe I can help you become more familiar with it. Now we will take a look at the days again.

A. Yes.

Q. You see, there are other people in the same column right ahead of yours; William Bowie, 5 days.

A. Yes.

Q. And that doesn't tell what days he worked, does it?

A. Just says 5 days.

Q. Five days. And underneath yourself is another man who gets credit for 10 days, isn't that right?

A. Yes.

Q. Doesn't say what days, does it?

A. I don't know.

Q. Well, you are looking at it now.

A. Yes, but I don't know if it is the days from the 1st to the 10th, it doesn't say that.

Q. It doesn't say which days.

A. No.

Q. It just says 10 days, isn't that right?

Richard Hauptmann

A. But I figure—

Q. Now, please answer the question. We will let you figure a little later. You have testified that you worked the 1st and the 2nd.

A. Yes.

Q. What I want to know now is not what you say but what the record shows as you see it. It says 2 days, but doesn't say which days, isn't that right?

A. That's right.

Q. All right. Now, while you look at it will you tell us what the rate of pay is as shown on that page?

A. A hundred dollar rate.

Q. Now, let's see. Oh, yes, you have already told us about the "resigned."

A. Yes.

Q. All right, sir, thank you.

Q. Yesterday afternoon just before we adjourned Mr. Reilly started to ask you about this board and I think from his questions it was his impression that you answered here in court that "Yes, you did write the number." Now is that the fact that you did testify in this court that you did write the numbers but not the letters?

A. In this court, no.

Q. You did not?

A. I did not.

Q. That was in the Bronx Court?

MR. REILLY: I think I was referring to the record in the Bronx in my question.

MR. WILENTZ: But I looked at it this morning and I thought maybe you were confused about it.

Q. What you meant then was that you did testify that in the Bronx but not here, is that right?

A. I was—I mean for this court here—

Q. Yes, in this court you gave testimony of whatever the nature was, the jury will have to remember it, but in the Bronx you testified it was your handwriting, but not here, is that right?

A. In the Bronx I don't know.

Q. Mr. Reilly read the record to you yesterday.

A. Yes, but I was not sure always.

Q. When he was asking you, you weren't sure?

A. (Shakes head.)

Q. You weren't sure yesterday when he was asking you?

A. No, I mean in the Bronx.

Q. I do remember now that you answered his questions by saying "I don't remember."

MR. WILENTZ: Have we that record here?

Q. I will read you the question as I see it here:

"By Mr. Reilly:

"Q. Do you recall when the board was shown to you in the Bronx you were asked this question, bottom of page 83," and then Mr. Reilly read the question:

"'Q. And District Attorney Foley asked you if you recognized a certain piece of wood or lumber, do you remember that?' And you said 'Yes.'

"Then do you recall: 'So that when you looked at Exhibit A,'"—that is that board, 226—"which I assume was the piece of lumber which was presented to you by the District Attorney of Bronx County, and you looked at the handwriting thereon, you said that was your handwriting, isn't that so?' And you answer: 'I said that is my lumber, I could not make out the handwriting.' Is that right?"

And your answer—Now, yesterday Mr. Reilly said to you "Is that right?" And your answer is "Yes."

Is it still Yes?

A. When he was asking me about if it is my lumber?

Q. Yes. You said it was your lumber, and did you yesterday say again "Yes"?

A. This "Yes" was the "Yes" I said in the Bronx.

Q. Well, did you say "Yes" that it was your lumber in the Bronx?

A. I said "Yes, this is my lumber," in the Bronx.

Q. That was your answer?

A. In the Bronx.

Q. Is it your lumber?

323

Richard Hauptmann

A. I can't prove it if it is my lumber or not.

Q. I don't want you to prove it. You said in the Bronx it was your lumber. Now, you have a chance here today before the jury and the Court, if you want to say now it isn't your lumber, just say so; if you want to say it is your lumber, just say so?

A. It is a piece of trimming; in every house it is the same trimming.

Q. I know what it is. I want to know if it is your lumber, that is all. You said yes in the Bronx. Now, is it or isn't it?

A. I can't say yes or no.

Q. All right, sir.

A. This lumber—

Q. So that when you said yes in the Bronx—why did you say yes when you did not know? You were a carpenter then, too, of years standing, weren't you?

A. I didn't think. You could show me a piece of lumber, in every house it is the same.

Q. In every house it is the same, eh?

A. Practically.

Q. Every house it is the same. It hasn't got Condon's telephone number and address on it, though, has it?

A. I don't know.

Q. In every house it is the same—it hasn't got your handwriting on it either, has it?

A. I don't think so.

Q. Certainly not. So this lumber was different than any other lumber, wasn't it? It had writing on it, isn't that so? Wasn't this lumber different in that it had some writing on it?

A. No.

Q. Didn't you take a magnifying glass and look at it up there?

A. Yes.

Q. So you saw there was a writing on it, didn't you?

A. Yes.

Q. It was different than other boards then, wasn't it?

A. No, I cannot say it was different.

Classics of the Courtroom

Q. When you looked at this piece of wood—never mind looking over there, you answer the question. When you looked at this piece of wood, S-204—

MR. REILLY: Oh, now, I object to that. The inference that he is looking over at us.

MR. WILENTZ: Not at you, not at counsel.

THE COURT: The Attorney General does not attribute any looking toward counsel.

MR. REILLY: But your Honor doesn't—

THE COURT: I was saying that I see nothing objectionable in the examination in view of the Attorney General's explanation, he has a right to direct the witness' attention to the board and not to other places.

Q. When this board was brought to you in the Bronx and you saw this piece of lumber, you also were shown the writing on it, were you not?

A. Yes.

MR. REILLY: Now, is this proper redirect? It's been gone over seven or eight times. I didn't speak about any board in my redirect. I just directed his attention to new things. Now we are having what we had yesterday, for thirty hours in cross examination about this board.

THE COURT: Well, I am inclined myself to think that the subject matter has been very thoroughly covered either upon the direct or the cross examination, but if the Attorney General thinks that the evidence of this witness is in a state of confusion with respect to certain particular things, he may ask the questions necessary to clear up that confusion and that, I assume, he is now trying to do.

MR. REILLY: I didn't assume he was confused after all this examination.

THE COURT: Well, I don't know what is in the Attorney General's mind.

Q. When you were shown this piece of wood S-204—I will only be another minute or two, your Honor please, and it is only because of my notions of the importance of the matter that I am spending this time—I don't want to waste any time—when you were shown this piece of wood S-204 you were also given a magnifying glass and given an opportunity to look at the writing on there, weren't you?

A. Yes.

Richard Hauptmann

Q. And when you saw this piece of wood with that writing on it you said, "That's my lumber." Isn't that so—in the Bronx?

A. I did.

Q. You did. You couldn't tell that from just looking at the wood, you had to see the writing too, isn't that so?

A. The first time when they showed this piece of lumber I didn't see the writing at all. They put a piece of lumber and said "Is that your lumber?" I said, "Yes," without thinking of anything.

Q. You don't usually do things without thinking.

A. No, my physical condition was so bad this time I could hardly think.

Q. Your physical condition was so bad that time that it was easier for you to say Yes than No?

A. No, I was not thinking at all.

Q. Well, I say, you weren't thinking. You have a very good mind, haven't you?

A. Well, I don't think so, not so good.

Q. Oh, you really do think so, don't you?

A. (No answer.)

MR. WILENTZ: That is all.

CLASSICS OF THE COURTROOM

Series One - Eight Volumes

Max Steuer's Cross Examination of Kate Alterman in
People v. Harris & Blanck and
The Summations of Max Steuer and Joseph M. Proskauer in
Oppenheim v. Metropolitan Street Railways

Robert Hanley's Summation in *MCI v. AT&T I*

Clarence Darrow's Cross Examination of
William Jennings Bryan in
Tennessee v. John Thomas Scopes

Irving Younger's Opening Statement in
Tavoulareas v. The Washington Post Co.

Thomas Murphy's Cross-Examination of
Dr. Carl A. Binger in
United States v. Alger Hiss (Hiss II)

Edward Bennett Williams' Cross-Examination
of Jake Jacobson in *United States v. Connally*

Highlights from the Direct and Cross-Examination of
Herman Goering in *The Nuremberg Trial*

Clarence Darrow's Sentencing Speech in
State of Illinois v. Leopold and Loeb

Series Two - Eight Volumes

James Brosnahan's Summation in
U.S. v. Aguilar (The Sanctuary Trial)

William H. Wallace's Summation in
Missouri v. Frank James

The Direct and Cross-Examination of John Dean
in *U.S. v. Mitchell*

(continued on following page)

Vincent Fuller's Summation in
U.S. v. Hinckley

Highlights from the Direct and Cross-Examination
of Richard Hauptmann in *The State of New Jersey v. Hauptmann*
(The Lindbergh Kidnapping Trial)

Lantz Welch's Summation in
Firestone v. Crown Center Redevelopment Corporation
(Kansas City Hyatt Skywalk Case)

Ulysses in Court (Speech by
Irving Younger)

For a complete listing of continuing legal education
audio tapes, video tapes and manuals contact:

**The Professional Education Group, Inc.
12401 Minnetonka Boulevard
Minnetonka, Minnesota 55343
Phone 612/933-9990**